EQUIPPED FOR GOOD WORK

"That the man of God may be adequate, equipped
for every good work."(2 Timothy 3:17)

Also by Joe H. Cothen
Come to Bethlehem: The Christmas Story, Pelican (1975)
Preacher's Notebook on Isaiah, Pelican (1983)

EQUIPPED FOR GOOD WORK

Joe H. Cothen

PELICAN PUBLISHING COMPANY

GRETNA 1987

First printing, April 1981
Second printing, March 1987

Library of Congress Cataloging in Publication Data

Cothen, Joe.
   Equipped for good work : a guide for pastors.

   Bibliography: p.
   1. Pastoral theology.   I. Title.
BV4011.C65   253   80-27964
ISBN 0-88289-271-1   AACR1

Scripture quotations cited as NASV are from the *New American Standard Bible*, © The Lockman Foundation 1960, 1962, 1963, 1968, 1971, 1972, 1973, 1975.

Manufactured in the United States of America

Published by Pelican Publishing Company
1101 Monroe Street, Gretna, Louisiana 70053

To Hazel,
whose love never fails;
who always understands
and constantly sustains.

Contents

Chapter III   Communication in the Church   39

Preface

"The pastor is the key." These words or expressions very similar come across the pastor's desk hundreds of times. They may appear in correspondence, bulk mail, or periodicals, but the message is always the same: the man of God in the local church is told that he is the person who can get things done.

When such challenges or flatteries—interpret them as you will—move into his consideration, the minister must be honest with himself, his church, and the cause at hand. No man can meet all of the expectations of other people. If one is to lead in an effective pastoral ministry, he must recognize who he is, what the priorities should be, and where the "handles" are in getting the job done in the right way.

This is no easy or simple assignment. Many qualities must be resident in the pastor if he is to minister consistently and effectively. These gifts are to be discovered and developed in the lives of God's undershepherds, and when this has happened they will be recognized and appreciated by churches. Most congregations realize, however, that no single preacher can be strong in every area. Such an understanding is easier to find in the church when diligence is evident in the pastor.

The fact that problems often arise between pastors and congregations has been documented throughout Christian history. The debris of heartbreak and disillusionment lines the roads of church development. The stories of hurt and discouragement are too numerous to tell. Churches seem to survive and recover to work another day, but the minister does not always fare so well. Some have died discouraged and sick at heart, while others have left the ministry to languish in the limbo of unfulfilled dreams.

No one has a final answer to this problem, but some help along the way is available. The purpose of this work is to provide insight, encouragement, and practical suggestions for those who are beginning their ministries and for those who continue in spite of the problems encountered. Somewhere between Elijah's juniper tree (1 Kings 19:4–8) and Simon Peter's proposed three tabernacles on the Mount of Transfiguration (Matthew 17:1–8) can be found the realm of constructive, daily work in ministry. For every prophet there is an occasional juniper tree and cave of loneliness, but he must never fail to hear the "voice" that urges him on after the stormy winds of pressure, the shattering earthquakes of crises, and the testing fires of adversity have run their courses. In the midst of every problem and doubt, there is God.

The false impression that the ministry is a constant, spiritual mountaintop experience is even more dangerous than the time of discouragement. One must be reminded that while our Lord blessed His closest followers in allowing them to go with Him to the mountain, He did not allow them to remain long enough to establish squatter's rights. Life is not to be lived always on the peaks or in the deep valleys. Both are to be experienced periodically, but between them are to be found the hills and plains of daily work in the master's vineyard.

There is an old cliché that reminds us: "The test of a man's spirituality is not in how high he can jump but in how straight he can walk when he hits the ground." The purpose of this book is to help the pastor find his footing and direction in a path that leads to purposeful, constructive ministry. A right understanding of himself—his weaknesses, strengths, and opportunities—is prerequisite to successful service. The responsibility of each day must be faced in the light of what God will be able to do through the ministry of a truthful and committed man.

This writer makes no claim to have discovered anything that is exclusively his own. The converging influences of growing up in a pastor's home, marrying a preacher's daughter, and pursuing thirty-three years of ministry together with many of God's elect have come to focus on these pages. The lives of many have made their contributions and are shared here in the hope that they, in His name, may continue to bless.

The Baptist background of these sources and influences will unapologetically come through. A great group of people has made its investment, and it will always be deeply appreciated. Such an investment can never be repaid, but if a token of gratitude to those who have meant so much can be of help to others, it is here offered with a grateful and hopeful heart.

EQUIPPED FOR GOOD WORK

CHAPTER I

The Pastor and His Work

The Pastor as a Person

The call of a pastor is an awesome experience. When God lays His burden on the heart of a man, He intends to lead the church through that undershepherd. The fact that the call is awesome in its source and ultimate intention necessitates faithful and honest reflection on its meaning and cost. Such signal honor is not handed out carelessly by the Great Shepherd. He chooses whom He wills to do that which is His will.

The initial experience may come in great and dramatic circumstance:

> In the year that king Uzziah died, I saw also the Lord sitting upon a throne, high and lifted up, and His train filled the temple. . . . Also I heard the voice of the Lord, saying, whom shall I send, and who will go for us? Then said I, Here am I; send me. (Isaiah 6:1, 8)

On the other hand it may be in humble surroundings and not so eagerly heard. In the case of Jeremiah the call fell on reluctant ears and a reticent heart:

> Then said I, Ah, Lord God! behold, I cannot speak: for I am a child. But the Lord said unto me, Say not, I am a child: for thou

3

shalt go to all that I shall send thee, and whatsoever I command thee thou shalt speak. . . . Thou therefore gird up thy loins, and arise, and speak unto them all that I command thee: be not dismayed at their faces, lest I confound thee before them. (Jeremiah 1:6–7, 17)

In each case the tone of the call and response is different, but the purpose of God to use a man to rebuke, warn, and exhort His people is the same. Regardless of whether the call comes while one worships in the temple or looks at the new buds of an almond bush, the living out of that call comes where God encounters men through His servants.

The pastor lives where the action is. Only those who know nothing of his life would ever say that God's man lives in an ivory tower far removed from reality. In fact, he lives with people, working through the deepest forms of human need. No matter what a person's station in life, there are times when he hurts and needs a friend. To the side of the great and the small, the rich and the poor, the believer and the nonbeliever the pastor is called. When he arrives, he hears life as it really is.

The face that smiles before the public often weeps before the pastor. Marriage on the threshold of divorce, economic disaster, children in rebellion against parents, alcoholism, drug addiction, serious illness, or loss of loved ones—any of these or a score of other problems can strip away the needy person's mask of pride when the pastor arrives. When people hurt the pastor must be there, because there is no one else who can fill his place in their lives.

On one occasion this writer was the pastor of a strong city church that was attended by many who worked in executive positions. One of these men called for an appointment. This man, who guided the business pursuits of hundreds of other people, said he was in need of personal help. As the pastor thought about the appointment, he wondered what he could contribute to such an influential church member. When the visit was over, however, the pastor had been reminded that regardless of a man's wealth or position, his spiritual needs are like those of all people. Money and position are not enough when a real friend is needed.

As he works with the people of God, the minister deals with matters both temporal and eternal in their nature. He must lead in planning the church budget, building new buildings, forming and operating adequate organizations, and guiding a staff; but he must do more. The pastor must lead those who are not Christians to a right relationship to God through faith in Jesus Christ, and he must instruct others how to do the same thing. Not only is he to devise ways and means of making disciples, but he is also under divine mandate to disciple those who accept Christ. His is an irreplaceable role in the lives of many people. God has endowed each servant in unique ways to do certain things that another may not be able to do. The thought that a given person will respond to the witness of one pastor and perhaps to no other is both frightening and humbling.

The pastor has a place in the epochal events of human life. In a recent seminary survey, no student had any problem remembering the names of the ministers presiding at his baptism and wedding, and at the funerals for his loved ones. In these times of great importance the pastor is asked to play a vital part, and he is enshrined in the affections of those whose lives he helps.

The unique man and his call

God told Jeremiah that he had been set aside for the ministry before he was born (Jeremiah 1:5). The intention of the Lord is firm in His mind for each of us from the beginning of life to its end. This does not, of course, preclude choice on man's part, but determines that his refusal to do God's will will result in the waste of much native endowment.

To say that each person is special is not enough. In the divine economy there is only one of a kind. No two people are designed to be exactly alike, and no two can do the same job with equal facility. Since there is only one of a kind, the importance of the individual whom God has designed, endowed, and chosen for service can hardly be overemphasized.

In the realm of providence each man accumulates experience and knowledge that equip him for ministry. A pastor's background affects all that he is and all that he is able to do. A person is truly able to improve and grow, but his action is colored in many ways by his past. His geographical origin, the cultural level of his family, the economic factors of his life, his education, military experience, and a multitude of other influences make their contributions. All of this affects his personal attitude, decisions, ability to relate to people, preaching style, word choices, and the types of illustrations used in sermons and in conversation. In a word, he is a part of all that he has met; all of his encounters with life have made him the person he is.

Whether or not a pastor is able to communicate with people depends in part on their background and his own. One pastor was invited to speak to a group of ten-year-old Sunday school children on how to become a Christian. He chose to begin with Matthew 7:13–14 and then began talking about two possible roads that life can follow. Being from a strong rural background, the pastor spoke of the time for personal decision as the time when a young person reaches a "fork in the road" and must choose either God's way or the way to destruction. The message moved along well until he used the expression "fork in the road." One child with questions written all over his face timidly raised his hand and asked why the fork was lying in the road in the first place. Not until he changed his analogy to a "street intersection" was the pastor able to communicate the proper message. His rural background had not provided the right word picture for urban children.

All ministers must be willing to grow and to adjust to times, places, and conditions where they serve. Each must look at himself and his people and make those adjustments necessary for effective communication and ministry.

The pastor and his family in light of his call

A strong and secure family base is essential for effective pastoral work. The pressures of working with others are too great for a man to endure over extended periods unless he has a refuge at the end of each day.

Extra care must be taken by the minister to be the kind of husband and father that he pictures as the ideal of the Scripture. This is no easy task. Wives and children do not understand all that goes on in the average working day of a pastor. Tensions from the church are too frequently imported into the home. If one is not careful at this point the children may see a loving, kind man at the church and a growling tyrant at home. A wife may see a smiling, affable type in the pulpit and a caustic critic at the table with the family. These differences will not be easily understood or accepted by those who see the pastor not as a professional man but as a husband and a father.

During the years that this writer has taught in the seminary, he has tried to caution young preachers about giving adequate attention and love to their families. In the anxiety to get through with school and move out to a church, the students sometimes forget that there is a constant and ongoing responsibility to those whom they love. A man must take the time and care necessary to help his wife develop with him as he grows in the Lord's work. It would not be fair for her to work all day in a secular job to enable him to go to school and then be criticized for not knowing much about the Bible or the work of the church. The task is not simple, but the pastor and his wife must devise ways for the two of them to grow together. The wife must feel included in her husband's life if she is to avoid developing feelings of resentment toward him and his work.

The preacher must always remember that regardless of how successful he may appear to the outside world, if he is not loved and respected by those in his home, who know him for what he really is, he is a failure. No man can afford to fail at this point. The cost of failure is too severe, and the incentive for success is too great. The man of God must be Christlike wherever he finds himself, and especially when he finds himself at home.

The assurance that comes with the call

The minister may be set apart, uniquely endowed, and heartily supported by his family and yet have times of doubt and discouragement. For a minister to endure with all that is involved there must be within his soul a bedrock assurance that this whole business is from God. Without such a sense of certainty there are too many reasons and opportunities to quit.

Those who believe the ministry to be easy have never served as pastors. The very nature of the position calls upon the shepherd to bear burdens that are not his own. The average man may see a church member on the street and think of him only as a friend and neighbor. The pastor sees the same person and is immediately conscious of a whole set of problems or heartaches known only to the two of them.

A deacon once light-heartedly greeted his pastor, "Preacher, tell me what you know." The pastor responded in similar tone but with weighted words, "Deacon, if I told you what I know we would both have to leave town." That pastor was keenly aware of burdens that could not be shared with anyone. Without the abiding assurance that this is all in the hands of Him who has placed the pastor in the ministry, the weight of other people's problems can become oppressive.

Because a man is called of God does not always mean that he is accepted by all people. The pastor lives with the hostilities of others. Some people are difficult by nature, some are hostile because of temporary problems, and others are difficult because of unseen and perhaps unknown factors. One wise denominational leader says he tries to be patient when people are not very kind to him. "There is always a reason," he says. "It may be nothing more than a rock in his shoe or it may be a cancer in his stomach, but there is always a reason."

When he senses the animosity of another, a wise pastor finds good counsel in the words of Paul: "Let all bitterness, and wrath, and anger, and clamour and evil speaking, be put away from you, with all malice: And be ye kind to one another, tenderhearted, forgiving one another, even as God for Christ's sake hath forgiven you" (Ephesians 4: 31–32).

When a pastor moves from one church to another, he continues to serve the same God, but he quickly learns that all of God's churches are not alike. Of course, there are many similarities, but there are also great differences. Each church has its own personality, and programs that work well in one place may not be suitable for the next. Some churches are almost self-operating while others need far more direction and supervision by the pastor. One congregation may expect and demand many hours spent in pastoral visitation of the sick, aged, and shut-in, and another congregation may have very few such needs.

In one situation this writer found a great need and desire for a church-sponsored day care center for the children of working mothers. Such a work was begun and has enjoyed phenomenal success for almost twenty years. The need was there, resources were available, and a large reservoir of good staff people was in the area. Both the pastor and the church enjoyed operating the program. In his next church, however, that pastor investigated the need and found it minimal. Adequate facilities were not available, and the right kind of staff help was almost nonexistent in that community.

Each church must have its program tailored to minister effectively in its own area. While the pastor is learning by trial and error what will work in each situation, he needs the constant assurance that comes from knowing beyond a doubt that he is God's man in the place where God has sent him for that particular time.

The challenge of the pulpit demands the assurance of God's presence and power. No pastor can face such a responsibility alone and survive. How is one able to communicate with an audience that is diverse in background, education, culture, emotional temperament, vocational interests, age, sex, intellectual achievement, and spiritual development? Each person has a different set of needs, and each attends the worship service in hope of hearing something from God which will help with those needs. Apart from the genius of the Scripture and the ability of the Holy Spirit to inspire the preacher and the hearer, the equation of effective communication would be impossible.

Another need for the assurance that stems from the minister's call from God arises as he becomes aware of his position in society. Status seekers are not interested in the ministry. Most ministers recognize quickly that the place of the pastor in society is no longer as prestigious as it once was. In an earlier era a man was recognized in the community if he was the local minister. That is no longer the case. Any influence the preacher has must be earned on each individual scene of service. Respect is no longer automatic; on the contrary, the mere fact that a man is a member of the clergy may make him the target of criticism or humor of an uncomplimentary nature. If an ego trip is one's goal, the ministry is not the path to follow.

The realization of financial wealth is seldom found in the ministry. Most churches have made great strides of progress in recent years in upgrading salaries and benefits, but much remains to be done in this area for decades to come. In some places the resources or the will to provide for the minister's financial needs are lacking. Some men are forced to subsist at almost poverty level, and others have found it necessary to go bivocational in order to live. Even when a church makes every effort to pay a pastor adequately, he still finds it difficult to live and educate his children in the present days of spiraling inflation. Those who continue to serve under financial hardships must claim the promise of the Lord with a determined faith. His contract with His workers is found in Matthew 6:33: ". . . seek ye first the kingdom of God, and His righteousness; and all these things shall be added unto you." Under the provisions of this contract the man of God must strongly believe until he receives. Then with God's help he goes on.

The pastor and his theology

The servant of God must be very sure of his personal beliefs about God. Without a firm conviction of God's presence and power in his life the preacher will not dare to attempt more than a man can do in his own strength. Unless he is sure that the Bible is God's inspired word he may soon yield to the pressures and fads of the times and begin to preach "thus saith my opinion" rather than "thus saith the Lord." Only when he has experienced the living, victorious Christ can he share the faith that proclaims the living Savior who gives victory to all. If the conviction burns in his soul that sin is real and ruinous, he will be concerned for sinners. Evangelism will cease to be a burden and become a joy as the man of God develops a compassion like that of his Savior. The nurture of believers will not be an irksome chore if the pastor enjoys seeing growth in people who aspire to the likeness of Jesus Christ.

The theology of the pastor on the nature and mission of the church must be biblical if he is to be its leader. There are many good organizations—some with religious missions—but the church is the only institution established by Christ, and it is the only organism through which He has obligated Himself to work. The church is the body of Christ, and in it Christians are to function as integral parts.

When one clarifies and solidifies his personal theology, he must then seek divine strength to remain stedfast on scriptural teachings. The pendulum of popular opinion and faddism will swing back and forth across the position of the stable leader many times. This author has seen it happen a number of times. There have been periods when the social gospel advocates were in the ascendency and looked upon his position as being extremely right wing. When the pendulum moved in the direction of the emotional, charismatic persuasion, he was regarded as something of a moderate or liberal. His stance actually did not change at all. Basic biblical theology was followed, and an honest effort to emulate the spirit of Christ was made.

When one believes something very strongly he may not always be popular, but he can always be consistent. A world that is already head dizzy and soul weary is not attracted to a vacillating ministry.

The pastor's philosophy of ministry

The ministry of a pastor is a ministry of love. No man can perform this ministry without a shepherd's heart as a gift from God.

> And He gave some . . . as pastors and teachers, for the equipping of the saints for the work of service, to the building up of the body of Christ. (Ephesians 4:11–12 NASV)

Jesus pointed out that the disposition of a true shepherd is to lay down his life for his sheep. The "laying down of life" can occur in more than one way. There have been pastors who have become martyrs and heroes of the faith by sacrificing their own lives in the work of Christ. There have been far more who have given up life day by grueling day in selfless service. When a man has been given the heart of a true shepherd, he is there for the best interest of the flock regardless of personal cost. If one's life purpose is service to others, then he will not mind being needed.

The pastor's preparation

Before one can give he must first receive. A pastor is constantly asked to give of himself, his knowledge, his strength, and his experience. The drain is always there. Others come to him in private and in public seeking the word that he brings from God.

All that the minister has to offer stems from his own experience with God and His written and Incarnate Word. The preacher has no tangible goods for sale. Those who come to him can never carry away what he offers in shopping carts. The only vessel for transporting his wares is the human heart. For this reason, his faith must not be merely that of intellectual assent but must be a burning, heartfelt conviction.

The pastor must give evidence of three experiences in

his own life: a genuine experience of *regeneration*, a continuing experience of *sanctification*, and an anticipated *glorification*. These are basic to all that he professes and teaches. With the foundations in order, he faces a daily discipline of preparation as he leads the people. They will hear his voice and follow him who loves Christ supremely, loves the Book devotedly, loves the people sincerely, and loves the church and its ministry sacrificially. Only the pastor who so loves will be willing to keep on laying down his life for the sheep. Without repeated preparation "in the secret place with God" such love will wane and grow cold.

The Work to Be Done

The singular role of the pastor

The importance of the pastoral office is emphasized in Scripture. In both catalogues of ministries given by Paul in Romans 12:6–8 and in Ephesians 4:11–12 the function of the pastor is mentioned. The overarching purpose of ministry is spelled out in Ephesians 4:12–13:

> For the perfecting of the saints, for the work of the ministry, for the edifying of the body of Christ: Till we [the church] all come in the unity of the faith, and of the knowledge of the Son of God, unto a perfect man, unto the measure of the stature of the fullness of Christ.

The word *pastor* is one which indicates leadership of a group in similar fashion to the shepherd's leadership of his flock. The pastor is to be closely and constantly identified with the local church family.

The office may be perverted or exalted. The sacred role of the pastor may be perverted by those who are insensitive and pleasure loving (Isaiah 56:10–12), negligent and divisive (Jeremiah 23:2), filled with error (Jeremiah 50:6), selfish (Ezekiel 34:2–3), and unloving (John 10:12). The servant role of the minister is exalted and made effective by those who prove themselves wise and gentle (Matthew 10:16), given to selfless service (Matthew 20:26), diligent in work (2 Corinthians 4:1–2; 6:1–10), spiritually qualified (1 Timothy 3:1–7), and adequately equipped for the work (2 Timothy 3:16–17).

The gifts of God for functional ministry look to one purpose, and that is the building up of the body of Christ. The office of ministry is not designed to honor a man, but to provide responsible leadership in preparing all the people of God for service to others.

The duties of the pastor are varied but most can be grouped under three general headings. In the first place, the pastor must oversee and feed the flock of God:

> Take heed therefore unto yourselves, and to all the flock, over the which the Holy Ghost hath made you overseers, to feed the Church of God, which He hath purchased with his own blood. (Acts 20:28)

Secondly, he has the responsibility of guarding and instructing the people:

> I have set watchmen upon thy walls, O Jerusalem, which shall never hold their peace day nor night; ye that make mention of the Lord, keep not silence. (Isaiah 62:6)

Thirdly, the pastor must be a teacher of the Word by precept and example:

> Teaching them to observe all things whatsoever I have commanded you: and, lo, I am with you alway, even unto the end of the world. (Matthew 28:20)

> A bishop then must be blameless, the husband of one wife, vigilant, sober, of good behavior, given to hospitality, apt to teach. (1 Timothy 3:2)

One needs to do no more than give casual attention to these and other portions of scripture to note some rather comprehensive words. Terms such as *flock*, *Holy Spirit*, *overseers*, *feed*, *watchmen*, *teaching*, and *blameless* carry with them great depth and breadth of meaning.

The varied needs to be met

The longer a pastor lives with a given church the more he understands the varied needs of the people. As he ministers to them over a period of time he becomes many things to many people. During the writing of this book the author was preaching in a series of revival services in a church he had served in as pastor twenty years before. It was interesting to hear how they remembered him. Some commented on the preaching ministry; others remembered a mission which was established and has now become a growing church; one couple thought back to the time when their small child was critically ill and the pastor's car became an ambulance. The warmth of such memories serves as a fresh reminder of the multiple functions of a pastor.

While the man of God may be many things to different people, he cannot be all things to all people at all times. He must exercise personal discipline and decide what he wants most to be. If he is to be a strong preacher there is a price of isolation and study that must be paid. Early in his ministry he must establish some priorities and ration his time and energies accordingly. A preacher with no sense of direction in his own life cannot effectively lead others.

The privilege of burdens

The man of God frequently walks a lonely path in the midst of masses. There may be people who seek his counsel, listen to his preaching, learn from his instructions, and follow his administrative leadership, but there are few who really understand the nature, burdens, and complexity of his task. There are things known to him that can be shared with no one but God. The cares of others are never completely out of his mind. The fact that God has chosen him as one through whom He loves and ministers is a high honor and an awesome responsibility.

Another load that he carries originates in the nature of his message. His is a word that is frequently out of step with the times and contrary to human desires. The preacher is human. He would like to be popular, but that is not always possible. The fact that self-preservation is the first law of the human race must be challenged by what he has to say. Self-renunciation is one of the basic laws of the kingdom of God. The burden of preaching the latter when the former is more popular leaves the man of God in a unique and sometimes lonely position. He is strengthened, however, in the knowledge that he never stands completely alone. There is for every such time of estrangement that eternal reassurance: ". . . I am with you always, even to the end of the age."

CHAPTER II

The Building of the Church

The pastor's primary responsibility in life is the building of the Lord's church. His understanding of what the church is will have direct bearing on the effectiveness of his work. There are those who look upon the church as a necessary evil, an inherited encumbrance, a monstrous organization whose operation has held the preacher back in his pursuit of reaching the world for Christ. It is a serious mistake, however, to ignore or fail to appreciate the church in an effort to reach the masses.

In the purpose of God the church has a key role to play in reaching, teaching, evangelizing, and developing. Those who have circumvented the church have found themselves frustrated in noble ambitions without support in realization. Others who have predicted the death of the church have themselves been buried with the church serving as the pallbearer. No other institution has been given the stamp of eternity in such a unique fashion.

The Identity of the Church in Scripture

The word *church* has a different origin from the organism designated as the church of the New Testament. Most philologists agree that *church* was derived from the Greek word *kuriokan*, which means "belonging to the Lord or Master." The earliest use of this word by the Christians was in reference to the house of worship. When this use began is not known, but it probably started not later than the third century. From this word in Greek, other languages drew. The Old English word was *cirice*, in the German language the word is *kirche*, the Scottish word is *kirk*, and the Old Scandinavian is *kyrka*. (The long and interesting history of the word *church* is traced by H. E. Dana in *A Manual of Ecclesiology*.)

However, the organism, rather than the name, commands the major attention of the pastor. The word used in the New Testament to indicate the body of the believers is the word *ekklesia*. In the Septuagint, this was the word used to translate the Hebrew word *qahal*, which means an assembly, convocation, or congregation. *Ekklesia* occurs in the Septuagint ninety-six times.

In its use depicting the New Testament idea of the church, the word *ekklesia* refers to a "called-out" body of persons who assemble to carry out certain organized aims. "To be more specific, there were in the classical usage of this term four elements pertinent to its New Testament meaning: (1) the assembly was local; (2) it was autonomous; (3) it presupposed definite qualifications; (4) it was conducted on democratic principles." [1]

The word *ekklesia* occurs one hundred fourteen times in the New Testament. Eighty-five times the use is in a local sense, and twenty-six times the word may have other interpretation. Jesus used the term in Matthew 16:18 (ASV): "and I also say unto thee, that thou art Peter, and upon this rock I will build my church [*ekklesian*]; and the gates of Hades shall not prevail against it." In this He told the disciples that on the basis of lives transformed by their faith in Him as Messiah expressed in Peter's confession, He would build a new congregation, distinct from the old congregation of Israel. This points out that the Master's gospel would be proclaimed not by the historical nation of Israel, but by a body of believers who openly confess Him as Savior and Lord.

The strongest exponent of the church in the New Testament had a unique experience. Saul of Tarsus was "breathing threats" against the church and was on his way to Damascus to afflict the church when he met the risen Christ. In this never-to-be-forgotten encounter the Lord asked, "why persecutest thou me?" In this there was a message with two revelations. The first had to do with the character of Jesus, and the second had to do with the relation of Christ to His church. "To his amazement Paul discovered that Jesus is not only living, but that He is identified with His Church, and that it is impossible to slight, despise, or oppose the church without wounding the Son of God Himself."[2] From that time until the hour of his death Paul had two consuming subjects—Jesus Christ and His church.

The imagery used by Paul in referring to the relationship between Christ and church is both rich and meaningful. No closer bond could be implied, and no stronger feeling could be communicated than that which is found in the letter to the Ephesians.

> . . . Christ also loved the church, and gave himself up for it; that he might sanctify it, having cleansed it by the washing of water with the word, that he might present the church to himself a glorious church, not having spot or wrinkle or any such thing; but that it should be holy and without blemish. (Ephesians 5:25–27 ASV)

In the mind of the great apostle, the church stands beautiful and radiant in the hour of her greatest happiness as the bride of the world's Creator and Redeemer.

This writer finds it impossible to believe that the Christ

who gave Himself for the church and to the church will look favorably upon those who are her detractors. As a pastor he performed the wedding ceremony for a university football player and his bride. The pastor had watched the little girl grow up, seeing her in her mischievous times and now in this serene and beautiful time of her wedding day. As the bride started down the aisle toward the altar and her groom, the minister watched the smile on the young man's face as it widened. He had eyes for only one—his bride. This would not have been the time to call to mind any of her past mischievous pranks. So the Lord, while recognizing the weaknesses of the church, has committed Himself to her for time and eternity.

While Paul emphasizes the church as the bride, he does not stop with that figure. He refers to various God-given ministries which are to equip the believers "unto the building up of the body of Christ." At other times he thinks of the church as the household of faith, the family of God, the temple of God, and as the pillar and ground of truth. It is the medium of revelation, the organ through which divine wisdom speaks to men.

> Unto me, who am less than the least of all saints, was this grace given, to preach unto the Gentiles the unsearchable riches of Christ . . . to the intent that now unto the principalities and the powers in the heavenly places might be made known *through the Church* the manifold wisdom of God. (Ephesians 3:8, 10 ASV)

These and many other passages speak to the pastor's heart. This institution in which he is to invest his life is not a passing fancy. The stamp of eternity is upon it. It has not been left to its own devices; God is in it. The destiny of the church is not honorable mention in the museum of dead institutions. Instead, as a living, spirit-led body it moves through history toward the consummation of the age and its own glorification.

The Identity of the Church
in Its Immediate Environment

The pastor must be well grounded theologically on the doctrine of the church, but he must not fail to be knowledgeable on the pragmatics of the church. The church in the biblical sense is the fellowship of believers redeemed by Christ and made one in the family of God. In the local expression the church is a fellowship of baptized believers, voluntarily banded together for worship, nurture, and service.

Where is the church and what is it to its own community? The question of where is not asked in order to locate the address of its building. Where is it that God in His providence has seen fit to locate His church? What is its role in the area of its service? Some churches have been located in communities where they have prospered and built large and great fellowships. Others are in remote or difficult places of the earth where numerical growth has been difficult and the work discouraging. The planting of the churches is the province of God as He leads men who serve Him. If men run ahead of God or let their interests preempt His, mistakes are made that make the work difficult if not unsuccessful.

When a man is called by a church to become its pastor, he needs to know as much as possible about its location and circumstances. Some questions to be answered are:

1. Who lives here? The national origin, educational level, economic status, ethnic background, median age of adults, and sex distribution are all important factors.

2. How many people live here? The population density and distribution are vital matters of information. The local census office, chamber of commerce, govern-

mental planning or zoning boards, or the engineering office of a major utility may be helpful sources of such information.

3. How long have the residents lived in the community? Program requirements for a mobile constituency are vastly different from those in a static situation. Whether a person intends to spend the rest of his life in that place may determine how much of himself he is willing to invest in the local church.

4. How fast are people moving in or out? Some churches are made up primarily of people whose companies transfer them on a three- to five-year rotation. Other areas such as those near military bases have a one- to two-year rotation.

5. How large are the family units and what ages are the children? Churches with large, young families may have maximum needs with minimum resources to meet those needs. This might determine whether a special drive to raise funds for building would be feasible. Low incomes and large families may preclude such a possibility.

These characteristics of a local church are important if the new pastor is to determine what type of leadership and programming are to be attempted. Another consideration is that of the church's location. The section of the country and the type of community within that given geographic area are important. Churches vary from one area to another as do the customs of the people. Charles Jefferson has noted that

> the church has a disposition and temperament of its own, that its personality is as distinct and solid as the pastor's, that it is an organism with traditions which are sacred and customs which are hallowed, with notions and whims that must be respected, and with idiosyncrasies which cannot be safely ignored. Blessed is the preacher who realizes that he is only a sojourner as all his fathers

were. He stands in the line of long succession. Other men have labored and he is entering into their labors. It is not for him to start out as though the world were just beginning.[3]

In trying to identify certain churches as to location, one finds himself in a dangerous dilemma concerning word choices. Words like *average, typical, ordinary*, and so forth are fraught with problems. Communities are structured in such a variety of ways that it is not possible to find one word that will adequately describe where one is. However, in an attempt to share some very broad generalizations some choices must be made.

1. The rural church
   A. The church is usually smaller in membership and the facilities modest.
   B. In such churches the organization is frequently very stable; change comes slowly.
   C. The pastor is expected to do more social visiting among the membership than in other types of churches.
   D. Since the rate of pastoral change has probably been high, the pastor may experience some hesitancy in being fully accepted.
   E. In many rural communities large family groups are found.
   F. Because of the family relationships, new people in the community are not always quickly accepted.
   G. Some problems may stem from the familiarity factor in the membership.
   H. Rural churches are frequently more conservative theologically, emotionally, promotionally, and financially.
   I. Vast differences are to be noted in churches within this category.
   J. Mobility within the membership is usually low.

2. The village church
   A. Many of the characteristics of the rural church are also found in the village church. In most cases the churches are very similar in nature and disposition, but some important differences can be noted.
   B. The village may have a more cohesive community organization which finds its center in a small business district with a school and church nearby.
   C. Village politics may be a factor in the church.
   D. Many of the people may work outside the community, and commuter problems may affect the church programming.
   E. The role of the church in community life may be more obvious, and the influence of the community may be felt more in the church.

3. The small-town church
   A. The pace of life is usually slower than it is in larger cities.
   B. The pastor is generally better recognized as a leader in the community than in larger cities.
   C. Relationships with churches of other denominations are critical to effective ministry.
   D. The church has a better opportunity to relate to the business community. The schedule of the business establishments has a more direct effect on the program of the church.
   E. The pastor is likely to be called upon for more secular community projects.
   F. Privacy for the pastor and his family becomes a problem in a town where everyone knows everyone else.

4. The suburban church
   A. The suburb may be growing or it may be static or

even in decline, however, many suburbs are growing with the influx of young families.

B. A young church in a developing area has the excitement of large numbers of prospects coupled with the frustration of meeting great needs with limited resources.

C. Real estate prices and building costs may serve as deterrents to church growth.

D. If the church was previously in the open country but now finds itself in the sprawling suburbs, fellowship problems may result between those who are in established leadership positions and the new arrivals in the fellowship.

E. Many suburban churches have a great desire to see change and are more tolerant of church debt so that this can be effected.

5. The inner-city church

A. Most inner-city churches have problems resulting from their locations.

B. Demographic changes may have separated the church site from growing population centers.

C. The immediate environs of the church are usually in a state of transition from residential to commercial and industrial interests.

D. The population in the area of many such churches is made up of elderly men and women, low-income families, highly transient people, and young couples living in apartments.

E. The pastor of an inner-city church may find older buildings in need of repairs and renovation.

F. Many such churches are faced with the painful alternatives of staying in a vanishing community, moving to a growing area, or dissolving.

G. The immediate prospect for many such churches is gradual or accelerated decline.

H. Stability and growth depend upon exceptionally strong preaching, organization, and programming.

In his very useful volume, *Hey, That's Our Church,*[4] Lyle Schaller provides a number of church case studies. Many of them fit the above categories and some interesting observations are offered on the personalities of various types of congregations.

Whether the Lord's church is found in a remote rural area or in the heart of a bustling city, it is there for a good reason. The pastor's job is to discover that reason, accept the situation as he finds it, and set himself to the task of leading that congregation to fulfill its mission in its community.

The Legitimate and Necessary Functions of the Church

To say that churches are different is an understatement. Churches are as unique as their membership, but, with all their variety, there are some legitimate and necessary functions common to all churches. A consistent program of worship, preaching, teaching, evangelism, healing, and helping is vital to church health.

Worship

The worship service of the church is its most cherished experience. There is a magnetism in that hour when believers meet to sing, pray, read God's word, and hear its proclamation. In this time the mind has an opportunity to feed on God's truth; the heart can be opened anew to the love of God, and the life can be rededicated to the purpose of God.

As the pastor has primary responsibility for the worship services of the church, he must be careful to learn the needs of the people, and design experiences in worship that will best meet those needs. In order to accomplish this, several details must have attention.

1. The order of the service must be clearly in mind. A printed order is helpful so that the people may anticipate the sequence of events.

2. The place of worship must be clean, neat, and comfortable.

3. Ushers must be available at the entrances to give assistance in handing out bulletins, seating the people, taking the offering, and in taking care of whatever details may need attention. The pastor should train his church ushers so that they will be efficient in their work.

4. The people should be taught reverence as they enter the building. The prelude should be the signal for conversations to cease.

5. Before the service all equipment such as books, lecterns, and musical instruments should be in place and ready for use.

6. The music and the sermon should be planned to present a total message throughout the service.

7. Announcements and other matters not related to worship should be minimized or deleted entirely.

8. Careful attention to time should be a discipline for those responsible for worship leadership. A well-designed service which begins on time and ends on time will be appreciated by the members and guests.

9. The pastor and his associates are responsible for good taste in the selection and arrangement of materials for worship.

10. Friendliness with reverence should be encouraged following the service.

An old hymn has rung out many times across the nation and around the world. "Brethren, we have met to worship and adore the Lord our God." Let the pastor and the church honor that desire!

Preaching

This writer's father was a country preacher in south Mississippi. He never had the opportunity to receive a full formal education, but he learned the lessons of practical experience exceptionally well. His repeated warning to his three sons—all of whom are preachers—has been recalled every Sunday. "Boys," he would say, "your people will forgive a lot of your faults, but they won't forgive you if you waste their time between eleven-thirty and twelve noon on Sunday." In his unique way he was saying that the most important task of a pastor is to preach God's Word. Edgar N. Jackson writes, "People do not have to go to church. The fact that they are there is a vote of confidence in the minister. He should not prove unworthy of such confidence."[5]

Great churches are built around great preaching. When the pulpit is neglected, the work of the church suffers and the souls of men hunger. Matthew Simpson warns, "If you have ever looked at the ministry as a life of ease, either abandon the thought, or abandon the ministry. It is a busy hive with no place for drones. There is work in the pulpit, and work out of the pulpit; work in the study, and work out of the study; work publicly and work privately."[6] Great preaching requires hard work.

When the people gather on Sunday, they turn their faces toward the pastor with the question of Zedekiah. "Is there any word from the Lord?" (Jeremiah 37:17). They come to the church looking for that which is available in no other place. Entertainment is not what they seek; that is available in other places. When people leave their businesses, homes, and other interests to come to church, they want what the church has to offer. The pastor must set the pace. His job before God and the world has been spelled out by the apostle Paul. "I charge thee in the sight of God, and of Christ Jesus, who shall judge the living and the dead, and by his appearing and his kingdom: *preach the word;* be urgent in season, out of season; reprove, rebuke, exhort, with all longsuffering and teaching" (2 Timothy 4:1–2).

Teaching

The job of teaching in the church was mandated in the Great Commission. "Go ye therefore, and make disciples of all the nations, baptizing them into the name of the Father and of the Son and of the Holy Spirit: *teaching* them to observe all things whatsoever I commanded you: and lo, I am with you always, even unto the end of the world" (Matthew 28:19–20). Elton Trueblood has put his finger on the real need for an equipping ministry through teaching.

> We must understand that, whereas public worship is important, it is important only as the beginning of a total process. The matter of chief importance is the steady continuous ministry of all of the members, and the chief function of the pastor is to help people to get ready for this ministry. This cannot be done by a single twenty-five minute sermon. People cannot normally learn without a teacher and good teaching is intrinsically an unhurried business. The congregation must, accordingly, be reconstructed into the pattern of a small theological seminary with the pastor as the professor.[7]

The average church member has much to learn and few competent teachers. Most churches have some teaching program for those who will attend, but the quality of instruction is not always good. A minister of education gave his Sunday school teachers a test to determine where they were in Bible knowledge. The results of that simple examination given to church leaders were devastating. Obviously, little Bible teaching was taking place because those who taught had so little to offer. What steps could be taken? To rebuke his teachers would do nothing to solve the problem. Help was needed for these leaders if they were to be effective in instructing others. After some reflection on the problem and some prayer, a course of action was drafted.

The minister of education and his pastor decided to make available to all church leaders an Old Testament survey to be taught at college level for two hours each Monday evening. The calendar was cleared of conflicts and the course was planned to begin in September and continue through May. A visit was made to the campus of a Baptist college for advice and counsel on such matters as teaching methods and textbooks. Two books were selected: G. F. Maclear's *A Class-book of Old Testament History* and H. I. Hester's *The Heart of Hebrew History.*

Adequate publicity was begun in early August, and other preparations were complete by the first week in September. This was not to be an ordinary church study course but a survey of the Old Testament designed to equip teachers for teaching. On the opening night one hundred thirty adults enrolled. More than a hundred of these remained through the entire nine-month period. Each student was required to read the texts, attend the class sessions, and develop a notebook. This church found that people respond to a serious, well-prepared learning opportunity. The following school year a similar course in New Testament was offered with even better results.

When the church is led by the pastor to equip the saints for the work of the ministry, it discovers that serious teaching can result through teachers who are concerned about their work.

Evangelism

Evangelism is the reason for the church's establishment. The Lord left the church with the assignment to make disciples of all the nations. This task can never be accomplished until pastors become serious about being effective pastor-evangelists. The reaching of the unsaved for Christ is not an "on occasion for occasion" effort. Evangelism is not to be stressed just during times of crusade or revival preparation. This is a work to be done every week of the year.

There will never be a serious effort at winning others on the part of laymen unless the pastor leads the way by teaching, preaching, and personal work. Satan would like nothing better than to help a pastor to become so involved with "good things" in church work that he has no time or spiritual energy left for the best thing—witnessing to those who are lost.

If the pastor works at the job of winning people to Christ, the Holy Spirit will bless his ministry in ways too numerous to mention. If he only talks about it but does nothing, his preaching will begin to take on the hollow ring of insincerity. No evangelist or outside "expert" on evangelism can ever be as effective as a pastor who loves his people and wants to see them saved. People are far more likely to respond to one whom they know and respect than to a stranger. The pastor has the opportunity to minister to them in their times of great personal need. Because of this relationship his appeal is more likely to be heard than that of any other. To become specific in his approach the pastor can try some or all of the following:

1. Resolve to carry a New Testament at all times.
2. Make a prayer list on the book's fly leaf of the names of adults who are unsaved.

3. Take five minutes each day to pray for these lost people by name.
4. Set aside one evening each week as a minimum for nothing else except witnessing to lost people.
5. Enlist one layman to accompany the pastor as a trainee.
6. Covenant with that layman to pray for a week about those to be visited the next week.

One effective method of evangelism utilizes *Good News by a Man Named John,* which may be purchased from the American Bible Society. During a prayer meeting hour, the pastor can lead the church in marking these copies of the Gospel of John for witnessing or for use as missiles to be left in doctor's offices, hotels, bus stations, airline seats, and other public places.

A step-by-step notation is used, with key passages and captions marked in red in the books. The caption is written at the top of the page where the scripture is found; the passage is then circled and connected to the caption by an arrow. At the bottom of each marked page, the number of the next step and the page number are written (the page number of the first step should be written on the cover of the book).

Step 1   Everyone has a sin problem
         John 8:23–24, 34–36
Step 2   But God loves you
         John 3:16–18
Step 3   Consider your choice
         John 3:36
Step 4   How to come to God
         John 6:65–69
Step 5   What you should do
         John 6:27–29, 35

Step 6   What Christ does for you
          John 10:28–30
Step 7   Decide now to trust Jesus
          John 12:35–36, 48

A stamp giving the church name, phone number, and address should be placed on the back page. Each person should mark a pattern copy and then take as many others (furnished by the church) as he will mark and share during a three-month period. Even the most timid member can participate in this type of witnessing by leaving a marked gospel where someone may read it and be saved.

There are thousands of other ideas to be found. Some of them are very good, but none of them will ever work unless a faithful pastor leads a caring church to become involved in evangelism.

Ministry of Healing

There is much more to the healing process than attention to bodily illness or injury. This writer has no call to divine healing in the circus tent approach that some have used. In His wisdom God has provided skilled physicians and great hospitals to carry on the major part of physical healing. However, there are many hurts that go deeper than flesh and bone, and cause more suffering than imagination can tell.

One Tuesday night, this writing was interrupted for the purpose of church visitation. The writer and his wife received assignments in suburban New Orleans. The first address was a part of a fourplex apartment building. An eighty-year-old lady finally came to the door after having peeked out of a window to assure herself that all was well. When the visitors were seated in the modestly furnished living room, a veritable flood of conversation flowed from this lonesome person. She was in poor health, alone except for one daughter who was rarely able to be with her, and occupied with memories of a deceased husband and the loss of seven of her nine children. She needed someone to hear her. A troubled heart was helped a bit by two sympathetic listeners. This dear old lady will never be able to help the church very much, but the church can be helpful to her and hundreds of others like her in every community where God has located the healing, helping presence of His church.

The opportunities for healing are found in many different areas of life. A ladies' Sunday school class teacher was visiting for her class when she found a young mother and three children living in a dilapidated duplex. Abandoned by her husband, the young woman had almost lost hope in life. The children needed food and medical attention; the mother needed help with child care to enable her to go to work. In addition, she had a very limited education and no marketable skills. To say that she was despondent would be an understatement. Concerned Christians went to work to help her to help herself. One by one problems were worked through. Child care and a temporary job were found; soon she was enrolled in a federal training program to become a licensed practical nurse. She and her children became active in church, and all of them found new hope in life. A shattered dream and a broken heart began to be restored because of the healing ministry of a caring church.

Ministry of Helping

From its infancy the New Testament church has been in the business of extending a helping hand to those in legitimate need. Luke shares with us one of the earliest cases of Christians involving themselves in the needs of others:

> And the multitude of them that believed were of one heart and soul: and not one of them said that aught of the things which he possessed was his own; but they had all things common. And with

great power gave the apostles their witness of the resurrection of the Lord Jesus: and great grace was upon them all. For neither was there among them any that lacked: for as many as were possessors of lands or houses sold them, and brought the prices of the things that were sold, and laid them at the apostles' feet: and distribution was made unto each, according as any one had need. (Acts 4:32-35 ASV)

From this early beginning the church continued its efforts to help those who needed assistance. The first deacons were selected in order to give the apostles some help in the equitable distribution of the resources available through the church (Acts 6:1-7). Paul gave leadership and instructions in 1 Corinthians 16:1-3 concerning the need for help for the saints in Jerusalem. In this case he encouraged those believers in one church to reach out a helping hand to those in another church.

In the modern age, when governmental agencies have taken over many of the functions related to aiding the poor, the church may be tempted to ignore responsibility in a ministry of helping. There are many areas of human need yet untouched and crying out for attention. Weekday ministries conducted by churches have provided sewing classes, language classes, craft instruction, tutoring service for slow learners, cooking and nutritional classes, and prenatal classes. The opportunities are myriad, and the church can use its facilities and people in a ministry of helping others to help themselves.

Problem Motives in Church Programming

To do the right things for the wrong reasons leaves the church suspect in this discerning and critical generation. The difference in manipulation and legitimate spiritual leadership is found in motivation. There are some unworthy and frustrating motives in church programming.

1. The desire to surpass other churches for the sake of prestige and notoriety is not a good motive to be used in consistent church programming. This can be a subtle and unadmitted factor for both the pastor and the congregation.

2. The setting up and striving for statistical goals for the sake of breaking previous records may cause the church to lose sight of the importance of the individual. Numbers are important, but only because they represent people for whom Christ died.

3. The effort to grow a "big church" for bragging purposes is a poor reason for the expenditure of one's life. If a church merely becomes large without becoming great in compassion and spirit, it may have so many internal problems that boasting would not even be possible.

4. There are some churches that seek to maintain a status quo because of pride or heritage.

5. The promotion of irrelevant programs within a church in order to court denominational favor is dangerous. Not all suggestions by denominational leaders are intended to be implemented in every church. The pastor must be selective and use those program items that will best meet the needs of his own church.

6. The opposite attitude of noncooperation with denominational leaders for the sake of asserting one's independence is equally hazardous, and may lead to problems within a fellowship.

The Challenge of the Place and the Times

If one seeks a problem-free life, he is looking for an impossible dream. The very fact that one is a Christian says that he is a stranger and a sojourner in this world. Because people have problems churches have problems. *All churches have problems.* The reason they need pastors and other spiritual leaders is because they must work through the problems and needs of their times and locations. Admittedly, some churches have problems that seem to be more critical than others. In other cases the needs may seem greater because the pastor knows more about them than he does those of another church.

One of the greatest deterrents to church stability and development is the restlessness of pastors. Men are needed who are mature and strong enough to take a church where it is and live with it and in it until it can be better than it has been. These are not easy times, and the individual church may not be an easy place, but the One who calls forth His pastors never promised anything but a cross in this life. The crown comes later.

The Permanence of the Church

Many "para-church" organizations come and go, but the church moves on through history. It may not be as spectacular as some other groups, but it abides to do God's bidding when all others have departed the scene. Let the pastor who is impatient and tempted to turn to other avenues take a careful look before he leaps away from his church. The Lord has committed himself to only one human institution—the church. He has promised to return for only one group—those redeemed by His blood—His church. The life invested in the work of the church for Christ's sake will have its reward.

Communication in the Church

Communication Defined

How does one "determine the limits of and specify exactly" what communication means? The word *communication* comes from the Latin *communicare*, which means to share, to impart, or to partake. From this same root the word *communion* is derived. This close association of a word so important to the church is not accidental. The "sharing" of the Lord's life has made the Christian community a reality and a necessity.

How is it then that a word so close to the heart of the church also poses a chief problem among Christians? Why do churches divide and war against each other? Why are fellowships frequently stymied in their purposes for God? How do pastors and church leaders so often end up on opposite sides of an administrative or doctrinal fence?

The communication problem is at the heart of all these and many other difficulties for pastors and churches. The proclamation of the gospel deserves the best knowledge and effort the man of God can give it. In the last two decades authors in the field of preaching have begun to relate communication studies to the effective sharing of the

Word, and this is commendable. In no way does a knowledge of behavioral science diminish one's esteem for or dependence upon the Holy Spirit and His manifest power in the act of preaching. To the contrary, the more knowledgeable the pastor becomes about human response the better able is the Holy Spirit to use him. Men like Bauman,[1] Abbey,[2] Pennington,[3] and Sweazey[4] have helped to set the stage for more effective preaching as they have shared their work in communication science. Much remains to be done in relating such studies to Christian preaching, but there is another area of concern in communication that remains virtually untouched.

The church is not likely to make serious impact on an unbelieving world as long as it must devote a major part of its time and energy to getting along with itself. The matter of intrachurch communication is important if the pastor is to lead a cohesive spiritual force in its onslaught against the gates of hell. *The sharing of meaning between a source and a receiver with minimal loss in the process of transmission is no simple task.* In this sense communication is more a process than a mere act.

Models for communication

Theorists have attempted for quite a while to demonstrate what happens in communication by drawing and explaining diagrams. These are as varied as those authors who have written about them. They range from the well-known and simple Shannon-Weaver model, which grew out of research done at the Bell Telephone Laboratories, to the more sophisticated probability chain models used in organizational studies. Whatever the origin, such models are intended to illustrate the process and complexity of information and impression dissemination.

The pastor in a local church situation finds himself faced with a variety of communication needs outside his pulpit responsibility. There are those times when he is involved in a simple one-to-one conversation which is later shared by the receiver. Such an encounter may be illustrated as follows:

Initial communication

$$P \rightarrow M \rightarrow E \rightarrow T \rightarrow D \rightarrow M \rightarrow R$$
$$\uparrow \qquad\qquad\qquad\qquad\qquad\qquad \downarrow$$
$$M \leftarrow D \leftarrow T \leftarrow E \leftarrow M \leftarrow$$

Feedback communication response

In this simple model the pastor is in the process of communication with one person. The pastor (P) is the source of the communicated message. He sees a need to be met and begins a process. The message (M) may be instruction, inspiration, encouragement, exhortation, or any other form of information. The encoding (E) process is the pastor's mental selection of verbal and nonverbal symbols such as words, gestures, facial expressions, and body movements. Transmission (T) is the actual verbalization of the message, accompanied by chosen emphatic movements such as gestures.

The decoding (D) process begins with the transmission to the mind of the receiver. At this point certain filters come into action. The frame of reference of the receiver will affect the meanings he assigns to the symbols used by the pastor in the transmission. His group relationships, personal background, education, family influences, culture, vocation, and predispositions toward the pastor will all have a bearing on how he decodes the message. The decoding process in the receiver is never *exactly* the same as the encoding process in the sender.

The message received and interpreted through the filtering personality of the receiver may be approximately the intention of the pastor or it may be very different. The receiver (R) hears, sees, interprets meaning, responds through immediate or delayed feedback, and eventually becomes a secondary sender of the pastor's message to another church member. The further the message travels from its original source the greater the risk of distortion becomes.

The feedback process in this model may be concurrent with or subsequent to the initial process of communication. In this case the receiver of the pastor's message begins to send back to him certain verbal or nonverbal responses. The feedback may be nothing more than a smile and nod of approval, a frown of disapproval, a grimace of distaste, or a verbal response coupled with some appropriate nonverbal form of communication. Silence may also be used as feedback response.

As in the case of initial communication, the message of feedback may or may not be accurately interpreted by the receiver who in this case is the pastor who began the process. The secondary transmission of the pastor's message, that is the sharing with others by the original receiver, is subject to the same process. In looking at the various possibilities for understanding or misunderstanding, the pastor sees the need for prayerful concern and careful selection of his communicative stimuli. On a purely human level adequate communication is difficult if not impossible. The pastor, however, has a most important ally who must not be overlooked. The Holy Spirit can give wisdom in the selection of words by the pastor, and He can also help to overcome some of the filtering process in the receiver.

As the pastor communicates with various groups, the factors in the previous model are multiplied and additional factors come into play. Regardless of size each group has some members who serve as opinion leaders for others in the group and for individuals outside the primary group. These opinion leaders are to be found in every church or in any other group where people attempt to function together. By virtue of personality, education, and business, social, or family relationships these people have gained the respect of others within the group. The opinion leaders function in influencing the attitudes of the opinion followers. The wise pastor will learn as soon as possible who these people are and how they function. Much more can be accomplished with their help than with their opposition.

A possible model for the process of communicating with and through a group might be as follows:

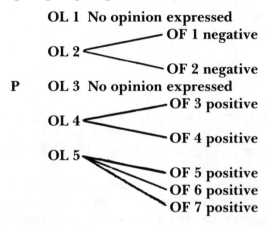

In this model the pastor is dealing with a group of twelve people. Five of these are basically opinion leader types, and seven are opinion followers, who are usually content to depend upon certain leaders whom they respect. Remembering the process illustrated in the previous model, look closely at what happens in the group situation.

As the pastor presents some facet of his program, he stimulates a variety of responses within the group. In this case 1 and 3 simply do not express themselves to followers or other leaders (opinion leaders do not always function). Opinion leader 2 has negative feelings and verbally or nonverbally communicates this to 1 and 2. Opinion leaders 4 and 5 have positive feelings and move with strength to affect opinion followers 3 through 7. If opinion leaders 1 and 3 maintained absolute neutrality (which is not likely when given time for interchange with others) the pastor's proposal would pass by a seven to three vote with two abstaining.

There is also a sequel to this group decision. Those who were neutral will probably not remain so, and those who were followers in the primary group will become leaders in other secondary groups, such as family units. Those who had negative feelings are likely to be more vocal than those who had positive feelings when they are among secondary groups. Other variables will doubtlessly enter the picture. For instance, there may be the possibility that one of those opinion leaders who remained neutral or nonfunctional may be influenced by a source outside the original group. The influence of a wife or an employer may serve to sway him into activity on one side or the other. The possibilities growing out of such a communication situation are almost infinite in number.

The two models shared indicate something of the potential and problem of communication. The process is often complex, but the dividends of good communication are worth the efforts put forth by pastor and people.

Communication as a process

The error most frequently found in church or business is the assumption that when a leader has spoken or written he has communicated. "The mere physical reception of a message (hearing sounds, or seeing objects) is not at all the same thing as understanding it. Understanding depends upon the *receiver's* translation. A useful axiom, then, for the organizational communicator is: only physical signals are literally transmitted, never meanings."[5] As the pastor attempts to communicate with various groups within the church, he must keep in mind certain factors within the hearers that affect the ways they receive messages. Psychologists agree that *attitudes* and *beliefs* are key indexes to human response and behavior.

According to G. W. Allport, an attitude is "a mental and neural state of readiness, organized through experience, exerting a directive or dynamic influence upon the individual's responses to all objects with which it is connected."[6] It is important for the pastor to understand that there are both dominant and latent attitudes to be found in each individual. The dominant attitude is that that is active at a given moment. The dominant attitudes of the hearer are those that control his psychological "set" or readiness to respond in a certain way when confronted with a message as a stimulus situation. The communicator hopes to appeal to the dominant attitudes in the hearer if he is to elicit favorable response. It is far more difficult to connect a proposition with the latent attitudes of the group members.[7]

Like attitudes, beliefs are learned. A belief is the acceptance of a specific proposition or set of propositions. Most beliefs are determined by social relationships. While some may be the result of personal experience, most of them are derived from the advice, testimony, and influence of others.[8]

There are some observations on attitudes and beliefs which are important for the pastor if he is to understand the challenge of communicating with individuals and groups within his church. The attitudes and beliefs of a person are colored by his frame of reference (total background), by facts as he perceives them, by his age, by opinions within his peer groups, and by the strength of his own personality.[9]

Given all of the above, it is understandable that different people get different meanings from what is said in a group meeting. No two people interpret a message in the same way. This emphasizes the pastor's need to know his people if he is to lead them effectively. To acquire such knowledge and understanding requires time, patience, perception, and the forbearance spawned by Christian love.

Another indispensable factor in the process of communication with the church is the *ethos*, the character or disposition, of the pastor. The character of the pastor and how he is perceived by his people may well be the most determinative factor in his communication with those who hear him. Every pastor will do well to mark the words of T. M. Higham, chief industrial psychologist for Rowntree and Company.

> We should remember the personal factor—the attitude of those giving and receiving communications—is the main influence in the reception of what is communicated. No matter how wooing our speech may be, it will not be very effective if no one trusts or believes us. For "though I speak with the tongues of men and of angels and have not charity [love] I am become as sounding brass or a tinkling cymbal." [10]

Communication Challenges

Communication is the major business of the church. God reaches out to man through His church as it seeks to proclaim, evangelize, and teach. Because of its commitment to Christ, the church must look closely at the vast amount of research and study that has been done in communication. The central message of the church is in hand, but the Bible will not be shared effectively in a modern age unless those devoted to its message sharpen knowledge and skills for the challenge ahead.

Fragmented society

The fragmentation of modern society is a major concern of leaders of every type. Only as people relate to each other in constructive and mutually helpful ways can a viable civilization exist. Not only does the church have a heavy responsibility in this area but all other institutions as well must play their parts.

A democratic society derives its strength from the effective functioning of the multitude of groups that it contains. Its most valuable resources are the groups of people found in its homes, communities, schools, churches, business concerns, union halls, and various branches of government. Now, more than ever before, it is recognized that these units must perform their functions well if the larger systems are to work successfully.[11]

This assertion is correct, but it must be remembered that no group is any stronger than the individuals that compose it. Without a high level of personal integrity and mutual respect, cooperation within the group becomes impossible. If suspicion, distrust, and dislike for each other becomes widespread, the group loses its power to function effectively and deterioration ensues.

The family and the church are basic to all other groups. Within these units, values are learned that are carried to all other groups in the society. If the right foundations are not built here, nothing else has much chance of success. Business, education, and government must be undergirded with strong moral bases. The fact that so many institutions are in trouble points out the serious "people problems" that are developing because of weakened home and church teaching. If society is to be saved, the home must be saved, and this will not happen until the church does its job in communicating the gospel of Jesus Christ in effective and meaningful ways.

The different worlds for a family

When the pastor looks at the congregation on Sunday morning, he may see a family of four seated on one of the pews. That pastor knows that he is looking at more than just four people. These are representatives of five different worlds. They have their world in common—home, church, recreational activities, work responsibilities, and an occasional vacation trip—but they also have their individual worlds.

If the children are teenaged or older, they have other worlds in which they also live. A college-aged son may be living away from home in a dormitory or apartment for a segment of the year. His problems and needs in the college environment are different from those of the others in his family. Peer group pressures, financial concerns, transportation, dating, academic demands, and social drives are all real factors in his college world.

A teenaged daughter who attends high school has quite a different world. She still lives at home, but her friends and social concerns are primarily elsewhere. Such a young person has numerous temptations to be involved in smoking, drinking, premarital sex, and drugs. Again, peer pressure is a major factor in her life. She wants to be accepted and finds herself facing the question "When is the price of acceptance reasonable and when is it too high?"

The mother in this family of four has her world. If she works outside the home, her world is filled with professional concerns, clothes, transportation, shopping for herself and the family, food preparation, domestic chores, and a generally hurried pace of living. If she does not work outside the home, her life is filled with family-oriented concerns, church or club work, shopping, volunteer work, social engagements, and in some cases boredom.

The father lives in a different world. He has a business or professional schedule to maintain. The pace is fast, the competition is stiff, the pressure to succeed is always present, and temptations to compromise are ever before him.

These four people live in four different worlds and share a fifth world together. When the pastor sees them in the pew, each of them has come to church seeking guidance and help from the Word of God as it is communicated by the Spirit through the man of God. How does one pastor speak to such a variety of needs with one sermon? The genius of the Scripture, the guidance of the Holy Spirit in both the speaking and the hearing processes, and the faithful purpose of both preacher and hearer make spiritual communication not only feasible but effective.

Common features in all churches

There is at the same time great variety and significant similarity among different churches. They are distinct because of their own personalities as congregations. They are similar in that all churches have many factors in common.

Most churches have different age groups represented in the congregation. There are children, youth, young adults, middle-aged adults, and elderly adults. With these differences in age there are also variations in socioeconomic status, intelligence levels, and educational backgrounds.

In each church there are families who are in trouble. It is not unlikely that of every one hundred family units in a given congregation, at least one third of them have problems serious enough to be causing real difficulty in daily living. It is an alarming fact that statistics are approaching the point where one of two marriages will end in divorce.

Wherever the church is found it is faced with the need to minister to people who are unhappy. A large number of people are not satisfied at work. The "starting over" phenomenon has, in recent years, received much attention. For each person who has made a dramatic break with the past and started on a second career there are probably hundreds who would if they dared. When a person has a feeling of dread about facing each day's work, he is susceptible to many other problems as well.

Others are overwhelmed by their own weaknesses. The great Apostle spoke for many when he said:

> For I know that in me, that is, in my flesh, dwelleth no good thing: for to will is present with me, but to do that which is good is not. For the good which I would I do not: but the evil which I would not, that I practice. (Romans 7:18–19 ASV)

There are those who live with feelings of guilt and low self esteem, those who struggle with bad habits, those who live with hostility, those who feel a sense of futility and discouragement, and those who are somewhat skeptical about the whole matter of attending church. At the same time, there are in every church some whose faith is a deep and profound experience. The pastor must minister to them all. When he preaches he must say something to each. To do so with meaning and power is his great privilege and responsibility.

Communication noise

That which distorts the communicated message is termed *noise*. In the electronic process this may be static or station override. In the person-to-person process, it may be lack of common ground of understanding, semantic differential, prejudice, cultural lag, group loyalty conflicts, or preconceived attitudes. The knowledgeable pastor recognizes that he never has a 100 percent clear channel of communication. There are always distractions and deterrents to effective communication, but the man who is motivated by a divine compulsion never quits trying. The stakes are too high and the rewards too great for him to be turned aside because of problems.

Communication problems of the receivers

In addition to those factors such as background, socioeconomic status, and educational level, the receiver may have perception problems. The person who views his own position as close to that of the pastor is likely to confuse his own thoughts with those communicated to him. This is a problem of *assimilation*. In other words, he may tend to "put words into the pastor's mouth" because he has a similar view. On the other hand, a receiver who sees himself as far removed from the pastor's position may perceive himself to be more distant than he actually is. Thus, in seeing no common ground between himself and the pastor, he may quarrel unnecessarily over perceived differences that are not, in fact, formidable at all.[12]

Audience Analysis

When the pastor is to speak to his church at worship, some subdivision of the church at work, a civic club, a denominational meeting, or any other group, he must ask himself some questions:

1. Who is to be in this audience? Are they old, young, professionals, workmen, businessmen, students, teachers, or preachers?
2. Why are these people present for this occasion? Is their attendance voluntary or dutiful?
3. What are the prevailing mores and attitudes?
4. In what ways are they homogeneous?
5. What does the audience already know about the speaker and the subject to be discussed?
6. Are they generally favorable or unfavorable to the speaker's position?
7. What degree of commitment or conviction exists?

Such questions will help the pastor to determine the level of knowledge so that he can then know what facts are essential in his presentation and what may be assumed to avoid boredom. Neither presumption nor tedium is conducive to good audience participation. The wise pastor will try to know his target audience and prepare to meet their needs.

Situation Analysis

Times and places for speaking are legion. The sensitive pastor will note that each event demands a different approach, different subject matter, and different delivery technique. As he plans to meet each situation, he will weigh the importance of four elements: the *time* of the meeting, the *place* of assembly, the prevailing *customs*, and the *purpose* of the gathering.

The time of a speaking responsibility is important in planning and preparation. A special time in the life of the speaker or the listeners may constitute the reason for the occasion. An anniversary, a building dedication, the amortization of a loan, a missionary emphasis, a regular church service, or any special event in the life of the church or community may have much to do with the preparation and delivery of the message.

The hour of the day for the meeting will have a bearing on what the pastor may choose to do. For instance, the message for the Sunday morning worship service would be structured differently from a message to be delivered at a Valentine Banquet.

The place of the meeting must be known and understood. Again, one of the best ways for a pastor to analyze this factor in the speaking situation is to ask himself or others some questions.

1. Will the meeting be indoors or outdoors?
2. In what type of community is the meeting to be held? Rural, urban, industrial, residential, poor, affluent?
3. What will the comforts of the auditors be like? Will

they be seated, standing, crowded, scattered, hot, or cold?
4. What are the lighting facilities? Will the audience face glare or gloom as they try to view the speaker?
5. What are the acoustical problems? Is there a P.A. system? Is it adjusted properly?
6. What are the speaker comforts? Is there a lectern? Will the speaker be on a platform or at floor level? How far removed from the audience is the speaker's stand?

If the pastor is to communicate effectively, any knowledge that he may gain concerning the prevailing customs of his hearers will be helpful. Each area and each church has its own ways of doing things, its own taboos, and other unique characteristics of organization and membership. To become familiar with such matters requires time and effort, but if a ministry is to be effective such knowledge is necessary.

The purpose of the gathering to which a pastor is to speak is of primary importance if the communicative act is to achieve its goal. Again, some pertinent questions are helpful in gaining an understanding of the reason for the speaking responsibility at hand.

1. Is the meeting one that is regularly held or is it a specially called affair?
2. Is the primary purpose instruction or inspiration?
3. Is entertainment a primary or secondary goal?
4. Does the meeting commemorate a special occasion?
5. Is persuasion expected or desirable?
6. What kind of audience response is desired?

With the answers to such questions the pastor may gain a good assessment of the situation at hand. The process of communication is largely dependent on the preparation of the communicator and the respondents, and its result is much more likely to be satisfactory if situation analysis has been a part of that preparation.

Persuasion as a Tool

There has been a strong aversion to the popularly held concept of persuasion among many modern pastors. Many have confused persuasion, which can be legitimate, with manipulation, which is not a technique worthy of the Christian ministry. As noted earlier, in the opinion of this writer the major difference in the two comes at the point of motivation. If the pastor's reasons are self-serving in any way, persuasion may result in manipulation. If his goals are Christ centered, legitimate persuasion that seeks the best interest of the respondent is valid. In fact, the definition of persuasive communication sounds very similar to some definitions of preaching. "In order to be persuasive in nature, a communication situation must involve a conscious attempt by one individual to change the behavior of another individual or group of individuals through the transmission of some message."[13] John A. Broadus, in evaluating the preaching of Jesus, pointed out the results and nature of this sort of preaching.

> Preaching in the meaning and purpose of Jesus included all elements calculated to stir the mind in all its functions and lead men to see, to feel, to evaluate, and to make moral decisions. Thus our Lord preached. And for their mission after him he bequeathed to his apostles the same strategy.[14]

The purpose of preaching incorporates a strong element of persuasion. The preacher is trying to motivate men to action in godly living. As the pastor employs persuasion he must be ever mindful of those elements which make it effective. The credibility of the source, organization of argument, group relationships, and individual personality traits of both the sender and receiver are all vital to the process of persuasion.[15] The same factors, plus high spiritual motivation and leadership, are found in effective preaching and pastoral leadership in the church.

The pastor is a leader, not an enforcer. His task is to convince men of their need for a better life in Jesus Christ. His skills in persuasion coupled with his dependence on the Holy Spirit make that task feasible.

The Unfinished Message in Church Communication

Until the end of the age the pastor and the community of believers are charged with the responsibility to communicate the good news of Jesus Christ. In order to do this job the church must be where the people are, and it must maintain the ability to relate the Word of God to the needs of men. Years ago this writer found a slogan for a church sign. "The Bible as it is for men as they are" spoke well of the message and target audience of church communications. "Preaching that is overly impressed with culture becomes weak and despairing and therefore incurs the scorn of the world. Preaching that is underimpressed with culture becomes arrogant and pharisaical, remote and cultic, and therefore incurs the hatred of the world."[16] The unfinished message in church communication is that those in Christ reach out in love to those in the world to share the good news of Jesus with all who will hear and respond.

CHAPTER IV

A Pastorate
from Start to Finish

There is an old adage which says, "If you would know about the success or failure of a man, look to his beginnings." For one to be successful as the pastor of a church he must begin well, proceed with care and compassion, and terminate with Christian grace. The purpose of this chapter is to give suggestions which will prove useful in the first few months—as well as the following years—of work with the Lord's people in a local church.

Qualifications for the Pastorate

In addition to those spiritual qualifications mentioned in Chapter I, the man who aspires to the work of a pastor must have a good background in several areas.

A good education

The congregation needs an educated ministry to meet its varied challenges. The ministerial student and practitioner must be equipped to meet people at many levels of education and culture, and, if he is to command the respect necessary for effective leadership, he must be well trained. The accumulation of degrees does not always mean that the holder is well educated. There is an essential difference in receiving a degree and an education. The former may be impressive on an office wall, but the latter is required if ministry is to be performed well in the complexity of human relationships in the pastorate.

The pastor must also recognize that the completion of seminary does not terminate his education. Life is a learning experience within itself. In formal training one learns how to find answers, and in life the process of discovery and assimilation continues. Education in the ministry is an ongoing process. The world is changing rapidly, and the pastor must be knowledgeable about what is happening in human lives if he is to apply God's message to their needs.

A good work record

The churches are looking for excellence in leadership. Pastor search committees are not only checking educational credentials, but they are also investigating each man's "track record." Where he has been and what he has done are very important matters when they are trying to determine his ability to lead their church.

Most church leaders recognize that the pastor has no immediate supervision to check on whether he works and how he works. Many people will depend on his leadership, but there is no one but God to guide him. He, of all people, must be a "self-starter." His call demands of him his best at all times, and his disposition must be such as will meet that demand.

Those with committee responsibility are likely to check with previous churches where a man has served. They will contact former deacons, staff members, and other leaders to see if the pastor practiced the same type of commitment that he preached. They know that men do not change greatly in this regard. The patterns of work in the past are likely to carry forward in another church community.

One of the chief sins attributed to ministers by laymen is that of laziness. If he wants to be lazy a pastor can find many opportunities to do less than he is really able to do. People in the churches who spend long hours in secular jobs and then *give* additional time to the work of the church do not appreciate or respect a pastor who is giving less than his best effort in the ministry. Each minister must be ever mindful of the fact that he is establishing records today for tomorrow's viewing. He cannot expect to become the master of many things without first proving himself faithful in a few things.

A good credit record

Some churches have been embarrassed to find out that their pastor does not pay his debts. No committee should seriously think of recommending a man to the church without running a credit check. The ministry of the church in its community is closely related to the attitudes and activities of its pastor. In the business world he is regarded as the church's representative, and every move is open to scrutiny. When he fails to meet his obligations, the influence of his congregation begins to suffer.

In more than one church there have been serious problems of fellowship at this point. Pastors have become so overloaded with financial problems that the church leadership has found it necessary to involve the church and its resources in order to prevent further damage to the organization's position in the community. When such situations reach this critical stage, division of opinion occurs among the people, and the work begins to suffer because of the indiscretion of the pastor.

One pastor became so heavily involved with personal debts that the creditors began contacting the lay leadership of the church in an effort to collect. Salary raises proved insufficient to meet the needs, and church intervention seemed necessary to prevent further loss of reputation in the community. Sharp dissension ensued in the membership as to whether the church was obligated legally or morally to take such steps. Humiliating and damaging investigations of the pastor's personal business and acrimonious discussion in church conferences finally resulted in the withdrawal of many families from the congregation and the pastor's resignation under pressure.

No church should ever be put through such an ordeal because of the carelessness of a pastor. To insure his own credibility at this point a minister must use great caution. In days of high inflation, spiraling automobile expenses, and easy credit, financial problems can reach the critical stage quickly. The man of God must be constantly aware of income versus expenses if he is to survive and remain a credible influence for his Lord.

A good attitude

Why is a man in the ministry? Most men are in the ministry because of a deep sense of call and a real desire to help people. When the pay is low and the demands are high, prayerful attention must be given to attitude. No matter how many hours he works, the pastor is never "caught up." There are always people who must be visited, sermons to prepare, administrative work to be done, and countless other needs to be met. The constant pressure of living in a "glass house" puts a strain on the minister and his family. When daily problems begin to mount and weariness with the work is starting to be felt, the wise pastor will once again return to the strength available to him in the Lord and in His Word. Paul gave young Timothy excellent counsel when he wrote:

> For to this end we labor and strive, because we have our hope set on the living God, who is the Savior of all men, specially of them that believe. These things command and teach. Let no man despise thy youth; but be thou an ensample to them that believe, in word, in manner of life, in love, in faith, in purity. Till I come, give heed to reading, to exhortation, to teaching. Neglect not the gift that is in thee, which was given thee by prophecy, with the laying on of the hands of the presbytery. Be diligent in these things; give thyself wholly to them; that thy progress may be manifest unto all. Take heed to thyself and to thy teaching. Continue in these things; for in so doing thou shalt both save thyself and them that hear thee. (1 Timothy 4 : 10–16 ASV)

In saying "take heed to thyself," Paul was pointing out that the pastor must take hold upon himself and to keep on paying attention to his own spirit and attitude toward the ministry. There is nothing that saps a man's devotion and destroys his enthusiasm any more than failing to appropriate God's encouragement and inspiration for himself. The preacher is so busy presenting God's Word to other people that he may begin to regard it as his stock in trade and forget to apply it to himself. If one's attitude is to be good, he must constantly return to the Lord for the refreshing presence of the Spirit.

Some ministers fail to do this, and self-pity sets in. There was a time in this writer's life when the pastorate became a burden. There was always more to do than could be done, and time off from church responsibility was almost nonexistent. His policy was to be available when needed, and the implementation of that self-imposed rule meant that he kept his secretary informed of his whereabouts at all times. After more than twenty years of this type of living, in which he was never completely out of touch with his office, he left the pastorate to teach in the seminary. Not many months after that he and his family were leaving campus for a Christmas vacation trip when he realized that he had not given anyone his itinerary.

Then the ego-shattering thought came: "Who cares where you're going?" For the first time in more than two decades there was no likelihood of his being needed, and he missed the feeling of being close to his own church people.

If attitude is good, the work of the pastor is more meaningful and more pleasant. When he enjoys his relationships, his efforts are more effective. Thus, the pastor's attitude is one of his most important qualifications.

Availability for the Pastorate

How is a minister to determine where God wants him to serve? This is no easy question, and its answer frequently involves soul-searching. Even the strongest men have some personal desires and inclinations toward decision making on a purely human level. That which appears logical and reasonable to man may not be the will of God.

> And they went through the region of Phrygia and Galatia, *having been forbidden* of the Holy Spirit to speak the word in Asia; and when they were come over against Mysia, they assayed to go into Bithynia; and the Spirit of Jesus *suffered them not* . . . (Acts 16:6–7 ASV)

A part of his call leads one to believe that God has a place of service for the man who is committed to His will. No man can be in more than one place at a time, and his effectiveness depends upon his being in the right place at the right time. For this reason many preachers pray that God will open only those doors through which He wants them to walk and close all others. With this degree of dedication and a sincere verbalization of it in prayer, the servant of God will not be found running ahead of the Spirit's leadership.

In the process of His leadership God uses human instrumentalities. An awareness of this should cause a young minister to make all the friends possible throughout his life. Preachers are great friends to have, and they can play an important role when they are led by the Holy Spirit to recommend a fellow pastor to a church. In light of this fact, a beginner's college and seminary friendships can be important to his ministry for years to come.

Additionally, the pastor's friendship with laymen can be helpful in his finding the place where he is to serve. In some cases the recommendation of a layman may carry as much weight as that of a fellow minister. In the final analysis, however, the pastor is his own best recommendation. Churches are looking for superior people as leaders. The man who does a good job where he is and remains open and available to the Lord will not lack for opportunities.

Dealing with the Pastor Search (Pulpit) Committee

When a pastor search committee shows interest in a preacher, there are some basic guidelines he should follow. First, he should *preach and behave normally*. The committee is interested in knowing the real man. To preach a "sugar stick" sermon for such an occasion may give a false impression. If a committee visits a pastor's church to hear him preach, he should not change his sermon for their benefit. His week-by-week, normal ministry is what interests them most because this is what he will do when and if he is called to their church. In fact, to guard against being overly impressed by one strong sermon many committees visit a man's church more than one time before interviewing him. As additional insurance against initial false impressions, many committees now invite a prospective pastor for a weekend revival in which he preaches several times instead of one "trial sermon." There is little to gain and much to be lost if one tries to be anything but himself under such circumstances.

Be gracious without being condescending or overly anxious. If the committee is considering a pastor, it is honoring him. Even if the church is much smaller than his present church and he has no real interest, he should be as gracious and kind as possible. On the other hand, if the church is a greater and more challenging field of service and the pastor is vitally interested, he should be gracious without appearing overly anxious.

Be open and honest. When a preacher is being interviewed, he may expect a variety of questions. A committee may ask about everything from his view on the inspiration of the Scriptures to the make, model, and color of his automobile. All of this is done to enable them to get a picture of the total man. They need to know about such things as his doctrinal position, past experience, administrative skills, priorities in ministry, personal work habits, family size and relationships, wife's attitude toward ministry, and interests in activities additional to church work. The committee may already have the answers to some of the questions, but verification from an open and honest man is always helpful.

Listen attentively and ask questions. This is a two-way street. The prospective pastor needs to know all he can about the church under consideration. What type of church is this? What do they need in a pastor? Do their needs and desires fit his disposition and qualifications? What are their priorities? What are their ideas on church programming? What resources—both human and material—are available for the work of the church?

No pastor wants to leave a good church where he has established himself in a leadership role to go to another place where he may be like the proverbial square peg in a round hole. The only way to prevent this is to listen carefully, ask the right questions and prayerfully evaluate the information in hand.

Ask for printed information. A well-prepared committee will usually have a file on the church. The most complete such file that this writer has seen was prepared by the pastor search committee of the Champion Forest Baptist Church in Houston, Texas, while he was interim pastor for that congregation. The folder included the following: a history of the church; characteristics of the congregation; profile of the community; population in close proximity; graphs on contributions, enrollment, and attendance; average weekly and average annual Sunday school attendance; financial program data; information and diagrams of physical plant; information on all church organizations; biographical sketches of church staff members and pulpit committee members; and informational references. Not all groups will be so thoroughly prepared, but most will have enough written material to give the prospective pastor a reasonable picture of the situation.

Deal with ministry—not money. The pastor who talks with a pastor search committee should let it be known that his first concern is the ministry to be performed and not the financial package to be offered. Can he provide the type of leadership needed? If the committee senses that the candidate is concerned first about the church and its needs, the matter of money is usually brought up at the proper time. Many times the printed material will give sufficient information for preliminary talks. To be sure, a time must come for a complete understanding on salary and benefits, but the early stages of conversation are hardly the occasion.

Visits to a Prospective Field of Service

What is expected of a pastor when he is invited to visit a church in view of a call? How he and his wife (who should accompany him) conduct themselves is of utmost importance both to themselves and to the church.

Accept with good grace whatever provisions are made for personal comfort. The church may provide hotel accommodations, or they may provide a room in a private home. Whether the provision is lavish or modest it is likely that it is the best that can be afforded and should be appreciated accordingly.

Be gracious and courteous at all times. The situation will be new and different, and both the preacher and the people will have a feeling of being on trial with each other. Forbearance, understanding, and courtesy are in order. Getting acquainted will be made easier when the pastor and his wife do their best to make others feel at ease.

Pay attention to good etiquette. In most cases the minister and his wife will be invited to dine with individuals or groups from the church. The fact that both are well informed about matters of etiquette helps all to be more comfortable. This may not sound like a matter of great importance, but no church wants a pastor who will be a source of embarrassment because he does not know simple social graces.

When invited to preach, *pray for the strength to preach normally and forcefully.* The "trial sermon" has been rightly labelled. It is a trial! The preacher should recognize the importance of doing well, but this may become his greatest problem. He may become so tense that he is not able to do as well as he ordinarily would, or he may prepare to the point that he preaches beyond his normal abilities. In the former case, he sells himself short, and in the latter he may oversell himself to the point that he is unable to maintain his own pace in preaching. The best approach is to seek the presence of God through prayer and preach as normally as possible under the circumstances. In the judgment of this writer, the current trend of a weekend of services, in which more than a single preaching opportunity is afforded, is a good thing and should be encouraged.

During the exploratory visit, *meet with church groups as requested.* The pastor search committee frequently will seek the opinions of other church leaders concerning a prospective pastor. They may have set several meetings with different representative groups to gain wider exposure for the preacher. Such meetings should be approached with the same candor as those meetings already held with the committee. Only as the minister and people get acquainted are they able to make the right decisions about each other.

If the committee or other groups do not initiate such "get acquainted" sessions, the prospective pastor should await their moves in such a direction. It would be presumptive for the minister to ask for such meetings.

Decide on availability before allowing a vote by the church. If the committee declares that it is ready to recommend a pastor for a vote by the congregation, it has taken a big step. The prospective pastor should give his feelings about acceptance before a vote is taken. Damage to both parties can take place if a church is asked to vote to call, and the pastor involved declines to accept. When the vote is taken the full count should be shared with the pastor. Not all churches give a unanimous vote to a minister. If there is opposition, the minister should know its nature and proportions in order to make his final decision. If the vote is strongly favorable and he accepts, the minister should look forward to years of service in his new church.

The Task Well Begun

When a church has extended a call and a pastor accepts and begins his work, the first few months are extremely important. A man can be the preacher in a church his first Sunday on the field, but it takes time to become the pastor in the full sense of that term. Only as the people come to know, love, and respect their minister do they regard him as a real pastor. To allow this to happen, the man of God in a new church must make wise decisions and show himself stable and trustworthy in the early months of his ministry.

The new minister must let it be known that he intends to shepherd *all* of the flock. When the people understand that the preacher loves all the people in the church, they begin to respond with love toward him. All parts of the body of Christ are important, and none should be relegated to places of insignificance. True, there will be some who are more easily loved than others, but all must have a place in the heart of a true pastor. As one pastor has said, "In the church everybody has to be somebody or soon nobody is anybody." No church fellowship is healthy when favoritism is practiced. "My brethren, hold not the faith of our Lord Jesus Christ, the Lord of Glory, with respect of persons. . . . if ye fulfill the royal law, according to the scripture, thou shalt love thy neighbor as thyself, ye do well: but if ye have respect of persons, ye commit sin, being convicted by the law as transgressors" (James 2:1, 8–9 ASV). Let the new pastor quickly recognize his responsibility to uphold the dignity and value of each individual regardless of his circumstances.

Take time to learn as much about the church as possible. One cannot understand the present without some knowledge of the past. A wise investment of time in the early months of a pastorate is a reading of all available records of the church. The history of the church, minutes of business meetings for several years, financial reports, attendance records, and any other written information can provide helpful insights into the life of the church in recent years. Sometimes what appears between the lines may be as important as what is written on the lines. The frequent appearance of certain names can tell more than the written record itself. The fact that records are available or unavailable may reveal much about the way business and programming have been conducted.

Another interesting and valuable source of information is the legal document file of the church. Deeds, mortgages, bond contracts, loan agreements, property easements, use permits, zoning regulations, paving liens, and other such documents can help the new pastor see where the church stands in its business life. This writer found one church that had two first mortgages outstanding on the same property and an incorrectly written bond contract that protected no one. In another community the church building was standing on property that was owned by a homeowner, and his home was located on land owned by the church. In both cases legal help was secured and the problems were rectified with no great harm being done. Unfortunately, not all such problems are so readily worked out. Some churches have been stymied in building plans for years because of an ancient "reversion clause" in a deed. Such a clause states that if the land ever ceases to be used for church purposes, it must revert to the donor or his estate. To the dismay of more than one pastor plans have been shelved for years until such problems could be resolved. The reading of existing legal papers helps the pastor in his orientation for future programming.

The "operating documents" of a church are its constitution, statements of policy and rules. The wise pastor will look through the church files and find such documents as early as possible. There may be real help in papers accepted by the congregation years before, even though they may not have been well implemented since their adoption. One pastor found the financial affairs of a church in a chaotic and deteriorating condition. Most of the financial authority was in the hands of one man; the church knew little about its business. General dissatisfaction was being expressed among the members. The new pastor was reading through the files of the church during his first week on the field and found a statement of financial policy. The document had been well prepared by a previous pastor several years before and had been officially adopted by the church. This paper was duplicated and presented to the deacons and to the church to be reaffirmed and implemented. In a matter of weeks a newly elected finance committee was at work and the problems were on the way toward solution. The key to the whole matter had been tucked away in a file drawer in the church office for years, but no one knew it was there. There is an old saying that "Everybody's business is nobody's business." This is frequently true in a church. A pastor must be sure that everybody's business is his business and care for it accordingly.

Before leaving this matter a word of caution is in order. Let the new pastor move judiciously if alterations are needed in the church's operating documents. Each document has a history, and even though it may not have been used recently, changing it can produce strong emotions.

Visit all families in the membership during the first year if possible. There is no substitute for pastoral visitation at any period in one's ministry, but it is indispensable in the getting-acquainted stage. A friendly call in the home of a church family will tell the new pastor much about that segment of his congregation. He is able to associate names and faces, put parents and children together in his mind, and determine the various relationships between families in the church.

During this process of visiting the pastor should spend much of his time looking and listening and a minimum of it talking. It is absolutely amazing to see how people respond to a man who will listen. Very few problems arise when one listens well to others before beginning to plan church programs that are designed to give guidance to human lives.

Another argument for pastoral visitation in each home is that people come to an early appreciation of a man who has a personal touch to his ministry. In an age of mass depersonalization people are hungry for the warmth and friendliness of a church leader who cares for them as individuals.

Keep an open mind. In the early stages of his relationship with a church the preacher has dealt primarily with the pastor search committee and other leadership groups. As he begins to visit in homes and other places where people are to be found, the new pastor comes into contact with a broader segment of the church. There are those of the fellowship yet unheard, and their input can be tremendously valuable.

If the pastor is to shepherd the flock effectively, he must learn all points of view. The old and the young, the active and the inactive, the educated and the uneducated, the affluent and the poor—all will have their peculiar needs and their private opinions. In some communities those who are long-term residents and those who are relative newcomers will constitute special needs for pastoral leadership in a ministry of accommodation and reconciliation. The wise leader will respect age with its experience and wisdom and cultivate youth with its energy and enthusiasm. If there are divisions between groups within the church, the pastor should see himself as an influence to bring the people together. This can be done by a man who takes the time to understand who his people are in the early months of his ministry.

Move cautiously in proposing major changes. The pastor must do his homework as he anticipates change in the church. Most churches are willing to follow the leadership of a man who really understands local needs and who knows what he is doing. Many preachers have gotten into trouble because they tried to go too far too fast.

As a new seminary graduate this writer was called to a small-town pastorate in Alabama. No one could have had a more pleasant relationship with such a loving congregation. After several delightful months of getting acquainted with the congregation, he drew up a three-phased program of development and renovation. Attention was given to every detail that he thought might be questioned. Several key opinion leaders were contacted as sounding boards and everything looked good. When the detailed plans were presented to the deacons, an elderly church treasurer inquired about how the projects were to be financed. The church had some of the money in reserve and was free of debt. The local bank had assured the pastor that the remaining funds could be borrowed at a favorable rate of interest. On the surface the pastor could see no problem, but the tone of the ensuing discussion told him there was a problem. He did not press for a decision in that meeting but asked the group to give the program some prayerful thought until the following month. He sensed that there was a problem that he had not discovered. More homework was required.

The following week the pastor visited the church treasurer in his office. The man was conservative but not against progress. When asked for his counsel on the matter at hand the deacon quickly suggested that the program be undertaken using available funds plus all that could be borrowed using the church-owned pastor's home for collateral. If this were not sufficient, his suggestion was to cease work on the last phase until the loan could be reduced enough to allow additional borrowing. He was willing to proceed on that basis but totally unwilling to place a mortgage on the church building. So firm was he in his opinion—an opinion shared by most of the elderly church members—that the pastor asked for his reasons. As he suspected there was some history involved.

During the Great Depression the church owed money on a new building that had been built in the late 1920s. While the town water system was under repair and water pressure was low, the church building caught fire one Sunday morning. All the people escaped to safety, but were forced to watch helplessly while the entire building was consumed by the flames. Existing insurance was not sufficient to satisfy the mortgage, so a discouraged congregation met in the school while the remainder of the mortgage was paid and a fund was started to rebuild. Great hardship and sacrifice faced the church members for several years, but they paid the debt and built a new building free of debt during the hardest years of the Depression. The new building was dedicated with a solemn promise that their church building would never again be mortgaged.

With this bit of very emotional history the pastor saw the reasons for the concern of the elderly church treasurer. The time schedule was modified, financing within acceptable limits was arranged, and the church moved forward harmoniously. When reasonable men take time to understand each other's reasons, they can usually work together, but understanding takes time and effort.

When someone differs in opinion, don't make it a personal matter. Preachers need to learn that those who disagree at times are not necessarily enemies. Problems arise because people fail to distinguish between principles and methods. Principles are nonnegotiable; a pastor cannot compromise on matters of *real* principle. Methods and procedures are negotiable. How and when things are to be done can be worked out amicably if the pastor and his people cooperate.

Necessities for Staying and Being Happy

Studies have shown that there is a great unrest and high mobility among ministers. Why are preachers changing churches each one and a half to two years? Some of these changes may be attempts to "climb," but many of them are due to a feeling of frustration and a desire to find a new beginning. There are some things that a pastor needs to consider if he wants to be able to be happy and remain in one church long enough to build a ministry with his people.

The pastor in the public eye

The preacher lives in a glass house. He is always before the public, and his every move is subject to scrutiny and criticism. *His option is not whether he will be criticized but by whom and for what.* Criticism of some type is a fact of life for the minister. Some of it hurts, some of it helps; he should not invite it but should be aware of it without letting it destroy him. The mature pastor must be critical of himself, admit his mistakes, and be able to laugh at himself occasionally if he is to survive emotionally.

Anything that moves creates some friction. When the friction is controlled and worthwhile in its purpose, it can be endured. There has never been a man of accomplishment in any area of life who did not have his critics. It is preferable to be criticized for being helpful and constructive in one's ministry instead of being criticized for being weak and ineffective.

The pastor who tries to grow with his people will be able to keep criticism within manageable limits. The pastor who is not growing in his ministry will not be happy in any church. He should remember that what he is to be in the future he is now becoming.

The pastor's visitation ministry

The pastor must visit if he is to do his job properly. Many different types of visitation demand his time and attention, and none should be totally neglected. In addition to initial "get acquainted" visits in each home and evangelistic visitation mentioned earlier, the pastor must maintain a schedule which will allow him to meet special needs. The shut-in ministry varies from church to church but is a real need in almost all communities. Additionally, the pastor must call in homes to comfort, to encourage, to solve problems within the church, to counsel, to reach unaffiliated people and dropouts, and to enlist workers for the church.

Leadership of visitation by the members is also a function of the minister. The people must be taught by encouragement and example to move out into the community where real human needs are to be found. There needs to be an active program of visitation for the entire church led and supported by the pastor. A regular time each week should be established when an organized effort will be put forth by pastor-trained visitors to reach the lost and the unenlisted.

In order to have a program of visitation there must be training opportunities, a good file of prospect cards, and a dedicated nucleus of workers. The time and methods to be used in making assignments will vary, but the pastor must make a disciplined effort to visit and to lead his people in this important phase of God's work. Good outreach efforts don't just happen; they are the result of hard work by people who care about other people.

The hospital ministry

The pastor is important to those who are ill. Their sense of need for God is probably deeper during a hospital confinement than at any other time, and the pastor can help them to meet this need through his ministry of prayer and encouragement. The office that the pastor holds seems to take on added significance at such times. For this reason the writer did most of his church's hospital visiting when in the pastorate. Although staff members were willing and capable, people appreciated the pastor's presence when they were sick.

Many good books have been written on this subject, so a brief list of some "Dos and Don'ts" for the pastor's hospital visitation ministry should be sufficient.

Don't awaken a patient who is asleep. Leave a card.

Don't enter a room with a "no visitors" sign without checking with a nurse.

Don't enter a room if the patient's physician is present.

Don't come into physical contact with a patient's bed.

Don't make a patient who has had surgery laugh.

Don't criticize any member of the medical team.

Don't enter *any* room on a psychiatric wing without checking with the nurse's station.

Do remember that the frequency of visits should be determined by the case and its needs.

Do stay in touch with critical cases.

Do have prayer with each patient when feasible.

Do try to calm and comfort those who are ill.

Do make friends with the medical team by showing sensitivity to and appreciation for what they are doing for the patient.

Do be pleasant, brief, helpful, and optimistic.

Do pay attention to the needs of the family of the ill person and help when needed.

The pastor as a counselor

Unless he has special training, a pastor is to counseling about what a general practitioner is to medicine. He will be faced with many counseling situations and should be able to deal with many in competent fashion, but there will be others beyond his expertise. Each pastor must recognize his own limitations and not hesitate to refer when the case dictates. Most pastors have some exposure to course work in this field in seminary, and since the subject is handled in other books, this work will offer only a word of caution to young pastors.

Some pastors have gotten into difficult circumstances because of their own indiscretions with counseling. This part of his work should be done by appointment and preferably at the church office during hours when others are nearby. The pastor should be aware of chronic cases and use good judgment in protecting himself as well as the persons counseled from gossip and criticism.

When a new pastor moves into a community, he should equip himself with some basic information about facilities and professional assistance available. He should know where the local mental health center is and should have the names of some *Christian* psychologists and psychiatrists. If there are private counseling centers nearby, the pastor should acquaint himself with these in case they are needed for later referrals. In no case should a pastor overextend himself in counseling. It is far better to refer to professionals skilled in the field than to risk the emotional health of his people.

Leaving a Pastorate with Grace

After a pastor has spent several years with a congregation, leaving to accept another position can be a painful experience. The way in which a ministry is terminated is important both to the man and the people. A pastor should have worked to make sure the church is in better condition than when he found it. In the process of moving he should be careful not to destroy the fruits of his labors.

When he has been contacted by another church, the minister should be discreet in his negotiations. He should be careful not to upset his people unnecessarily or prematurely. When the call to another place is in hand and he has decided to accept, he should discuss plans to resign with the deacons a short time in advance. He should write out a gracious letter of resignation and read it to the church at the conclusion of an evening service. In this letter he should be as Christlike as he has taught the people to be. Under no condition should he take parting shots at people or conditions he does not like.

Two weeks notice is normal in most churches. The advance notice of leaving should never be more than a month. If the pastor lives in a home owned by the church, he should vacate the home immediately upon termination of his service with the church. Extra care should be taken to make sure that all church-owned properties are properly accounted for and left in the hands of a responsible church leader such as the chairman of the deacons. The pastor's office and home should be left clean and in good repair for the next occupant.

The pastor and his family should be gracious and appreciative for any farewell functions provided by the people. If he has served well, he and his family will be greatly loved by most of the church, and he will be missed. Christian love developed over a period of years does not terminate with a letter of resignation, and this is to be remembered. A good pastor will earn the affection of a people, and they will be reluctant to see him go.

After leaving a church a pastor should be careful about returning. There may be some special cases in which it would be impolite not to return, but visits should be kept to a minimum. If he must return, it should be with the knowledge and approval of the new pastor. When this is necessary he should take pains to support his successor in every way possible and stedfastly refuse to exercise any voice in the current affairs of the church.

The faithful pastor should be able to say to his church in leaving, "In all things I gave you an example, that so laboring ye ought to help the weak, and to remember the words of the Lord Jesus, that he himself said, It is more blessed to give than to receive" (Acts 20:35 ASV).

CHAPTER V

The Need for Pastoral Preaching

Is there a real need for preaching and preachers? Many have contended that the preaching of the gospel is out of date and superfluous in a technological age. What impact can a local pastor, preaching to the same congregation every Sunday, have? Is the pastor-preacher an anachronism in modern society? Why should he continue his labors, though sometimes discouraging, with a limited group in an era of mass communications? These are hard questions asked about the pastor and, at times, they are asked by the pastor about himself.

With his great variety of duties the pastor faces some definite limitations. He will not have the time to become a professional theologian and make a mark upon the religious world by some special insight or profound work in print. Nor will he be able to devote endless hours to textual criticism in an effort to achieve a name for himself through scholarship. If he recognizes the true source of human problems, he cannot give his life to the illusive dream that human ills can be cured by education, good jobs, and homes in middle-class, suburban neighborhoods. As the pastor faces life where he finds it, he soon discovers that people are hurting and need help wherever they are found, and the kind of help they need requires the personal attention of someone who knows them and who cares.

Constant Needs in Changing Circumstances

This writer has been privileged to serve in the poorest of rural communities and in the most affluent suburban neighborhoods. The economic and social conditions were different, but the basic needs were the same.

Time, circumstances, frugality, hard work, good fortune, a reasonable degree of prosperity, and education may combine to keep people out of the slums, but affluence does not always keep the slums out of the people. People may not be concerned about their next meal, but this does not mean they have no concerns. Some do not live in the confusion of a ghetto, but they do live in confusion. Need in a man's life is not determined by the condition of his stomach alone; emptiness describes more than the digestive system. Housing may be adequate or even luxurious while the home is falling apart. Income may be above average and morals still below par. The minister who watches human life and behavior is not long in realizing that destitution describes more than the condition of one's bank account or kitchen pantry. Neither place, prestige, nor property will still the pastor's jangling telephone or the anxious voices seeking help of any kind from someone who cares enough to listen.

Problems are real and those who live with them need a pastor. Human nature is basically the same wherever and whenever it is found. Ambition is just as real for the man in a stylish business suit as it was for Lot as he pitched his tent toward Sodom. Bitterness can be found in the life of an unwed mother today just as it was found in the heart of

Hagar by the spring on the way to Shur. Fear is real whether it be found in the heart of a senior citizen in a modern city or in the mind of Elijah as he fled from the wrath of Jezebel. Hatred can blight the soul of an Arab refugee in this century just as it did the heart of a Jew as he looked at the Samaritan of the first century. Jealousy impedes growth in the life of a minister now in the same way that it darkened the minds of the twelve as they argued over who was to be first in the kingdom. Loneliness is just as real to a young widow of the Vietnamese war as it was to Ruth in the fields of Boaz. Lust can destroy happiness for the college student at a pot party in the same way it did for David as he looked upon Bathsheba. Sickness is a stark reality for the cancer victim in the surgical suite just as it was for Naaman on the muddy banks of the Jordan. Futility can overcome whether one be in a ghetto without hope or a penthouse without purpose. With all the weaknesses, temptations, and personal trials of living, people are in need of spiritual help no matter where they live or when they come upon the scene.

As he faces his preaching ministry, the pastor must not be discouraged by some of the common fallacies of the age. First is a mistaken idea that human nature cannot be changed. If this were true, there would be little point in preaching at all. God can change lives, and He does so through the preaching of His word. Paul said, "For seeing that in the wisdom of God the world through its wisdom knew not God, it was God's good pleasure through the foolishness of the preaching [literally 'the thing preached'] to save them that believe" (1 Corinthians 1:21 ASV). Second is the fallacy that people can change people. The pastor alone can save no one, but he is the emissary of Him who can make all things new. Realizing this, he is able to proclaim, "And my speech and my preaching were not in persuasive words of wisdom, but in demonstration of the

Spirit and of power: that your faith should not stand in the wisdom of men, but in the power of God" (I Corinthians 2:4–5 ASV)

Third is the mistake of believing that the pastor must solve all the problems or answer all the questions. It isn't the problem or the province of the pastor to justify human suffering or meet all needs by means of his own wisdom or energy. He is there to preach not himself but Christ Jesus as the Lord. The message must be compassionate, inclusive, and delivered from a concerned and convicted heart. His every effort must be directed toward bringing men out of themselves and into the merciful presence of a loving God.

Orientation for Effective Pastoral Preaching

Pastoral preaching requires a man to begin where he is with people as they are and share the Word of God in the strength of the Spirit to help them to become what they can be. The attitude of the pastor toward this task controls much of what can be accomplished in all phases of his ministry. There is no substitute to be found for a concerned pastor who pays the price to preach effectively.

Preaching is the catalyst that brings all of the pastor's knowledge and skills into focus on the needs of the people. His theology may be correct, his ethics above question, and his zeal unflagging, but if he does not come across well from the pulpit, much of the impact of his ministry is lost. The pastor has an opportunity that no one else has in modern life. People leave off what they are doing, come to the church, pray for the speaker, and dedicate a block of their time to listening to what he has to say. The responsibility is awesome. The pastor who preaches a thirty-minute sermon to two hundred people has consumed one hundred man-hours of time. When this happens two or three times per week with the same congregation, the man of God has commanded a great deal of time and attention to what he has to say.

For the pastor to do his job well on Sunday he must touch the lives of his people during the week. Real preaching comes from a love for God's Book and a deep concern for His people. To be a student of the Scripture is not enough; the minister must be a student of human nature as well. When he has been with the people in their times of need, a pastor has little problem in getting their attention in the time of his exhortation.

The real power in pastoral preaching does not come from the man alone, but by the presence of the Holy Spirit in his life and message. Effective preaching is not to be realized in mere human knowledge and technique. God's Spirit must garner all of the man's abilities and experience and provide guidance in their use. He must lead in the selection of passages of Scripture, in giving insight and discernment, in the organization of ideas and illustrative materials, and in providing boldness in delivery.

While He works with the messenger, the Holy Spirit also works with the congregation as He unifies and creates attention, convicts of sin, righteousness, and judgment, and plants the Word in mind and memory in such ways as to make it productive. The pastor should never entertain the idea that he stands alone in the pulpit. The One who has called him forth and placed him in the ministry is always ready to bless and encourage.

Needs and Problems to Be Addressed in Pastoral Preaching

The preaching of the pastor must correspond to the needs and potential of the church. It should be of such quality that the church will be built through the pulpit ministry of its shepherd. The influence of the church in its community will not likely be stronger than its pulpit. If the challenge is to be met the sermons must be Bible based, life oriented, and Christ centered. The pastor will speak to his people in times of moral breakdown, political and economic stress, doctrinal confusion, lethargic efforts in missions and evangelism, difficulty in the fellowship, domestic crises, and problems among the youth. Because churches are made up of people he will find "the deeds of the flesh which are: immorality, impurity, sensuality, idolatry, sorcery, enmities, strife, jealousy, outbursts of anger, disputes, dissensions, factions, envyings, drunkenness, carousing, and things like these" (Galatians 5:19-21a NASV). Because the pastor wishes something better for his flock, he will encourage the fruit of the Spirit which is "love, joy, peace, patience, kindness, goodness, faithfulness, gentleness, and self-control" (Galatians 5:22-23a NASV). To take human weakness in one hand and divine power in the other and bring them together through a strong pulpit ministry is the consuming passion of a faithful pastor.

Questions to Be Answered through Preaching

Problems and discouragements in life bring an unceasing stream of questions to the minister from his congregation. What is life? Why live? Why should I try to live for God? Is there really life after death? Am I worth anything? Does God care about what I do? How can I know His will and be sure about it? Why does this happen to me? Why have a church? Why should I go to church? The questions come thick and fast from every corner of life. The answers are not quick and easy, nor are they even possible apart from the Bible.

As he tries to answer these and many other pressing

questions, the pastor is under instructions from God. "Tend the flock of God which is among you, exercising the oversight, not of constraint, but willingly, according to the will of God; nor yet for filthy lucre, but of a ready mind" (1 Peter 5:2 NASV). To fulfill this charge and to bring relevant scriptural answers to life's questions demands of the pastor unceasing prayer and a rigid discipline of study and preparation.

Preaching and Pastoral Work

The work of a pastor is never done. There is a degree of frustration in spite of his best efforts and attitudes toward his responsibilities. When he sits down to read and study, the faces of people to be visited and counseled sometimes make it difficult to concentrate on the task at hand. Many of them have needs that are urgent, and it is not easy to let them wait while he tries to prepare his sermons. On the other hand, when he is out among his people he might remember books to be read, Scriptures to be studied, materials to be organized, writing to be done, and messages to be polished. Times will come when the pastor wishes he could do one or the other. However, as frustrating as the tension between preaching and other ministerial tasks may be, it is not all bad. The preacher needs to be among his people to know their needs and to keep from becoming remote and unrealistic in his messages. Also, the pastor needs some time to himself in study, prayer, and meditation if there is to be real substance to his pulpit work.

The fact remains that no man can ride two horses unless he can keep them going in the same direction, and even then he will likely lean more heavily in one direction than in the other. Most pastors favor one aspect of the work more than the other. There is a price to be paid for excellence in anything. If he concentrates on his preaching, he may not be able to give all the time and attention that some would expect to other things. The minister should do all that he can to maintain a wholesome balance, but the church must understand that strength may not be equal in all areas of his work.

Purposes in Pastoral Preaching

When a man gives his life to a ministry, there should be some well-defined purposes in what he is doing. J. Daniel Bauman defines preaching as "the communication of Biblical truth by man to men with the explicit purpose of eliciting behavioral change."[1] He then concentrates his attention on the three important elements in the definition: communication, biblical truth, and behavioral change. As a pastor looks at what he proposes to accomplish, he finds these three elements essential.

The preacher tries to focus the teaching of Scripture on everyday life for different reasons at different times. Evangelism should be one of the major notes in preaching. A shepherd who cares will reach out in his efforts to find the lost sheep. On other occasions he may have in mind inspiration, edification, instruction, guidance in conduct, and the general building of Christian character. In some messages he may seek to heal the brokenhearted and to promote intimate personal fellowship with God. To make man aware of God's presence and love is one of the chief aims of good preaching.

In his hand the pastor has a sourcebook that touches every area of need. He is reassured in his purpose by the reminder within this marvelous book: "Every scripture inspired of God is also profitable for teaching, for reproof, for correction, for instruction which is in righteousness: that the man of God may be complete, furnished completely unto every good work" (2 Timothy 3:16–17 ASV).

With such a tool in his possession and with abiding love in his heart the pastor preaches for response in each life.

The Ceaseless Quest for Materials

The pastor who speaks to the same people two or three times per week must "go to the well" frequently. Unless he studies constantly he dooms his listeners to boredom. There is no way a man can stay fresh, interesting, and helpful without working at the job of developing good materials. Admittedly, he cannot stay in his study all of the time, nor should he, but when he is able to be alone with God and his working tools, he should make the time count. In fact, the pastor needs to study in his study and outside his study. Sound strange? Yes, the pastor can do much gathering of material outside the study as well as in it if he learns to "think preaching" all of the time.

One of the great frustrations of this preacher's early ministry was his difficulty in following the neatly packaged schedule he received in the seminary classroom. The preaching professor said that a pastor should use his morning hours for study, afternoons for visitation, and evenings for necessary church meetings and administrative duties. It sounded so good and so reasonable that he gave it his best effort. For three years in a small-town pastorate it worked fairly well. Of course, there were exceptions when the schedule was disrupted. Pastors soon discover that people don't always die during the scheduled hours for such things, family counseling cannot wait in some cases, and pressing church functions don't always fit the pattern. But by working hard and enduring some interruptions he was able to keep a reasonable schedule.

After those blissful years, however, his carefully devised plans and schedules received a devastating blow. There appeared in his congregation a pastor search committee

from a struggling suburban church in a rapidly growing city. The chairman of that group spoke the unvar-
nished truth in describing their church situation. He said,
"Preacher, you name it; we need it!" The young pastor
soon found himself living with that challenge. Everything
that could be needed in a church was needed. There were
problems of space, staff, finances, fellowship, organization, and debt. The schedule was shot. Some things would
not wait until the preacher got out of his study. For-
tunately, he had begun some habits in the earlier pastorate
that helped him to survive in this one. (This will be discussed further in the following chapter on the planned
preaching ministry.)

Regardless of his schedule the pastor must study some
of the time in some way. He cannot preach effectively without it. To do this he must devise a general program of
study and reading, a program of Bible study, and a program of sermon preparation. For this he must acquire
some suitable working tools and develop some working
habits.

There are some basic tools of his work that the pastor
must have. No carpenter can do his work without tools,
and no preacher can prepare to preach without his books.
Books are expensive and budgets are frequently limited.
Unless a pastor invests wisely he can have a fortune tied up
in a library that does him very little good. It is not how
many but what kind of books that really counts. This
preacher has the privilege of visiting many churches and
pastors' studies. To see what is on their shelves as working
tools is often a sad experience. It is no wonder that some
of them are having problems with their preaching; they
have nothing with which to work!

What should the pastor buy? First, purchase a good
study Bible with wide margins for notes. The preacher's

"working Bible" should be a good one capable of lasting through years of constant use. A loose-leaf Bible or one that has interleaved capability can be bought at good religious book stores. Such a Bible can become a growing treasure for a pastor as he incorporates his own notes in it from his study, Bible conferences, and conventions. Along with this "working Bible" there should be a number of good translations for comparative study. The Revised Standard Version, the New American Standard Version, and the Amplified Bible are among the most helpful. If the pastor can work with Hebrew and Greek, he certainly should have a good lexicon for each language close at hand. A Bible dictionary, either in a single- or multi-volume edition, is needed. *The Interpreter's Dictionary of the Bible*, a five volume set, is one of the best of its kind. *Young's Analytical Concordance to the Bible*, or a similar work, is very important. A topical reference work such as *Nave's Topical Bible* can be a very helpful timesaver. This writer has found the five-volume *International Standard Bible Encyclopaedia* to be an invaluable source of background material.

There should be a good introduction or two for both the Old and New Testaments on the shelf. Clyde Francisco's *Introducing the Old Testament* and Bruce Metzger's *The New Testament: Its Background, Growth, and Content* are both good for starters. At least one good set of commentaries on each Testament should be purchased as early as possible. Instead of buying several expensive sets, the purchase of individual volumes as needed might conserve funds and build better quality into a limited personal library.

Halley's Bible Handbook is a good general work on the entire Bible. In the New Testament area one or two harmonies of the gospels are needed along with some books on New Testament backgrounds. If the pastor can handle Greek, he will enjoy the ten-volume work edited by Kittel, *Theological Dictionary of the New Testament.*

Books on theology, hermeneutics, geography, archaeology, philosophy of religion, ethics, church history, missions, comparative religions, pastoral work, preaching, evangelism, worship, administration, religious education, and devotional subjects should all be included in a pastor's library. A good list for the building of the minister's library, developed by the faculty of the New Orleans Baptist Theological Seminary in 1978, is *The Minister's Library, A Selected Bibliography.* Each professor listed books that were available in print in the order of their importance.[2] The pastor would do well to begin the purchasing of suggested books on a regular basis. Remember, it is not how many books but what type of books that gives working value to the pastor's library.

A good filing system may become almost as important as a library. Most pastors are exposed to a wealth of good material that they never use because they have developed no system for its conservation and organization. Many preachers have only a "piling system" instead of a filing system; there is a real difference. Expensive equipment is not necessary for a beginning. A cardboard box with some index tabs will do for starters. The important thing is that the preacher get started with some kind of orderly system without further delay. Each day of procrastination adds to his "piling system" and to his frustration in trying to find what he wants for his message from that pile.

Dr. Paul Gericke has developed a system called the Minister's Filing System. His book under the same title is available through Baptist Book Stores and gives detailed instructions on what is needed and how to get started. The pastor may develop his own system, but if he does, the key words to remember are simplicity and efficiency.

With a good working library and a system for organizing and conserving materials gathered from a multitude of other sources, a pastor should have the resources available to provide good materials for sermon building and teaching.

Books on the shelves and materials in the files are worthless unless used. The pastor must find time to study. It may not be easy, but it must be done. There must be some specific time when he can be alone with God and his books. Whatever it takes and whenever it can be done, he must set himself to a program of study and stay with it as best he can. When the regular time suffers from interruption, make it up by getting up earlier or staying up later. Study is not optional for the preacher; it is mandatory. "Study to show thyself approved unto God, a workman that needeth not to be ashamed, rightly dividing the word of truth." (2 Timothy 2 : 15)

A man who really wants to excel in his pastoral preaching ministry will keep a book available in his car, on his bedside table, on his office desk, or wherever he might have a few minutes to read. He must learn to "think preaching" every waking hour, and let no opportunity for preparation escape him.

CHAPTER VI

The Planned Preaching Ministry

"Blessed is he that goeth in circles, for he shall be called a wheel." If this were true, there would be many real "wheels" in the pastorate. It is not uncommon for a pastor to find himself going in circles. This is especially true in the preaching ministry. When this writer had the luxury of a small town pastorate, he decided to take a critical look at his own preaching. Through several years of student pastorates he had preached whatever sermon ideas he could find. After graduation he found himself in a new church still preaching the old sermons. Upon taking a careful and honest look, he discovered that he was actually covering a small number of themes over and over. Of course, he had a different text, a different outline, and different illustrations, but the ideas were the same. For a well-educated and knowledgeable congregation this was not good enough. Neither they nor the pastor would grow with such repetitious pulpit fare. He decided that something had to be done. After reading what he could find in such books as Blackwood's *Planning a Year's Pulpit Work* and Winston Pierce's *Planning Your Preaching*, he determined to do something to break out of his tight circle of ideas. The best single decision of his ministerial life was to begin planning to preach.

More than anything else, preaching according to a plan has taken the dread and drudgery out of preparation and replaced it with a thrill and a challenge. This one decision has helped to open the Scripture and all of life as sermon material. The Bible became an inexhaustible source of fresh ideas, the Holy Spirit became a guide who could see much further into the future than the pastor could antici- pate, and daily living began to reveal needs and illustrative materials that demanded attention.

Whether a man turns to planned, biblical preaching as a regular discipline depends upon his answer to several very personal questions. How does he regard the Bible? Is it adequate to speak to human need? What does he think of the Holy Spirit? Is He wise and discerning enough to lead the preacher's thoughts for several months or years in ad- vance, or is He only able to lead for a week at a time? Does the man of God have a real desire to grow in his own knowledge of God, the Scriptures, and human need? Is there a concern in his heart for the steady growth of his people? Is he willing to settle down to some hard week-by- week work on his preaching?

If he is happy as he is, he will not be willing to pay such a price, but if he wants to see things begin to develop and come together in his own life and in his church, he may well take up the challenge of planned preaching.

Long-Range Preparation for Preaching

There must be a point of beginning for any worthy ven- ture. The Bible is that point for the pastor who wants to feed his flock and see them grow over the years. The supernatural nature of the Scripture has enabled it to cover the broad spectrum of human need in a variety of ways. Exposition of its message will command the best efforts of the preacher and the sustained interest of the congregation.

Several things are necessary for a good start. First, let the pastor secure a good working Bible with wide margins and some space at top and bottom of each page for notes. Second, a pen and notebook should be at his side on the desk for quick notations of passages that stir his interest and imagination. Third, he should have a quiet time and place in which to read and study.

Three different types of Bible reading should be done at each session. The first type should be purely *devotional* in its nature. Perhaps thirty minutes of reading the Scripture and praying may seem to be lost time, but this is not the case. If he is to represent God and speak for him, the preacher needs to spend some time in the nurture of his own spirit. During this period no sermon work should be done. This time is for divine input to the pastor's personal life. He may read through several psalms or some book of the New Testament or he may involve himself with some program of reading through the Bible within a specified period. Remember, don't sermonize at this time. Let the man of God receive for himself.

The second half hour should be given to a careful, studious reading of other Scriptures with the specific purpose of finding and *making brief preliminary notes for sermons.* One of the best ways to do this is to select a book in the Bible for building a course of sermons. The reading should be slow and thoughtful, and time should be taken to underline or otherwise mark passages for consideration in detailed study. A loose-leaf notebook with a good supply of sermon worksheets (see Appendix A) should be readily at hand. When a passage begins to speak to the preacher's heart, he should immediately start a worksheet on that portion of Scripture. The section may be a whole chapter, a paragraph or two, a single verse, or a section of a few verses or several chapters. First impressions should be written down. A subject or title—no matter how sketchily developed—should be noted and if possible a few notes of a skeleton outline. Several sermon ideas may begin with a single reading period of thirty minutes. Remember, these are not for use next Sunday! File the worksheets so they will be available for further notes as more thoughts on that passage continue to flow. This second period of "sermonic reading" may produce ideas that will not become a part of the preaching program for a year or more. The work will not be lost; the Holy Spirit will help the subconscious mind to brood over these Scriptural seeds and bring them to fruition at the most appropriate time. For sermon ideas to grow and ripen they must be planted, cultivated, prayed over, thought through, and brought to organized form during a period of months or years. Remember, one of the most important aspects of this phase of study is to begin writing down some notes on thoughts and impressions. The conscious memory of a pastor has too many other concerns to be able to retain all the sermon ideas that are gathered during such a study session. An orderly system of conserving ideas in written form must be worked out if planned preaching is to work well.

As the pastor reads for sermon ideas in the Scripture, he must keep in mind the seriousness of what is before him. God is speaking to mortal man on these pages, and the preacher becomes the means of sharing the divine revelation. The words of the Word become vital, powerful, and active in the mind of the messenger through the energizing power of the Holy Spirit. The process of deciding what to preach from this rich treasure should be a prayerful and studious undertaking. It must not be done carelessly or hastily. The pastor becomes a responsible interpreter when he tries to discover what God is saying, what it meant to the original recipient or to those who first heard it, and its application to the needs and problems of modern man.

As he reads, marks certain passages, and makes preliminary notes on his worksheets, the man of God should ask himself some questions. What does this say to the congregation in its present status? Is there a message here that meets some community need? What national problem or need may be touched upon? What personal or family situations can be improved by the teaching of this segment of the Scripture? What encouragement to good or discouragement of evil is present here? What instruction in doctrine do the people need? What denunciation of wrong is involved? What is said to help a lost person to find Christ? What hope is offered to believers? What reverent worship of God is inspired? These and many other questions are faced by a pastor as he prepares to preach. When he begins his sermon preparation in the Bible, he finds answers and ample material to help solve problems.

The third type of Bible study is the working out of an *outline for preaching* in the immediate future. The pastor must prepare to preach each sermon in an organized schedule. The principles of sermon building found in a number of good books on expository preaching should be followed. At this point an adequate library is indispensable. Good introductions, commentaries, books on theology, Bible dictionaries, encyclopedias, and devotional books must be used in a thorough study of the passage selected. The sermon worksheet previously begun will serve as a good place to make detailed notes of the study being done. When copious notes have been made, the preacher can develop a complete outline and choose appropriate illustrations from materials already on hand in his file system. When a pastor prepares to preach in this fashion, his problem is that of the selection of ideas and materials, not their discovery.

The work on the sermon for any given Sunday should begin early in the week. All materials for the sermon should be gotten out and organized into an outline not later than Tuesday night. If this is done, the pastor can spend Wednesday morning preparing for prayer meeting, Thursday for background reading, Friday as a day with the family, and Saturday morning or evening for a last minute review of the message. Sound idealistic? It can be done if the pastor puts some system into his preaching.

Church Identity and the Preaching Ministry

Pastoral preaching must be planned with the local church in mind. Because churches are different, preaching must be varied. The sermons that went over well in the last pastorate may or may not be appropriate for the present church. Evangelistic preaching is great, but it may not be needed twice each Sunday in a small church where no prospects are present in the services. Conversely, in a church where there are many lost people and a large number of new converts, evangelism and basic doctrinal preaching may be the primary need. As already indicated, the intelligent pastor will spend his first few months in a new field getting acquainted. He can learn much by visiting in the homes, reviewing church records, and listening to church leaders. Soon the picture of the real needs will begin to fall into place. He will be able to get a sense of direction and know how to plan his pulpit work both for the short and long term.

Until he is thoroughly oriented, the new pastor can feed the flock from rich passages that meet a variety of needs. A course of preaching through Acts on Sunday mornings linked with a series of messages on Bible personalities on Sunday nights could be helpful. Wednesday evenings could be devoted to a study of some of the great prayers of the Bible. Another good approach to preaching in the early months might include a short series on prayer and another on the church for Sunday mornings coupled with an extended course of preaching on the life of Christ on Sunday evenings. Wednesday evenings could be used for expositions of selected psalms. (See Appendix B for sample sermon subjects and texts for the early months of a ministry.)

Since impressions about the work and its needs will be growing in the early stages of ministry, perhaps a schedule for three months at a time will be sufficient. Remember, the schedule is for the pastor's discipline. It is his working tool and need not be advertised to the congregation. The people will soon detect that he has a particular system of preparation as he consistently meets their needs through biblical preaching.

Good preaching does not happen in a vacuum or in isolation from reality. The Bible is a living book that speaks to every conceivable need of man. With this sourcebook before him and an awareness of where his people are in their spiritual lives, a pastor can plan a preaching program that will enhance personal and church growth.

The Church Calendar in the Planning Process

As the pastor begins to project his preaching ministry for the months ahead he will want to keep in mind his church calendar of activities. The pulpit work of a dedicated, disciplined pastor can set the stage for much that is to come in the program of the church. The long- and short-term goals of the program should always be kept in mind and scheduled activities designed to enhance the goals should be undergirded by well-planned sermons. This is not to say that the pastor should use preaching time for program promotion as such, but the consistent sharing of appropriate biblical materials will form a solid foundation of instruction, inspiration, and motivation. Never forget that the pulpit sets the pace and direction for church programming. If there is no plan or design at that point all the rest of the work will suffer accordingly. When the pastor knows where he is going, the church finds it much easier to follow.

Preaching toward a revival

When a major emphasis appears on the church calendar, the pastor should keep it in mind as he prepares his preaching schedule for the preceding months. If a revival is planned for early April, careful attention should be given to what is preached in the Sunday morning worship services January through March. People learn and remember when they are taught line upon line, precept upon precept. In other words, good biblical preaching has a cumulative effect in the lives of the church members. In preparation for a revival there is more involved than merely advertising to get good attendance in the special series of services. Minds should be stimulated and hearts should be warmed so that maximum spiritual results can ensue. This process can be guided and aided by prerevival sermons that point toward the desired results to come later.

As he looks toward an April revival, the alert pastor already knows what he hopes will happen. Basic themes such as the church, prayer, and the ministry of the Holy Spirit should be given concerted attention as he preaches. Perhaps a three-part series of sermons would be useful in the quarter before the revival. The first four weeks might be devoted to a biblical investigation of the character of the church.

Sunday 1   "Christian Fellowship" (Acts 2:42–47)
        I. The basis for fellowship (2:41–42)
       II. The need for fellowship (2:43–45)
     III. The blessedness of fellowship
          (2:46–47)

Sunday 2   "The Importance of the Church"
Paul addresses himself to churches in Romans 1, 1 Corinthians 1, Galatians 1, Ephesians 1, Philippians 1, Colossians 1, and the two letters to the Thessalonians.

  I. The Character of the Church
    1. It is a distinct body
    2. It is the Lord's own work (Matthew 16:18)
    3. It is filled with His fullness

  II. The Present Privileges of the Church
    1. It occupies until He comes (Luke 19:12–15)
    2. It suffers with Him (1 Peter 2:20–21)
    3. It works with Him (1 Corinthians 3:9)

 III. The Future Prospects of the Church
    1. It looks for His return (1 Thessalonians 1:10)
    2. It expects to be caught up by Him (1 Thessalonians 4:16)
    3. It expects to be made like Him (1 John 3:1–3)
    4. It expects to reign with Him (Revelation 20:6)

Sunday 3   "A Spiritual House" (1 Peter 2:1–8)
      I. A Holy House (2:1–3)
     II. Spiritual Sacrifices (2:4–5)
    III. Stone of Stumbling (2:6–8)

Sunday 4   "Talk Your Church" (Psalm 137:1–6)
      The church can only be what its members make it.
      I. Paths of Pessimism and Poverty
        1. The story of Judah's fall
        2. The cry of anguish over lost blessings
     II. Paths of Perseverance and Power
        1. Perseverance in the church (Galatians 6:9–10)
        2. Power in love for the church (Psalms 102–4)
        3. Power in tears for the church (Psalm 126:5)
        4. Power in prayer for the church (Psalm 2:8)
        5. Power in assured victory (Isaiah 2:2–3)

The brief series on the church can be followed by discussion of what the church needs most in order to experience real revival. There is much talk about prayer, but there is also minimal understanding and practice. Without genuine contrition, repentance, and supplication there will not be the spiritual refreshing that is so much needed. Prayer does far more to prepare people than does promotion. To center the church's attention on this indispensable part of its preparation, the pastor might concentrate on prayer for the second set of sermons.

Sunday 5   "The Parts of Prayer" (Matthew 6:9–15)
    I. Recognition (6:9–10)
    II. Supplication (6:11–13a)
    III. Praise (6:13b)

Sunday 6   "The Duty of Prayer" (Jeremiah 33:3)
    I. Prayer Is Prescribed ("Call unto me")
    II. Prayer Has Promise ("I will show thee great and mighty things")
    III. Prayer Is Pioneering ("which thou knowest not")

Sunday 7   "How to Pray Successfully" (Daniel 9:17–23)
    I. Where to Pray (Matthew 6:6)
    II. When to Pray (1 Thessalonians 5:17–18)
    III. What to Say in Prayer (Daniel 9:16–19)
    IV. How to Look for Answers (1 Kings 19:11–12)

Sunday 8   "Things Happen in Answer to Prayer"
    I. Prayer and the Holy Spirit in the Life of Jesus (Luke 3:21)
    II. Prayer and Change in Jesus (Luke 9:29)
    III. Prayer in the Ministry of Jesus (Luke 6:12)
    IV. Prayer in Crisis Times with Jesus (John 11:41)
    V. Prayer in Times of Decision for Jesus (John 12:27)

Meaningful and lasting spiritual revival comes because of what God can do. In answer to prayer the Holy Spirit begins to do His work in human lives. The people must come to a fresh awareness and appreciation of what He can do in them and through them. Following the short series on the church to remind the people of who they are and the series on prayer to indicate what they must do, a series on the Holy Spirit helps the church to remember what God must do for revival to come.

Sunday 9   "Meet My Friend" (John 16:7–15)
     I. Who Is the Holy Spirit?
       1. The author of the Bible (2 Timothy 3:16)
       2. The teacher of God's people (Ezekiel 36:27)
       3. The person of power (Zechariah 4:6)
     II. What Does the Holy Spirit Do?
       1. Convicts the lost (John 16:8–9)
       2. Brings about the new birth (John 3:5)
       3. Inspires witnessing (Isaiah 61:1)
       4. Instructs in what to say (Luke 12:12)
       5. Gives power to believers (Acts 4:31)
       6. Gives assurance (Romans 8:9, 14, 16)
     III. How Do We Know Him in Our Lives?
       1. He bestows gifts (1 Corinthians 12:3–11)
       2. He produces fruits (Galatians 5:22–23)
Sunday 10   "The Promise of God" (John 16:7–15)
     I. The Personality of the Holy Spirit
       1. He is God (John 14:6)

    2. He is sovereign

    3. He feels with the heart of God (Ephesians 4:30)

  II. The Practicality of the Spirit

    1. The church needs Him (Revelation 3:6)

    2. The leaders need Him (Ezekiel 13:3)

    3. Individuals need Him (Acts 15:28)

  III. The Promise of the Spirit

    1. He is the pledge of Jesus (Luke 24:49)

    2. He is the authority of God (John 16:8, 13, 14)

Sunday 11   "Help Is Near" (Romans 8:26–28)

  I. Spiritual Help, Our Greatest Need

    1. Help is needed with our mind set (Romans 8:7)

    2. Help is needed with rebellious hearts (Mark 7:21–23)

    3. Help is needed with wrong deeds (Galatians 5:19–21)

  II. The Holy Spirit, Our Sufficient Helper

    1. The neglected friend is ready to help

    2. The ignored power is available

    3. The understanding intercessor is at hand (Romans 8:27)

    4. The wise planner will help us (Romans 8:28)

With pulpit work having been done on the church and its needs, prayer and its potential, and the Holy Spirit and

His power, the preacher needs to focus the attention of his sermons on the responsibility of each believer in the approaching revival. The final two Sundays before the special services begin may be devoted to the motivation of the Christian workers.

Sunday 12   "Privilege and Responsibility" (Ezekiel 33:1–19)

    I. Spiritual Privilege (33:1–2, 7, 10–11)

        1. The revelation of God (33:1)

        2. The important work (33:7)

        3. The spiritual vantage point (33:2)

        4. The recognition of man's problem (33:10)

        5. The presentation of a solution (33:11)

    II. Spiritual Responsibility (33:8–9)

        1. The received message (33:8a)

        2. The appointed responsibility (33:8b)

        3. The discharged duty (33:9)

Sunday 13   "One to One" (John 1:40–42)

    I. Church Responsibility in Revival Preparation

        1. To recapture simplicity

        2. To recapture courage and purpose

        3. To recapture confidence

    II. Personal Responsibility in Revival Preparation

        1. To hear and to heed (1:40a)

        2. To follow Jesus obediently (1:40b)

        3. To find others who need Jesus (1:41)

        4. To bring them to Jesus (1:42)

When the calendar of activities shows a revival in early April, the pastor can help the cause greatly by pointing toward it with a preaching approach like the one above. One might ask, "Why use the Sunday morning services for such spiritual preparation?" First, there are more people present at that hour, and second, those members who are not deeply committed to the work are most likely to attend only the morning service. These are the people who need most what the revival is intended to do.

What about the Sunday evening messages and the prayer meeting services during such a period of planned preaching? An exposition of the Gospel of John on Sunday evenings (see Appendix C for possible subjects and texts) coupled with messages on basic doctrines of the faith on Wednesday nights might be used with good effect.

Whatever the approach to preaching in preparation for revivals, let the pastor make sure that he puts prayerful planning into the several Sundays prior to such an effort. God has committed Himself to honoring His Word, and the pastor who faithfully preaches it will see what the Lord can do among his people.

Preaching and stewardship

The responsible use of life, talents, energies, and resources is a vital part of Christian growth. The church that never hears messages on stewardship will not be a growing church. The pastor who avoids such subjects in his pulpit work is not doing his people a favor. The narrow concept that stewardship should be reserved for budget promotion time deprives the preacher and the congregation of a well-rounded diet for Christian development. Sermons dealing with such themes should be incorporated in the preaching plan throughout the year. Individual messages, short series, and longer courses of messages may be utilized with good results.

Some individual message subjects and texts that could be used throughout the year are "Christian Commitment" (Romans 6:12–16), "Attitude before Amount" (Mark 12:41–44), "Is Money Master or Minister?" (Matthew 26:6–16), "Giving: The Will and the Way" (Exodus 35:1–35), "The Greater Blessing" (Acts 20:35), and "You and Yours" (Deuteronomy 14:22–25). Short series subjects to be preached during a given month might be "Required of the Redeemed" (1 Corinthians 4:15), "God's Financial Plan" (Psalm 24:1–5; 1 Corinthians 14:40), "The Way to Tithe" (1 Corinthians 16:2), and "Our Obligation to Others" (2 Corinthians 8:1–15). A longer course of sermon subjects for a special stewardship awareness promotion could be taken from the book of Malachi: "The Burden of the Word" (1:1–5), "Where Is My Honor?" (1:6–11), "The Profane and Polluted" (1:12–14), "Wearied with Words" (2:17), "Our Changeless God" (3:1–6), "Reciprocal Agreement" (3:7–12), "The Day Cometh" (4:1–6).

The church that hears strong, positive, biblical preaching on matters related to stewardship is likely to be a growing and generous people. Such preaching must be well planned, carefully prepared, and preached with love. The results are not always obvious at invitation time, but they will come as the years pass and as faithful sharing of the Scripture persists.

Preaching for special purposes

Opinions on what is "special" will vary with each pastor and each church. Some regard a calendar of the Christian year to be indispensable while others pay little or no attention to it. There are, however, some occasions that should receive attention in a planned preaching calendar. At this point an obvious question arises: What should the pastor do if he is involved in a series of sermons or is preaching through a book of the Bible and does not find an appropriate passage for the special occasion? Remember, the planned preaching calendar is primarily a working tool for the pastor. It has not been published for the people's use and is not to be regarded as a binding contract. As he does his planning, the preacher may interrupt what he is doing for a particular Sunday and return to it the next week with little or no harmful effect. It is far better to have a plan which is interrupted momentarily than to have no system at all.

Some of the basic occasions common to most churches can be observed with real profit. At such times the people already have their minds on the special day, and a relevant message which capitalizes on that preconditioned state will receive a good hearing.

The *new year* should be recognized with a message of real optimism and challenge. Some even dare to make personal resolutions and talk about them, but almost all of the people find themselves with a fresh spirit of anticipation. It is a time for beginning again, and a pastor would do well to speak to such emotions by speaking on a subject like "And Now, Tomorrow" (Philippians 3).

Easter is perhaps the most signal day of the year. People who come to church at no other time are likely to be present on that day. Apart from special music programs even Christmas rarely equals Easter Sunday in church attendance. An approach to preaching that includes both the crucifixion and the resurrection can be very effective. A note of victory must be sounded because of the unique nature of the day. There is nothing else in world history that compares to it, and its significance for the church cannot be overemphasized.

The Gospel of John gives an excellent narration of the death, burial, and resurrection. If the preacher can spend some time in study and reflection upon this moving narrative, he can bring himself to empathize with those who were present at the time. A narrative sermon using the people, emotions, and events found in John 18:28 through 20:18 can be made to dramatize the most touching and meaningful event of human history. This writer has preached this passage under the title, "Until the Third Day." The message was developed by taking the role of each of the major personalities and looking at the crucifixion, burial, days of waiting and wondering, and the glorious resurrection event through the eyes of each.

Mother's Day gives the pastor an excellent opportunity to speak to the needs of the home. The sermon should not be a mere sentimental tribute to mothers, but should challenge Christian parents in the building of a good home for the Lord. There has never been a time when the home has had so many problems. The pulpit must not fail to offer scriptural guidance in such a crisis period. One possible preaching approach for this occasion might be to deal with "Unsuccessful versus Successful Mothers" in the Bible. Those who were unsuccessful failed their children because of disobedience to God (Eve in Genesis 3) and selfish immorality (Herodias in Matthew 14). There are others who were godly and successful, such as the mother of Moses (Exodus 2), the mother of Samuel (1 Samuel 1), and the mother of Jesus. More than ample materials can be found within such passages, and a moderate amount of study and organization can make it live in the minds of the people.

Many pastors do not give much pulpit attention to *Father's Day*. In a day when the media tend to present the male American as some sort of clown or buffoon, the church needs to challenge the men of the nation to stand forth in a responsible, spiritual role. While much of the material depicting men as clumsy simpletons is done in jest, it is having devastatingly harmful effects on the father's image and leadership position in the family. It is time for another side of the picture to be seen. The father must not abdicate his place of leadership as the head of the household. A passage such as Colossians 3:19–21 can be preached under the title, "The Duty of a Dad," with great profit.

Independence Day provides an opportunity for the pastor to speak on "Christian Citizenship." Romans 13:1–14 speaks loudly and effectively on this important subject. This country needs its Christians to act like Christians, pray like Christians, and love like Christians more now than at any other time.

Thanksgiving may afford one of the best opportunities for the church to meet in fellowship with other churches. Doctrinal differences are not usually a problem on the subject of giving thanks to God for His blessings. Several churches can meet at one place and enjoy a period of worship and fellowship if this is desirable and feasible. Whether this happens or not, however, the pastor should lead his people in a time of real thanksgiving. Scripture is replete with texts for such sermons. Psalms has scores of passages that will almost "preach themselves." Among many songs of praise for God's goodness to His people, Psalms 9, 18, 19, 30, 32, 46, 65, 66, 81, 92, 98, 103, 111, and 118 stand out as "preachable" passages for Thanksgiving. Adequate exegetical work will make such Scriptures open up to the heart of the preacher like a budding flower. One cannot even casually read them without catching their mood of praise.

Christmas presents a challenge each year for the pastor who would like to brush away some of the commercialism, lights, and tinsel in order to help his people understand the real significance of the birth of Christ. When God became flesh, He chose to do it in humble surroundings and circumstances. This writer has attempted to go back to the real event in preaching at Christmas time. Some reading and research, thorough textual investigation, and moderate amounts of creativity have produced several messages to help people understand how the first Christmas took place. The first attempt, "Come To Bethlehem," was later published as a small book. Such preaching has met with excellent response and seems to have done some real good. The effort to place oneself at the scene of the Lord's birth is often a real blessing for the preacher and congregation. The fact that God loved enough to become a man is awesome, but the way in which He did it is beyond doubt the miracle of the ages!

In addition to the special days, the pastor will face numerous special events and occasions which demand his attention. In the church he will need to include in his preaching schedule such things as deacon ordination and installation, leadership installation, ordination for ministers, dedications of buildings, organs, special gifts, and homes, and church anniversaries. In the community he will be invited to speak to civic clubs, school functions, business people's meetings, and ladies' clubs. For his denomination he may be asked to preach in associational meetings, evangelism conferences, state assemblies, college and seminary chapel services, and youth retreats and camps. How is a man to meet such a wide variety of challenges? There is no better sourcebook than the Bible. The ideas and materials therein are inexhaustible and always worth hearing.

Preaching for long-term goals

The wise pastor who knows his people realizes that many problems and needs cannot be worked out in a short period of time. Preachers who have attempted to change attitudes and customs of long duration with a short-term approach have usually met with frustration and grief.

Those who have had faith in the efficacy of God's Word and who have faithfully and lovingly preached it have lasted to see the miraculous nature of what God can do through time in human lives.

All churches have problems because all churches are made up of people. God knows this, and the pastor will soon understand it. If the people were perfect and without problems, they would not need a pastor. Since they do have needs, they are seeking help—not castigation. To rebuke and scold constantly does not solve problems. For sake of illustration consider some of the usual problems and some biblical passages that will speak to them in a constructive way.

In some situations a pastor may discover serious problems in a church fellowship due to the fact that the church was once a "one family" church and new people were not made to feel welcome; problems may also have arisen because it is an old church in a rapidly growing area, and the makeup of the membership is changing. Some tensions may have stemmed from moral problems in the lives of some of the members or because some want to "run the church." Whatever the source or reason for friction it is likely to take time to quiet tensions and assuage hurts that have taken place. No opinionated approach to preaching is likely to help, but a sound, biblical message Sunday after Sunday that speaks to the spiritual illness instead of its symptoms can begin to have an effect. When this type of problem faced this writer's church, he began a course of Sunday morning messages entitled "The Spirit of the Cross versus the Spirit of the Age." He did not scold the people for their bad attitudes but simply let God's Spirit deal with them as the Scriptures from the letters to the Corinthians were expounded. After six months of this, marked changes in attitude and improvements in the fellowship became evident. He did no fussing and no taking sides—just compassionate biblical preaching.

In more than one case the pastor may find a discouraged people who lack the faith to launch out in significant programs of work. A series of narrative sermons from the book of Joshua can do marvels in helping people to become more optimistic and willing to undertake the new and difficult tasks ahead.

Doctrinal problems can often be worked out by preaching through Romans, Ephesians, and Hebrews. Christian immaturity can be partially alleviated with an extended series on the Sermon on the Mount, and feelings of pessimism can be counteracted with messages from Philippians. A congregation with a wrong set of values may receive help from a Sunday night course of messages from Ecclesiastes.

The choices available are almost without number. The pastor must be willing to take the people where they are and the Bible as it is and become the catalyst to bring the two together with Christian love.

Conservation of Ideas and Materials

When the pastor has settled upon the passages of Scripture and the themes to be developed, he must then begin to gather materials that will illustrate and elucidate them. There is a simple and easy way to do this so that efforts in visiting, reading newspapers, books, and magazines, and regular activities in living can become usable materials for sermons. Secure enough letter-sized folders to have one for each message to be preached during a quarter. This should be approximately thirty-nine folders. Organize them into three groups of thirteen each for Sunday mornings, Sunday evenings, and Wednesday evenings. The sermon subjects and texts should be written on each group with a different colored pen and these should be kept at a convenient spot near his desk or in one of the drawers. Easy access is essential because he will be placing materials in the folders on a regular basis. This should be done from one to two months before the first sermon is to be preached.

Once the folders are ready, a sermon worksheet should be placed in each folder with subject, text, and any previously developed notes written upon it. The pastor should supply himself with an ample stock of three-by-five cards to be carried with him at all times. When he sees, reads, hears, or thinks of something that will fit one of the projected messages, he should stop and make a written note of it immediately. Promptness is absolutely essential because materials left to memory are often lost. Those cards can be dropped into the appropriate folders at the end of the day, and they will be ready and available when he needs them for his final stage of sermon building. Materials from newspapers and magazines can be clipped out, and materials found in books can be noted on the cards. Nothing must be left for a later time. The discipline of making notes as materials are discovered will serve to keep the preaching task on the pastor's mind. When this is consistently done, he will be amazed at how much he has accumulated for a given message, and will have eliminated the irksome waste of time in hunting for materials.

The pastor who disciplines himself to "think preaching" all of the time learns to make time outside of his study work for him instead of against him in sermon preparation. Good sermon illustrations are all around him everywhere he goes. The best materials of this type come from life—not from books of rehashed stories by other preachers. *Look, listen, and think.* Let the things and people around you come to life in and through the preaching ministry. Discretion must of course be used and confidence never violated; there is still far more usable material than one has ever imagined if he is alert to capture it.

As one gathers material he will often find much that does not fit one of his sermons under construction at the time. He must not overlook such gems but make a place for them in an orderly filing system until they are needed months or years later. When this becomes the pattern of a life, the minister's file system will soon be as valuable as his library, and it will have cost nothing but his own effort.

The Layout of the Preaching Schedule

The whole sweep of the preaching program must be before the preacher if his mind is to stay fresh on what he intends to do. All sermon subjects and texts for the entire quarter should be written on a schedule form for quick and easy reference (a sample form for a quarter's preaching schedule is supplied in Appendix D). Copies should be made for the secretary who types the order of worship, the minister of music, and one for the pastor to keep on the sun visor in his automobile.

In summary, for planned preaching to be effective the pastor must:

1. Know the people and their needs.
2. Pray about immediate and long-range goals.
3. Have definite ideas about a program for winning and developing people.
4. Give himself to continuous study and evaluation of needs.
5. Begin with the Scripture—not with personal ideas or pet themes.

6. Develop a system of Bible reading, noting the message and purpose of each passage as it relates to his church.
7. Mark passages for future study and use.
8. Develop attractive (but not sensational) subjects for the portions selected.
9. Vary the type of messages preached on Sunday morning and evening.
10. Do careful exegesis of each passage to be used.
11. Avoid becoming bound to one method of outlining. No set number of points is required.
12. Study different types of sermons. Biographical, textual, paragraph, chapter, book, and narrative sermons aid variety and interest.
13. Use the church calendar in laying out the schedule.
14. Maintain flexibility. It is usually not best to announce the preaching program in advance. The whole idea of planned preaching is to provide the preacher with a systematic way to feed his people. It is not to enslave him, but to serve him.

With the discipline of a plan the pastor can capture the thrill and excitement of the preaching ministry, and the people can have real confidence in a man who knows what he is doing with the time they spend with him in worship.

CHAPTER VII

Pastoral Evangelism

The pastor lives and works in the midst of opportunity and change. As in the days of the Exodus, new nations are emerging; as in the age of the Renaissance, there is a battle of ideas, a struggle for the minds of the people; as in the days of the Reformation, a fresh gospel must be preached in the face of opposition and indifference. As he looks about him, the undershepherd sees some who are devoid of moral and spiritual strength and others who are caught up in the lusts of the times and who live out their lives in the domain of spiritual poverty under the tyrannical influence of the Evil One. A man with a heart that is sensitive to spiritual needs and problems cannot help but think as did Paul when he wrote:

> And you were dead in your trespasses and sins, in which you formerly walked according to the course of this world, according to the prince of the power of the air, of the spirit that is now working in the sons of disobedience. Among them we too all formerly lived in the lusts of our flesh, indulging the desires of the flesh and of the mind, and were by nature children of wrath, even as the rest. (Ephesians 2:1–3 NASV)

Because the man of God knows both the blight of sin and the blessedness of salvation, he covets for every person the experience of redemptive love to be found in Christ Jesus. In a time when many changes are being made for the worse, a real pastor longs to see the kind of difference in life that God can make.

> But God, being rich in mercy, because of His great love with which He loved us, even when we were dead in our transgressions, made us alive together with Christ (by grace you have been saved), and raised us up with Him, and seated us with Him in the heavenly places, in Christ Jesus, in order that in the ages to come He might show the surpassing riches of His grace in kindness toward us in Christ Jesus. (Ephesians 2:4–7 NASV)

Since the Lord has made every provision for salvation and since His presence in life can make such a difference, the concerned pastor should desire the genuine experience of grace for every person in the community.

The Pastor's Theology of Evangelism

The worth of the individual in the plan of God is one of the central teachings of the Scripture. Nothing else in all God's creation has been given the place of importance that man occupies. His original position and privileges were unique, and even after his disobedience man still holds a special place in the plan of God. Since the beginning of history God has initiated contact with man in numberless ways in an effort to restore the fellowship of love which has been broken by sin. The supreme move in this direction was the coming of Christ to reconcile man through His own death and resurrection. God is not satisfied apart from the redemption of the whole man; He continues to reach out to all through evangelism and missions. On the local scene, God's most prominent medium of outreach is the pastor who is concerned for lost people.

The shepherd's heart

As a pastor faces each new day, his prayer should always be that the Lord will renew the gift of a shepherd's heart for him. The sheep has been a favorite symbol of man as the object of God's deep and abiding love. Each sheep is important to the Shepherd as He indicates conditions and the need for faithful and true shepherds.

> My people have become lost sheep; their shepherds have led them astray. They have made them turn aside on the mountains; they have gone along from mountain to hill and have forgotten their resting place. (Jeremiah 50:6 NASV)

Not only were false leaders a problem in the mind of God as He reached out to His flock, but the lack of any shepherds at all was often even more serious. Those who demonstrate a willingness to lay down their lives seem to be in short supply. Selfless devotion and service are rare in any age.

> And they were scattered for lack of a shepherd, and they became food for every beast of the field and were scattered. My flock wandered through all the mountains and on every high hill, and my flock was scattered over all the surface of the earth; and there was no one to search or seek for them. (Ezekiel 34:5–6 NASV)

The model for pastoral concern for people was given in Matthew's Gospel. Jesus was moving about among the throngs of people healing, casting out demons, teaching in the synagogues, and preaching the good news of the kingdom. He was under the pressures that came from people, and His every move was watched by those who wanted to misunderstand and criticize Him. In the midst of all of this He was still moved by the spiritual needs of the masses.

> And seeing the multitudes He felt compassion for them, because they were distressed and downcast like sheep without a shepherd. Then He said to His disciples, the harvest is plentiful, but the

workers are few. Therefore beseech the Lord of the harvest to send out workers into His harvest. (Matthew 9:36–38 NASV)

This text has been used for sermons throughout the history of the church, and the people have listened politely and gone away unchanged. Perhaps if the pastor began to set the example of witnessing to the lost the lesson would be better understood. To talk about a lost world and the need for many workers is good, but pointed illustrations can frequently teach best. The only way a real beginning will be made is for the pastor to zero in on winning individuals to Christ.

When this writer was a boy, his father taught him to hunt quail. It took time and patience to learn not to shoot at the whole covey of birds as they roared out of the brush. In the excitement many shots were gotten off on a "to whom it may concern" basis. All such efforts were in vain and frustration was the inevitable result. He never got a single bird by shooting wildly at the quail. Only when he disciplined himself to take calm, deliberate aim on one bird did he begin to find success.

The pastor may never be able to bag the whole world, but he can learn to deal effectively with selected individuals. The only way that the masses can be won to Christ is one at a time. Each person is important to God, and to win just one is cause for rejoicing in heaven.

Peter and John learned the importance of the individual on the way to the temple. There were hundreds of people all around, but they took time to meet the need of one. For the crippled man it was business as usual. He had seen religious people come and go for years, and no one had ever really shown any love for him. The most that he expected from life was a meager, miserable existence. The thoughtless crowds had taught him not to anticipate too much.

When the two apostles came near, he cried out in his

usual beggar's voice, but this time the response was different. They did not drop a penny and hurry along past him. These men actually stopped to spend a moment with him. This was different. Others had been in too much of a rush to give him any time; they had more to do than to waste time on beggars. The followers of Jesus could not provide him with money, but they had something better to offer. In the name of Jesus Christ of Nazareth, they shared a miracle with him. This was almost more than he could have hoped for, and it was made possible by men who cared enough to devote time and attention to one single person.

The lostness of the sheep

While Jesus was visiting with a group of the disreputables of His time, His enemies paid Him one of the greatest of all tributes. They said, "This man receives sinners and eats with them." In answer the Master shared three parables which illustrate God's concern for the lost. The first was the story of a shepherd who owned one hundred sheep and lost one of them. When the discovery was made that one was missing the shepherd did not rest until he had found it.

This passage has had sermons without number based upon it, but two observations are necessary for the purpose of this section. First, the shepherd was concerned about the lost sheep for the sheep's sake. The animal was helpless and would not have survived long without the shepherd's love. Second, the shepherd's concern stemmed from his own needs and from the needs of the flock. Each sheep was special to the owner and to the others of the group.

In the lostness of man a similar double tragedy is involved. Apart from the love of God in Jesus Christ, man has no real future in time or eternity. Because his own sin has separated him from God, man is doomed to eternal death unless he is found by the Good Shepherd and brought back to the love and mercy of God's fold. To be lost in the position spoken of by Paul is a dread condition. "You were at that time separate from Christ, excluded from the commonwealth of Israel, and strangers to the covenants of promise, having no hope and without God in the world" (Ephesians 2:12 NASV).

From the perspective of God the lostness of man is also tragic. In the economy of the loving Creator, each person is unique and special. There is only one of each, and there will not be another. God has designed each life with a special purpose in mind, and if that goal is missed by the one individual who alone can achieve it, God's hope is thwarted. Each person has his own place in the Lord's plan, each has the Savior offered, each is of infinite value, and each has a contribution to make to others. As long as man remains lost, both he and God are losing much that would give them joy.

The Great Shepherd's instructions

Jesus spent His earthly ministry training witnesses. With divine wisdom, patience, and forbearance He worked to weld an unlikely group of prospects into an effective, cohesive force. He talked, prayed, coached, rebuked, demonstrated compassion, and exemplified obedience for over three years. After all his best efforts they still had problems, and it looked as though all His work had gone for naught. On the morning of the Ascension they were still looking for a kingdom on their own terms. He gave one last word of explanation about the nature of the kingdom and left them with this parting: "It is not for you to know times or epochs which the Father has fixed by His own authority; but you shall receive power when the Holy Spirit has come upon you; and you shall be my witnesses both in

Jerusalem, and in all Judea and Samaria, and even to the remotest part of the earth" (Acts 1:7–8 NASV). With these words ringing in their ears they returned to pray and to wait for the power of the Holy Spirit. After He came in a special manifestation of power, they were never to be without guidance and strength for the task assigned.

In some respects the choices of the first-century believers were clearer—if not easier—than those of today. The lines were more clearly drawn, and the opposing ideals were not hard to identify. When their enemies demanded that they no longer preach in the name of Jesus (Acts 5:28), they were faced with an ungodly but explicit command. They could choose either to obey or disobey. There was no doubt as to what was demanded of them by men, nor was there uncertainty about what God wanted.

Nineteen centuries later one finds that God's will for His people has not changed, but the opposition has grown more subtle. The issues are deliberately muddled and confused. The world does not demand that the Christian deny God or reject His commandments and obey those of the world. He is not asked to turn away from God and embrace the world but is tactfully advised to hold on to both.

Whatever the nature of the opposition, God still urges His messengers on as He did in the early days of the church:

> An angel of the Lord during the night opened the gates of the prison, and taking them out he said, Go your way, stand and speak to the people in the temple the whole message of this Life. (Acts 5:19–20 NASV)

When the preacher responds to such marching orders, he may expect opposition and criticism. The apostles were threatened with death, but they found the courage to respond in a most admirable way.

> But Peter and the apostles answered and said, we must obey God
> rather than men. The God of our fathers raised up Jesus, whom
> you put to death by hanging Him on a cross. He is the one whom
> God exalted to His right hand as a Prince and a Savior, to grant
> repentance to Israel, and forgiveness of sins. And we are wit-
> nesses of these things: and so is the Holy Spirit, whom God has
> given to those who obey Him. (Acts 5:29–32 NASV)

The proper choice of each pastor is clearly spelled out,
"we must obey God." It is not always the choice of pru-
dence but of divine persuasion, not the choice of safety
but of service; it may not be the choice of human wisdom,
but it is the choice of a Spirit-led servant and witness.

The compulsion of compassion

The best service is born from personal concern. The
coming of the Holy Spirit upon the early church brought
about life-changing miracles that affected the whole
course of history. In a matter of days God allowed His people to see how totally dependent they were upon strength
greater than their own. The drama of Pentecost transformed a group of self-seekers into a set of self-givers such
as the world has never known. Those who formerly looked
out for number one suddenly found themselves deeply
concerned for others. Those who had been told to "feed
my sheep" became servants in the urgent work of the
Shepherd of Israel, who had promised to show His love
and compassion for His flock.

> For thus says the Lord God, Behold, I myself will search for my
> sheep and seek them out. As a shepherd cares for his herd in the
> day when he is among his scattered sheep, so I will care for My
> sheep and will deliver them from all the places to which they were
> scattered on a cloudy and gloomy day. And I will bring them out
> from the peoples and gather them from the countries and bring
> them to their own land; and I will feed them on the mountains of
> Israel, by the streams, and in all the inhabited places of the land. I
> will feed them in a good pasture, and their grazing ground will be
> on the mountain heights of Israel. There they will lie down in

good grazing ground, and they will feed in rich pasture on the mountains of Israel. I will feed my flock and I will lead them to rest, declares the Lord God. I will seek the lost, bring back the scattered, bind up the broken, and strengthen the sick . . . (Ezekiel 34:11–16 NASV)

The compassion of God to find and save the lost can only be manifested through those who serve in His Name. He teaches the undershepherd to care in the same way that He cares. The pastor who shares the good news of Jesus Christ because he is convinced that this is the only hope for the lost will make every possible effort in developing personal and church ministries of evangelism.

The Pastor's Motives in Evangelism

Is it possible that a man of God might do the right things for wrong reasons? Generally, the diligent pastor knows what needs to be done in an honest effort to reach the lost. Those who have such understanding are found in varying stages of involvement in outreach, but the reasons for their work may need some careful evaluation.

Wrong motives for good work

The pastor who has been in the work very long knows something about pressure. Society is success oriented, and the church is not exempt from the expectations brought on by this psychology. All laymen have heard glowing stories about what is happening in other places, and most of them have a desire to see their own churches succeed. They are not alone in such wishes; the conscientious pastor also wants to see things happen in the work of the kingdom.

In his zeal to succeed, however, he must beware lest he make serious mistakes. If the expectations of people are the driving force behind his efforts, they are destined to failure in the sight of God. Let each pastor retreat to the privacy of the secret prayer chamber and listen again to the Wonderful Counselor:

> Beware of practicing your righteousness before men to be noticed by them; otherwise you have no reward with your Father who is in heaven. When therefore you give alms [or do your work], do not sound a trumpet before you, as the hypocrites do in the synagogues and in the streets, that they may be honored by men. Truly I say to you, they have their reward in full. But when you give alms, do not let your left hand know what your right hand is doing that your alms may be in secret; and your Father who sees in secret will repay you. (Matthew 6:1–4 NASV)

For the preacher conceit is an insidious thing. It can come upon him slowly, stealthily, and in imperceptible ways. He would not consciously try to win someone to Christ purely for the sake of beating last year's record, but that reason may ease in unawares. Merely to exceed the record of a predecessor, a neighbor, or another pastor in the denomination is not the right reason to undertake such a noble and serious task.

Right motives for good work

There are good and bad models for pastoral evangelism. Paul sent a report and a reminder of the way he had worked when at Ephesus. As he spoke to the elders of the church, he gave an excellent example of the work of a faithful pastor and evangelist.

> You yourselves know, from the first day that I set foot in Asia how I was with you the whole time, serving the Lord with all humility and with tears and with trials which came upon me through the plots of the Jews; how I did not shrink from declaring to you anything that was profitable, and teaching you publicly and from house to house, solemnly testifying to both Jews and Greeks of repentance toward God and faith in our Lord Jesus Christ. (Acts 20:17–21 NASV)

The man of God must witness with a sense of real, personal obligation. Because of the gift that he has received in

Christ Jesus, the pastor is living "in the red." In Romans
1:14 Paul said, "I am under obligation both to Greeks and
to barbarians, both to the wise and to the foolish." His feeling was that God's man has a responsibility to the mer-
chant, the artisan, the teacher, or any other professional of
his own kind (Greeks); he also must demonstrate his concern for those who are not of his type and who have little
or no background of understanding (barbarians); he must
share with the "up-and-outs" (the wise) and the "down-
and-outs" (the foolish).

The debt is large. Shakespeare writes of "seas incar-
nadine," or seas of red ink. Those are seas that have been
navigated by most preachers. Its dashing waves break
heavily over him at the first of each month. The greater
indebtedness, however, comes at the point of his spiritual
obligation. It is a responsibility to be faced with determination and courage. Let the pastor gather himself up and
stand tall as he says, "Thus, for my part, I am eager to
preach the gospel to you also. . . . For I am not ashamed of
the gospel, for it is the power of God for salvation to every
one who believes" (Romans 1:15–16 NASV).

The Pastor's Practice of Evangelism

In his parting words Christ told the disciples where and
when to start the process of witnessing. He told them that
they must tarry until the Holy Spirit came upon them, and
then they were to start where they were—in Jerusalem.
The instructions were to preach in the hardest place first.
To do this required total reliance upon the Holy Spirit.
After all, Jerusalem not only rejected Christ in person, it
killed Him. The Lord knew that a beginning here would
require utmost trust, complete commitment, total forgiveness, and godly daring.

When they had done their best where they were, they

were to move into Judea where frightened people had been intimidated by those who sought to destroy Christ; after that, they were to witness in Samaria where racial hatred defied description. Once they had trusted God enough to witness in the difficult "here and now," they were ordered out to an unbelieving world in which the faith they shared would be viewed as an illegal religion.

This was a big order. So few were commanded to do so much with so little. The task was not easy nor the path smooth, but God takes little note of difficulty. He asks only the faithfulness of His followers, while He takes total responsibility for the results.

Commitment to the task

The local church is not likely to be evangelistic unless the pastor is personally committed to the task. There must be in the heart of the undershepherd a burning desire to see people saved. So great was the desire to see his people come to Christ that Paul was ready to sacrifice himself if that would do the job.

> I am telling the truth in Christ, I am not lying, my conscience bearing me witness in the Holy Spirit, that I have great sorrow and unceasing grief in my heart. For I could wish that I myself were accursed, separated from Christ for the sake of my brethren, my kinsmen according to the flesh. . . . Brethren, my heart's desire and my prayer to God for them is for their salvation. (Romans 9:1–3; 10:1 NASV).

Friendship evangelism

How many adults are ever won to Christ apart from some meaningful relationship with the person who shares the gospel with them? Admittedly, there are some, but the vast majority must have an opportunity to know and trust the witness as a personal friend before a decision comes.

The Christian who can accept a person as he is and try to be his friend will have more opportunities to get a hearing for what he has to say. The Lord said, "Greater love has no one than this, that one lay down his life for his friends." No one would suggest that the believers of today need to become martyrs for their friends. However, the suggestion is made that there is need to "lay down" some of the stuff that life is made of—time and energy—for lost friends.

If a pastor or any other Christian is serious about what this writer has chosen to term "friendship evangelism," there are some things that should be attempted:

1. Make friends with an unsaved person.
2. Place that person on a personal prayer list and pray for him each day.
3. Cultivate a wholesome relationship.
4. Witness by life-style and attitude.
5. Share the Christian faith as the opportunity arises.
6. Make the Scriptures available.
7. Seek a commitment to Christ when the time is right.

Some want to see instant results in every evangelistic effort. In some cases this is possible, but usually much time, patience, love, and prayer will be necessary. There is no time like the present to begin, and it is desirable to work with a number of persons simultaneously. While there can be no specific timetable for visible results, the pastor should always remember that the planting and watering of seeds must precede the spiritual harvest. Friendship evangelism can result in the reconciliation of man to God through Jesus Christ, the greatest of all friends.

Working with children

One of the most rewarding things this writer has ever done as a pastor has been to help parents learn how to lead their own children to faith in Christ as personal Savior.

Most parents want to be a part of the important events in the lives of their children, but many have little knowledge about how to deal with them in spiritual matters. Those who have taken the time to learn and then have followed through with prayerful efforts in this experience have come through with hearts aglow and faces beaming with happiness. There is no greater joy in a Christian home than for parents to lead their own children to Christ.

There are several suggestions that the pastor may make to the parents. To begin with, they should not take the child's salvation for granted. Church and Sunday school attendance is good but not good enough. Do not underestimate the child's ability to understand the plan of salvation. Point out that if they put off talking to the child, someone else may rob them of the joy of leading the child to Christ.

Have the parents prepare themselves spiritually through prayer for the very important responsibility of sharing Christ with the child. Discuss a time when they can be alone, with everything quiet, while they talk. Remember that the decision for or against the Lord will affect every other decision in the child's life.

Use the Bible to show God's love and concern. Point out that every person must choose which road he is going to travel in life (Matthew 7:13–14). Make it clear that if he chooses the "broad" road that leads to "destruction" he must face the penalty of wrongdoing (Romans 6:23). On the other hand, if he will choose the "narrow way" that leads to "life" he can have God's forgiveness (1 John 1:9). Point out the fact of God's love for us as individuals (John 3:16). Show him that he can be saved by inviting Christ to come into his heart (Revelation 3:20). After he has accepted Christ as his Savior, he needs to make a public commitment of himself to Christ and His church (Matthew 10:32–33).

The Pastor's Church in Evangelism

There is general recognition of the duty of the Christian to minister to those in the community outside the church. Evangelism, the primary function of the church, is one subject upon which most evangelicals quickly agree in principle if not in practice.

There are, however, some internal considerations for the church that must receive attention if efforts in evangelism are to be effective. A climate of love, concern, and mutual helpfulness is needed in the church if people are to be reached for Christ and nurtured in His love. Paul admonishes all church people as he says,

> Now we who are strong ought to hear the weaknesses of those without strength and not just please ourselves. Let each of us please his neighbor for his good, to his edification. For even Christ did not please Himself; but as it is written, the reproaches of those who reproached thee fell upon me. For whatever was written for our instruction, that through perseverance and the encouragement of the Scripture we might have hope. Now may the God who gives perseverance and encouragement grant you to be of the same mind with one another according to Christ Jesus; that with one accord you may with one voice glorify the God and Father of our Lord Jesus Christ. (Romans 15:1–6 NASV)

In these verses Paul deals with the duties of those within the Christian fellowship to one another and especially with the duty of the stronger to the weaker brother. When men live in a world of competition where success means outmaneuvering or disabling the other fellow, it is sometimes difficult to be considerate within the church.

One of the marks of a church fellowship that can minister in evangelism is the consideration the members have for each other. There must be an attitude that leads others to a fuller faith in an atmosphere of love instead of a spirit of criticism.

Another mark of a church that is effective in total evangelism is the consistent study of the Scripture within the fellowship. Outreach efforts will not be effective in bringing in new converts unless they receive something worthwhile when they attend. People are hungry for the Word of God, and those churches that preach and teach it faithfully grow and continue to win the lost.

A third mark of a congregation that can reach people for Christ is that it is characterized by hope. The hope of the Christian does not come easily or cheaply. Its optimism does not develop because it has never encountered the difficulties in life, but because it has met them all and triumphed. Real hope that attracts people is not just in the human spirit, or human goodness, or human endurance, or even in human achievement; all of these can fail. The hope that attracts is that which is centered in the power of God.

If the message of Christ given by the church is to be effective, it must contain more than man can provide. A confused and pessimistic generation not only needs hope for tomorrow but needs also joy, peace, and strength for today. The word in the mouth of the church for a lost world is "Christ." In Him the man who is a walking civil war can find the peace and hope he needs.

The Pastor's Preaching of Evangelism

The Bible is replete with texts for preaching on the entire scope of evangelism. It is a book divinely inspired to cover the total spectrum of human need. Obviously all of the Scriptures that can be used to preach on winning and developing people cannot be covered in such a volume as this. In searching for a fair and manageable sample the author decided to share some materials for preaching from the book of Ephesians. The outlines are skeletal in form, and, of course, any pastor who might be interested in using these starter or "seed" thoughts would want to do his own exegetical work in order to "flesh out" the outlines into preachable form.

One will note some of the great doctrines of total evangelism are present in these passages under consideration. Paul deals with such matters as election, faith, atonement, repentance, and justification. He also gives guidance on subjects like love, the church, assurance, forgiveness, sanctification, and glorification.

The pastor might want to introduce a series of sermons from Ephesians by dealing with the times and circumstances of Paul when he wrote this epistle.

"The Prison Preacher" (Ephesians 3:1; 4:1; 6:20)

Some of the greatest messages in our Bible came from behind prison doors. The gospel cannot be confined except in a selfish heart.

    I. Locked Up For a Cause (3:1; Acts 26:6–23)
    II. Locked Up With a Concern (4:1; Philippians 2:12–18)
    III. Locked Up With a Challenge (6:20; Acts 23:11)

A little Jew from a prison cell shook the world (Philippians 4:22).

After the introduction of the book through its author, the pastor may want to devote one message to the theme as found in Ephesians 4:13. Another approach would be to preach one introductory message from the life of the author and join with it a section on this key verse.

"The Goal of God" (Ephesians 4:13)

What is the purpose of churches, colleges, seminaries, and mission undertakings? Where do they all point? What is God thinking, hoping, and seeking?

    I. Unity ("unity of the faith")
   II. Experiential Knowledge ("knowledge of the Son of God")
  III. Christian Maturity ("unto a full grown man")

Once he has introduced his series by emphasizing the author and his purpose, the pastor may then preach one message from each of the six chapters.

"Blessings With a Purpose" (Ephesians 1:1–23)

Whether we read the covenant agreement with Abraham, the instructions for implementation given to Moses, the prophetic interpretations, or the words and acts of Christ as He fulfilled God's part of that covenant, we are forced to see and admit that all of God's blessings have a purpose.

    I. The Love of the Father and His Purpose (1:3–6)
   II. The Work of the Son and His Purpose (1:7–12)
  III. The Earnest of the Spirit and His Purpose (1:13–14)

"What Does God Have to Offer?" (Ephesians 2:1–22)

For those who have no status or rightful claim on God and good, God has much to offer. For a man in great pain any relief is welcome, but a cure is wonderful.

    I. God Offers Grace to Redeem (2:1–10)
       1. The way it was with us (2:1–3)
       2. The way it is with God (2:4–7)
       3. The way it can be through Christ (2:8–10)

   II. God Offers Peace to Sustain (2:11–22)
       1. Peace of heart because of a new status (2:11–13)
       2. Peace through a person (2:14a)
       3. Peace in changed relationships (2:14b–18)
       4. Peace in union with God (2:19–22)

"The Stewardship of Grace" (Ephesians 3:1–21)

The fact that Paul uses the word "stewardship" (verse 2) says that the grace that has been given to us is not ours to hoard. We have no right and no reason to break the line of communication between God and the lost world.

 I. Prisoner (3:1–6)
 II. Preacher (3:7–13)
 III. Persuader (3:14–19)
 IV. Perfecter (3:20–21)

"Worthy Living" (Ephesians 4:1–32)

Paul admonishes Christians to "lead a life worthy of the calling to which you have been called." John Wesley once said, "Give me ten men who hate nothing but sin, who fear nothing but God, and who seek nothing but the salvation of their fellow men, and I will set the world on fire for God."

 I. Unity (4:1–7)
 II. Understanding (4:8–16)
 III. Unction (4:25–32)

"Imitators of God" (Ephesians 5:1–20)

The poet has said, "I am a part of all that I have met." We have met Him and He is a part of us. Our lives must take on His mold.

 I. Compassion (5:1–2)
 II. Cleanness (5:3–7)
 III. Conviction (5:8–13)
 IV. Compulsion (5:14–21)

"How to Live and Win" (Ephesians 6:1–24)

Christians must demonstrate their convictions and concern. Since the days of Paul, times, places, and names have changed, but problems and needs are much the same. Gear yourselves to live as the Lord teaches.

 I. Service above Status (6:1–9)
 1. In the lives of young people (6:1–3)
 2. In the lives of parents (6:4)
 3. In the lives of employees (6:6–8)
 4. In the lives of employers (6:8–9)

 II. Strength with Supplication (6:10–20)
 1. The source of strength (6:10)
 2. The call to arms (6:11)
 3. The enemy and his nature (6:12)
 4. The resources of the Christian (6:14–17)
 5. The attitude and need of the Christian (6:18)
 6. The condition and ambitions of a winner (6:20)

In the event that the pastor wants to develop prayer meeting Bible studies on evangelism or an extended "course of preaching" to guide his people, a more complete treatment of Ephesians is included in Appendix E of this work. Equally effective approaches to preaching on evangelistic themes could be worked out from several other New Testament books such as John, Romans, or Hebrews. This writer has found more material than he could find time to preach.

Let the pastor always remember that he must be personally involved in evangelism if he is to develop his people in this primary task of the church. Pastoral evangelism is important business. It is the Lord's business and it is not finished until He returns. When He arrives in great glory, He wants to find His undershepherds faithfully working at the job He assigned to them.

CHAPTER VIII

The Pastor and Weddings

There are many happy opportunities for service in a pastor's life. To be with his people and to be of real help in connection with a wedding for two young Christians is a real privilege. When such times come the pastor must remember that he is performing a ministry that will be either a fond or unpleasant memory for the couple, their families, and their friends for years to come. His sensitivity to their needs and desires and his wise counsel can endear him to the people involved for life. The variety of demands and expectations for weddings makes each case a new challenge. While there are many common factors, no two are exactly alike.

When the pastor is first asked to perform a wedding, he should schedule a counseling session with the couple to determine their qualifications for marriage and their desires for the service. This writer long ago determined not to let himself be a party to "quicky marriages." There must be enough time for deliberate consideration of all that is involved for a Christian home to ensue.

Premarital counseling

The first counseling session should include several things. The pastor should spend some time getting acquainted with the couple. Are these two people qualified for Christian marriage? Has either person been involved in a previous marriage? Are both Christians? What are their views and feelings on establishing a Christian home? Are they willing to receive guidance in solving any problem ideas? What type of wedding ceremony is anticipated? How many people will be in the wedding party? What type of rehearsal is needed or expected? Do they have a copy of the church policies on use of the buildings and facilities? Have they contacted and made necessary arrangements with other staff personnel such as the organist and the janitor? Has the wedding been scheduled on the church calendar? Is the pastor to do the wedding alone, or is some other minister to assist? What sort of clothing will be worn by the groom and his attendants? Is any special attire expected for the pastor? Has the couple applied for and received a marriage license? Are they aware of any required waiting period between the time the license is issued and the time for the wedding? Is the license from the state where the minister resides and holds legal authority to perform such ceremonies? Is the couple willing to meet for at least one other counseling session on the meaning of Christian marriage?

Many young couples have stars in their eyes and such happiness in their hearts that they simply do not think about the details for a good wedding ceremony. Most families do not know all that is involved in making their dreams become a reality. The first counseling session is designed to help them know what they need to think about as they pursue their plans. It is not intended to dampen their spirits or to discourage them but to give guidance in how to work through all that needs to be done.

The second session with the couple assumes that the pastor is willing to work with them. If he is not able to do so because of his personal convictions and policies, no such session should be scheduled. In those cases where the pastor must exclude himself, it is usually evident to him early in the first session; this fact would normally eliminate the need for many of the questions listed above.

When the pastor is able and willing to perform the ceremony, he should have at least one more session with the couple to help them to understand what is necessary to establish a Christian marriage and a happy home. There are many books on counseling which the minister may find useful for such a procedure. This writer has tried to keep such sessions simple, biblical, and somewhat directive in nature. A number of items should be discussed under three general headings.

I. Spiritual Relationships in Marriage
    1. Try to lead each party to personal faith in Christ.
    2. Encourage membership in the same church if this does not violate convictions.
    3. Point out the value of regular church attendance.
    4. Indicate the wisdom of their making friends with couples in their church.
    5. Emphasize the need for a family devotion from the beginning of the marriage.

II. Emotional Relationships in Marriage
    1. Point out the need for continuing courtship after marriage. Many marriages deteriorate because partners begin to take each other for granted.
    2. Work to cultivate a growing love for each other.

3. Recognize each other's limitations and learn to accept some things with love and understanding.
4. Develop mutual interests and do things together for recreation.
5. Be wise enough not to discuss major decisions when physical and mental fatigue is present.
6. Seek guidance before problems get beyond repair.

III. Physical Relationships in Marriage
1. Prepare for the marriage experience by reading responsible books on marriage and sex. Be informed.
2. Consult a physician for a physical checkup before marriage.
3. Develop wholesome attitudes toward the sexual relationship. It is not dirty but sacred.
4. Be patient. Full adjustment takes time.
5. Be considerate. Selfishness can destroy a relationship quickly.
6. Seek professional help if some hang-up deters the quest for adjustment and mutual fulfillment.

The Pastor's Personal Policies on Weddings

When one deals with an area as sensitive and complex as marriage, there is no way he can make everyone happy all the time. The pastor must give careful study and thought to his own interpretation of the Scripture and to his own convictions. No one else can ever outline the right course of action or give the correct answers. There are too many different needs and human problems for solutions to come easily or simply. The pastor will frequently go through great struggles and agony of spirit in trying to determine the right thing to do.

Regardless of what position he takes, he will suffer some criticism. This is one of those situations when the man of God must work out a position he can live with in good conscience and stick with it even if he becomes unpopular in the process. After all, he must be able to live with himself and with his Lord.

In this writer's judgment, no pastor should allow himself to become a mere convenience for people who have no thought of marrying to develop a Christian home. Any preacher can pick up extra money in fees if he cheapens his ministry by becoming a "marrying Sam." This should not be done.

The question of divorce and remarriage presents a growing problem for pastors. The answers are not simple or easy. Some say a rigid position against any remarriage is the solution while others contend that this is much too harsh, and that the minister should take a "redemptive" approach to the question. The "never-under-any-circumstances" position is one end of the continuum, and the indiscriminate performance of ceremonies regardless of circumstance is the other end. One cannot impose his position upon another. This problem has caused the author great agony of soul. The only position he has been able to live with is to take each case in the light of the Scripture, upon its own merits. It has made some people very unhappy when he was not able to perform their marriage ceremony. On the other hand, it is his hope that the seriousness and sanctity of marriage may have been emphasized to the young people of the churches in which he has served, who have yet to come to the altar. The decision can be painful, and the pastor must be prepared to accept whatever criticism may come.

Church Policies on Weddings

Policies of churches vary from place to place. Some written policies, however, should be available for prospective couples and their families so that a clear understanding of church regulations can be secured early in the planning process. (If the church does not have a printed statement of policy, the sample wedding application and policy statement included in Appendix F might be helpful.)

Legal Requirements Affecting Pastors

When a pastor performs a marriage ceremony he becomes, to some degree, a state official in that what he does has serious legal implications. Laws and regulations governing this function of the minister vary widely from state to state. Some states have strict laws requiring the pastor to establish residence, provide a bond, and register in the county where his church is located. At least one state (Maine) requires registration to conduct funerals. Many states require only that the minister meet the qualifications set up by his denomination.

The minister has the responsibility of finding out for himself the regulations of the state in which he works. He owes it to himself, the state, and the couples he marries to make sure that he has fulfilled all legal requirements so there will be no shadow over the legality of the weddings he performs. (For a state-by-state listing of requirements and further information, see Appendix F.)

The Wedding Rehearsal

As early as possible the pastor should know what is expected of him at the wedding rehearsal. In some cases a consultant, friend, or relative will take responsibility for directing the rehearsal. If such a person is trained and competent, the pastor's job is easy. In the event that no adequate help is available, the pastor may find himself with complete or partial responsibility. When this is the case, he should learn from the bride and her mother their wishes concerning the positions of the attendants and other members of the wedding party. Some will have definite ideas about where each person will stand, and others will be completely dependent upon the pastor's advice.

The major reason for having a rehearsal is to help each person involved know what to do and when to move. In consultation with the bride and her mother the minister should line up the wedding party at the front of the church in the configuration desired by the bride. At this point it would be a good thing to have a "stand in" for the bride so that she can stand in the rear of the auditorium to see how it looks. Each wedding will vary, but a general pattern for positions should be set up first and then altered to suit the taste of the wedding group. Once each person is in the proper location, the minister can simplify matters by placing a very small piece of masking tape at the spot for each attendant. With this aid each can find his place when the "walk through" of the ceremony begins. The tape is usually not seen from the audience and is easily removed from the carpet after the wedding.

Although the sequence of events in a wedding service does not follow an exact pattern for all cases, there is usually a certain order. Fifteen to thirty minutes before the service is scheduled to begin, the organist should begin to play soft music. Five minutes before time, the ushers are to stop formally seating guests and light the candles. The pattern of the service itself, and of the rehearsal, follows this general form:

The groom's mother is ushered in and seated on the second pew, center section, on the right end (as one faces the front).

Suggested Positions for Wedding Party

The bride's mother is ushered in last and seated on the opposite end of the same pew.

Wedding music is played; the organist begins the wedding march.

The minister enters, followed by the groom and best man.

Bridesmaids and groomsmen enter.

The bride enters, escorted by her father.

The introduction to the ceremony is read by the minister.

The father gives the bride in marriage.

Wedding ceremony.

The couple kneels for closing prayer.

The groom kisses the bride.

As the organist begins the recessional, the groom escorts the bride out down the aisle to their left (past the groom's mother). Each groomsman meets a bridesmaid at the center of the stage and escorts her out.

Ushers escort the bride's mother, and then the groom's mother, out.

As the pastor leaves the platform, the congregation is dismissed.

The pastor should lead the wedding party to walk through the whole procedure during the rehearsal until every person feels comfortable in what he is to do. This is the time to work out details and solve problems. Patience may be needed in abundant measure, but a beautiful wedding makes all of the hard work worthwhile.

The above rehearsal obviously assumes a rather involved, formal church wedding with several attendants in addition to the bride and groom. Smaller weddings should be done in basically the same way but with fewer people in the party. Generally, small, informal weddings do not require rehearsals. A moment of instruction by the pastor prior to the ceremony is usually sufficient.

Sample Wedding Ceremonies

Much of the beauty of the wedding ceremony should be found in the words spoken by the minister. If people do not want a distinctly Christian wedding, they usually go to a justice of the peace. The pastor must refrain from preaching, but in the reading of the marriage service he has the opportunity to speak to the couple and others present on the seriousness and the permanence of what is taking place.

A number of wedding ceremonies may be found in books such as J. R. Hobb's *Pastor's Manual* and Franklin Segler's *Broadman Minister's Manual*. The author has written a number of others for special occasions and offers three for the possible consideration by the pastor seeking additional ideas. These may be used in their present form or altered to suit varying needs.

Informal marriage ceremony

Friends and family have gathered to share a moment of great joy in the lives of _____(groom) and _____(bride). Their testimony is that they love each other and wish to be united in the marriage bond for the rest of their lives. Such a commitment has not been made without careful thought, planning, guidance, and prayer. The seriousness of such a step must never be overlooked or minimized. After these moments their lives will be permanently altered. There must be no thought of turning back.

_____(groom) and _____(bride), if you are willing and ready to embark upon the remainder of life's pilgrimage together, will you please indicate this desire by joining your right hands.

You have spoken to each other, to God, and to me of your love. It is a beautiful word and will become a growing, enduring blessing if you cultivate it and make it the foundation of your marriage. Love is strong and lasting. "Love is patient, love is kind, and is not jealous; love does not brag and is not arrogant, does not act unbecomingly; it does not seek its own, is not provoked, does not take into account a wrong suffered, does not rejoice in unrighteousness, but rejoices with the truth; bears all things, believes all things, hopes all things, endures all things. Love never fails. . . . now abide faith, hope, love, these three; but the greatest of these is love" (1 Corinthians 13:4–8a, 13 NASV).

As you grow in Christ and in His type of love you will grow in the happiness and fulfillment ordained by God for the marriage union.

_____(groom), as you hold _____(bride) by the hand, do you promise her, God, and these who love you both that you will love, honor, cherish, and sustain her as your wife? Do you solemnly commit yourself to be her faithful and devoted husband so long as you both shall live?

_____(bride), as you hold _____(groom) by the hand, do you promise him, God, and these who love you both that you will love, honor, cherish, and sustain him as your husband? Do you solemnly commit yourself to be his faithful and devoted wife so long as you both shall live?

The wedding ring is a beautiful symbol of a great and wonderful reality. It pictures a love not to be broken, tarnished, or denied. When you accept it you are identified as belonging to another in an inviolable relationship. Please place the ring on the finger of your bride and hold it in place as you repeat after me. (The following words should be repeated by the groom and then the bride as rings are exchanged.)

> *I give you this ring as a token of my love for you and as a symbol of our marriage union. Please wear it as a reminder of the promises and the love we now share. It says, "I love you as my very own."*

Because _____(groom) and _____(bride) have consented to become one in Christian marriage, I now pronounce them husband and wife, so long as they both shall live. What God has joined together, let not man put asunder.

When the ceremony is completed, the pastor should lead a prayer asking God's blessings on the couple and the Christian home that will begin with this marriage.

Small formal marriage ceremony
   We have come to the house of God as friends to rejoice with friends. No problem or need should dim the joy of such an hour when two Christian young people come to unite their lives in scriptural marriage. The prayers of godly parents are answered and the dreams of youth realized at this altar. From this hour, we trust that the purposes of God for a new home will begin to be achieved in the union of _____ and _____. The presence of both families indicates that those who have given birth and nurture to you are now ready to share you with each other and with Him who has given you life. If this is your intention and hope, who then gives _____(bride) in marriage to _____(groom)?

   _____ and _____, you stand before God and your loved ones to witness your love for each other. The word of God would have you to understand the nature, quality, and spirit of the love that will make your lives together rich and profitable. "Love is patient and kind; love is not jealous, or conceited, or proud; love is not ill-mannered, or selfish, or irritable; love does not keep a record of wrongs; love is not happy with evil, but is happy with the truth. Love never gives up: its faith, hope and patience never fail. Love is eternal" (1 Corinthians 13:4–8 TEV).

   _____(groom), the Scripture instructs you in your obligations to _____(bride) and this marriage.

   For this cause shall a man leave his father and mother and shall cleave to his wife; and they shall be one flesh. (Ephesians 5:31 ASV)
   Husbands, love your wives even as Christ also loved the church and gave himself for it. (Ephesians 5:25 ASV)

   With this and other biblical directions, _____(groom), do you take _____(bride) to be your wedded wife, to live together after God's ordinance, in the holy estate of matrimony? Do you promise to love her, comfort her, honor and keep her, in sickness and in health; and, forsaking all others, keep only to her, so long as you both shall live?

_____(bride), you are also guided by the Scripture in your role as a wife:

The wives shall give to their husbands honor.
The wife must be serious, not slanderous, sober, faithful in all things.
Wives, submit yourselves unto your own husbands as unto the Lord.

In keeping with God's purposes, _____(bride), do you take _____(groom) to be your wedded husband, to live together after God's ordinance, in the holy estate of matrimony? Do you promise to cherish him and serve him; love, honor, and keep him in sickness and in health; and, forsaking all others, keep only to him as long as you both shall live?

I ask you to join hands as you address each other in sharing your marriage vows. (At this point the bride and groom face each other with both hands clasped together as they repeat the following.)

We share our vows to become one in Christ with our hearts, our minds, our souls, and our spirits. From this day forward, we pledge our love and trust to one another completely, until death do us part. "For whither thou goest, I will go; whither thou lodgest, I will lodge; thy people shall be my people, and thy God my God" (Ruth 1:16).

The ring is a symbol of your love and your promises. As you place the ring on in love, please share your promise in truth. (The groom repeats these words, followed by the bride.)

I give this ring as a token of my love for you. I want us to be together from this day forward; for better, for worse; for richer, for poorer; in sickness and in health; to love and to cherish as long as we live. To you, I give all that I am and have.

Because _____ and _____ have expressed their love for each other, and because they have solemnly pledged themselves to keep these vows, I pronounce them man and wife. "What God hath joined together, let not man put asunder."

As we share your joys, we all share a heartfelt prayer for your abiding health and happiness. May God's choice blessings be with you now and always.

Large formal marriage ceremony

Sacred is the hour when two Christians come in love to be made one in marriage. This is the purpose of the Heavenly Father for his own. In the beginning God saw that it was not good for the man to be alone. He took part of the man and created a helpmate at his side to love, encourage, and strengthen in every test and circumstance of life. With the coming of each generation the Creator and Author of life has said, "Whoso findeth a wife findeth a good thing and obtaineth favor of the Lord."

_____, you and _____ have found each other in the providence and will of God. You have come before God, your loved ones, and your friends to be united in the bonds of holy matrimony. Because of your love for each other you have expressed your wish to leave your parents and all others in order to share life together. The happiness of this moment is enhanced by the approval, blessings, and prayers of your families.

_____(bride) has agreed to become the wife of _____(groom). The testimony of favor toward this union is given by her family. So that the friends may know of this, I shall ask, "Who gives _____(bride) in marriage to _____(groom)?"

As the two of you come to this marriage altar you profess your love for each other. God's word will serve as a constant help in understanding what love really is and how it conducts itself in making life rich and beautiful. "Love is patient and kind; love is not jealous, or conceited or proud; love is not ill-mannered, or selfish, or irritable; love does not keep a record of wrongs; love is not happy with evil, but is happy with the truth. Love never gives up: its faith, hope, and patience never fail. Love is eternal" (1 Corinthians 13:4–8 TEV).

The love that you now feel will grow stronger through the years if you give yourselves to its nurture and care. This must have the attention and commitment of both husband and wife.

_____(groom), you are instructed:

Husbands love your wives even as Christ also loved the church and gave himself for it.

In the same way you married men should live considerately with your *wives, with an intelligent recognition of the marriage relation, honoring the woman as physically the weaker, but realizing that you are joint heirs of the grace of life in order that your prayers may not be hindered.*

_____(bride), *you are instructed:*

In like manner you married women must reverence your husbands. That is, you are to feel for him all that reverence includes, to respect, defer to, to honor, appreciate, admire, and be deeply devoted to him as your husband. Wives submit yourselves unto your own husbands as unto the Lord.

Are the two of you now prepared to accept these and other applicable instructions from the Scriptures as binding upon each as long as you both shall live? (The bride and groom then repeat the following vow in unison.)

Entreat me not to leave thee, or to return from following after thee; for whither thou goest, I will go; and where thou lodgest, I will lodge; thy people shall be my people, and thy God my God. Where thou diest, will I die, and there will I be buried: The Lord do so to me, and more also, if aught but death part Thee and me. (Ruth 1:16–17)

(Exchange rings.)

I give you this ring as a token of my love for you. With it will go all the devotion and loyalty of my life. My promise to you is that we shall be together for better or for worse, for richer or for poorer, in sickness and in health; to love and to cherish till death do us part.

Because you have expressed your love for each other and your desire to leave all others and become one in Christ, and because you have here pledged yourselves to each other in unending loyalty and devotion, I now pronounce you man and wife in the name of the Father, and of the Son, and of the Holy Spirit.

What therefore God hath joined together let not man put asunder.

In conclusion, let the pastor be reminded that while counseling, rehearsing, and performing ceremonies take time, he also has an opportunity to make a real contribution to the lives of his people. To be remembered with love by Christian friends for showing real concern for them is one of the great joys of the minister.

CHAPTER IX

The Pastor's Ministry
to the Bereaved

When a call comes telling the pastor that a death has occurred, he moves into a unique opportunity for ministry. Seldom do people feel the need for a friend with a shepherd's heart as much as they do in the passing of a loved one. Many families have had no previous experience with such loss and find themselves in need of guidance as well as comfort. The man of God with a sensitive spirit, a compassionate heart, and a clear mind can be of inestimable value.

The Pastor's Personal Ministry at the Time of Death

Each case of grief is different and demands special attention. In most cases the faithful pastor who has visited during an illness will know the circumstances surrounding the death and the needs of family. When there has been a terminal illness leading to death, the shock factor is not extremely severe. The end has been expected, and in some cases of prolonged suffering, may be welcomed as a release. The sudden death of a loved one, however, does not allow for any preparation at all, and the shock factor is tremendous.

The pastor must take into account the circumstances leading to the death, and he must also be mindful of the relationships involved if he is to minister effectively. Was the deceased young, middle aged, or old? What family members have been left behind? What is the state of health of the surviving spouse? What are the ages of the children? What is the spiritual status of the family? Are they prepared to cope with grief, financial responsibility, and other demands to be met in a time of stress?

If the pastor is not present at the time of death, he should go to the family as soon as possible after receiving word. He will then be able to note the emotional condition of the family and do what he can to calm and to comfort. Usually friends and neighbors will be present, and his first visit can be relatively short. He should talk briefly with the family, share words of comfort and concern, and have prayer. Before leaving, the pastor should set a time when plans for the funeral may be discussed if he is expected to conduct the service. If his assistance is needed or desired in accompanying the family to the funeral home to make necessary arrangements, he should make himself available.

During the early hours following a death, how much a pastor says may not be the most important factor. Often his presence and manifest concern is sufficient. The fact that he is there and available is of great significance.

At an appropriate time the pastor should meet with the family to discuss the funeral service. The thoughtful pastor will ask questions about the music and Scripture preferred for the service. If the family has suggestions which befit the occasion, the minister should make every possible effort to meet their requests. Some may prefer that the minister simply take over and do what he deems appropriate.

In such a planning conference the pastor should determine whether he is to conduct the service alone or together with other pastors or organizations. If others are to be included, he must discuss with the family the role to be played by each. With this information in hand he can have an understanding about the place, time, order of service, facilities to be used, pallbearers, movement of the funeral party to the place of the service, and subsequent movement to the place of interment.

In planning the funeral service the pastor must have clear purposes in mind. Nothing that the minister says will affect the eternal destiny of the deceased. The real reason for the service is to give comfort and help to the survivors. Those who remain need to deal with their grief in a normal, Christian manner. Emotions must not be played upon unnecessarily. Morbid or highly emotional statements or music should be avoided. Scripture has an important place at such a time. The Bible has appropriate and helpful passages for every situation. More than any other sourcebook it helps the family to remember the true, spiritual nature of man and the great love of God.

The great truths of the faith are never more helpful than at such an hour. Those who mourn must have the assurance that is available to them through God's Word. The human tendency is to look at a still form and think of death as the end of everything. If the deceased was a Christian, nothing could be further from the truth. Man is not a body who has a soul. He is a living soul created and re-created in the spiritual image of God through Jesus Christ. For the child of God death is not the end. Eternal life begins the moment a person accepts Christ as his Savior, and it never ends. The resurrection of the Lord robs death of finality. The funeral message should offer such hope for believers.

In case the deceased was not a Christian, there is still help for those who remain. The pastor should not try to play the role of a judge in discussing the end of an unbeliever. He may not have all the facts, and if he does it is an exercise in painful futility. After death the funeral sermon does not determine heaven or hell for the departed. That is in the hands of God. However, the pastor does have the opportunity to help those whose grief may be complicated or intensified by uncertainty. Let God's servant be sure he shares comfort for the suffering at such a distressing occasion.

The Church's Ministry to the Family and Friends

If the stricken family is a church family, there are usually many Christian friends who are concerned and available. Support is spontaneous, and in some cases it may be almost overwhelming. This writer has seen cases when family members were physically and emotionally exhausted by the press of a multitude of people offering service and words of comfort. In other cases, when the affected family was not well known, very few church people have appeared. The pastor and his deacons should make sure that appropriate assistance is available regardless of what the circumstances may be.

Ladies' groups or a special committee of the congregation should make sure that food is taken to the family and that other needs are met as they arise. Nothing can be more helpful than a church group that knows what to do and how to do it at such a time. If those affected are not church people, discreet and tactful concern by Christians can become a potent witness for Christ. Let the church be ready to minister in a variety of ways when people need help.

The Place and Time for the Funeral

In discussing the service with the family, the pastor should determine their wishes in regard to place and time. The time may be governed by the proximity of family members; travel is frequently a determining factor. If some relatives must come from distant places, the service may be delayed pending their arrival. In most cases the funeral is scheduled after one full night of delay. The family will want the evening hours to spend with friends and concerned acquaintances at the funeral home. Midmorning or afternoon hours are frequently selected for a variety of reasons. Occasionally an evening funeral service with interment the following day is necessary.

When the place for the funeral is discussed, a decision may be made from necessity, or it may be made on a purely emotional basis. Years ago services were conducted either in the home of the family or at the church. This writer can distinctly remember one service held in a crowded residence in July with no air conditioning or ventilation. For this and many other reasons the home is seldom the location of services in recent years. Most services are held either at the church or at the chapel of the funeral home.

The family should have the right to say where the funeral service is to be conducted. They may have strong feelings for one place as opposed to the other; each has its good points. One family felt very strongly in favor of holding the service at the church. As their wishes were carried out, however, a subsequent problem that they did not anticipate was created. For months afterwards the widow wept in every worship service because she could not erase from her memory the sight of her late husband's casket in front of the pulpit. If this is a likelihood for a family, perhaps they should choose the chapel at the funeral home for the service.

Services Designed for Individual Cases

Each service of comfort should be designed for the particular case involved. No two will be exactly alike, but some general services which can be adapted may be helpful. In the hope that some assistance may be offered, the author suggests orders of service and message outlines for use in the funerals of a child, a non-Christian, a victim of murder, suicide, or tragedy, and a Christian in adult years.

Service for a baby or small child
  Prelude
  Song or quiet organ music
  Scripture reading:

  And it came to pass on the seventh day, that the child died, and the servants of David feared to tell him that the child was dead: for they said, Behold, while the child was yet alive, we spoke unto him, and he would not hearken unto our voice: how will he then vex himself, if we tell him that the child is dead? But when David saw that his servants whispered, David said unto his servants. Is the child dead? And they said, He is dead. Then David arose from the earth, and washed, and anointed himself, and changed his apparel, and came into the house of the Lord, and worshipped: then he came to his own house; and when he required, they set bread before him, and he did eat. Then said his servants unto him, what thing is this that thou hast done? Thou didst fast and weep for the child, while it was alive; but when the child was dead, thou didst rise and eat bread. And he said, while the child was yet alive, I fasted and wept: for I said, who can tell whether God will be gracious to me that the child may live? But now he is dead, wherefore should I fast? Can I bring him back again? I shall go to him, but he shall not return to me. (2 Samuel 12:18–23)

Prayer
Very soft organ music during the message
Funeral message: "The Loss of a Lamb"
David had a shepherd's background and heart. He knew that if the shepherd picked up a baby lamb and carried it in his arms, the sheep would follow closely. He was human enough to want his child to live, and he prayed earnestly that it might. However, when the child died, he realized that the Great Shepherd of the sheep does no wrong. Doubtless he remembered what he himself had thought on the Judean hillside years before:

> *The Lord is my shepherd; I shall not want. He maketh me to lie down in green pastures: he leadeth me beside the still waters. He restoreth my soul: he leadeth me in the paths of righteousness for his name's sake. Yea, though I walk through the valley of the shadow of death, I will fear no evil: for thou art with me; thy rod and thy staff they comfort me. Thou preparest a table before me in the presence of mine enemies: Thou anointest my head with oil; my cup runneth over. Surely goodness and mercy shall follow me all the days of my life: and I will dwell in the house of the Lord forever. (Psalm 23)*

The first lesson to be learned from the Word of God is that your child is now secure with Jesus Christ, the Great Shepherd of the sheep.

> *Take heed that ye despise not one of these little ones; for I say unto you, that in heaven their angels do always behold the face of my Father which is in heaven. For the Son of man is come to save that which was lost. How think ye? If a man have an hundred sheep, and one of them be gone astray, doth he not leave the ninety and nine, and goeth into the mountains, and seeketh that which is gone astray? And if so be that he find it, verily I say unto you, he rejoineth more of that sheep, than of the ninety and nine which went not astray. Even so it is not the will of your Father which is in heaven, that one of these little ones should perish. (Matthew 18:10–14)*

If the Lord loves those who have gone astray enough to seek and save them, He certainly will take care of one who has made no conscious choice to go astray.

The second lesson to be learned from the Word of God is about the serenity of your child with Christ.

And they brought young children to him, that he should touch them: and his disciples rebuked those that brought them. But when Jesus saw it, he was much displeased, and said unto them, Suffer the little children to come unto me, and forbid them not: for of such is the kingdom of God. Verily, I say unto you, Whosoever shall not receive the kingdom of God as a little child, he shall not enter therein. And he took them up in his arms, put his hands upon them, and blessed them. (Mark 10:13–16)

The last lesson to be learned from this painful loss is that Christ has a place for you also where families can see each other again.

Let not your heart be troubled: ye believe in God, believe also in me. In my Father's house are many mansions: if it were not so, I would have told you. I go to prepare a place for you. And if I go and prepare a place for you, I will come again, and receive you unto myself; that where I am, there ye may be also. And whither I go ye know, and the way ye know. Thomas saith unto him, Lord, we know not whither thou goest; and how can we know the way? Jesus saith unto him, I am the way, the truth, and the life: no man cometh to the Father, but by me. (John 14:1–6)

There is no way that human words can assuage the hurt that is yours. However, you know that your Lord has not left you to suffer alone. He is near and He cares. Until the day of better understanding shall come, place your prayerful trust in Him and He will comfort and heal your hearts.

Prayer

Move to the cemetery. When the family is seated, the pastor may conclude the service with this reading.

Thou shalt guide me with thy counsel, and afterward receive me to glory. Whom have I in heaven but thee? And there is none upon earth that I desire beside thee. My flesh and my heart faileth: but God is the strength of my heart, and my portion forever. (Psalm 73:24–26)

Benediction

Service for a non-Christian

Prelude

Song or quiet organ music

Scripture reading:

Blessed be God, even the Father of our Lord Jesus Christ, and the Father of mercies, and the God of all comfort; who comforteth us in all our tribula-

tion, that we may be able to comfort them which are in any trouble, by the comfort wherewith we ourselves are comforted of God. For as the sufferings of Christ abound in us, so our consolation also aboundeth in Christ. And whether we be afflicted, it is for your consolation and salvation, which is effected in the enduring of the same sufferings which we also suffer: or whether we be comforted, it is for your consolation and salvation. And our hope of you is stedfast, knowing, that as ye are partakers of the sufferings, so shall ye be also of the consolation. (2 Corinthians 1:3–7)

Prayer
Song or quiet organ music

Funeral message: "God Is with Us Through the Shadows"
There are times when God allows us to walk in the valley of the shadow of death, but there is never a time when God is not with us. At such a time of sadness as this, the human heart, if left to its own resources, would find itself on the brink of despair. We may be ever grateful that He will not allow this to happen.
God is with us in the shadows of grief.

For the Lord will not cast off forever: But though He cause grief, yet will he have compassion according to the multitude of his mercies. For he doth not afflict willingly nor grieve the children of men. (Lamentations 3: 31–33)

God is with us in the shadows of doubt and weakness.

Like as a father pitieth his children, so the Lord pitieth them that fear him. For he knoweth our frame; he remembereth that we are dust. As for man, his days are as grass: as a flower of the field, so he flourisheth. For the wind passeth over it, and it is gone; and the place thereof shall know it no more. But the mercy of the Lord is from everlasting to everlasting upon them that fear him, and his righteousness unto children's children; to such as keep his covenant, and to those that remember his commandments to do them. (Psalm 103:13–18)

God is with us in the shadows of loneliness.

And I will pray the Father, and he shall give you another comforter, that he may abide with you forever; Even the Spirit of truth; whom the world cannot receive, because it seeth him not, neither knoweth him: but ye know him; for he dwelleth with you, and shall be in you. I will not leave you *comfortless: I will come to you. Yet a little while, and the world seeth me no more; but ye see me: because I live, ye shall live also. (John 14:16–19)*

W. S. McKenzie has written: *"Thy will, O God, my lot ordains, whate'er my lot in life may be; My faith in thee its grasp retains, However harsh seems thy decree. I know not what thy ways portend, But this I know, thou art my friend, and in my need thy help is near; I know that thou canst ne'er deceive the soul that will in thee believes—then what have I from thee to fear?"*

Prayer

Move to place of interment. When the family is seated at the grave site the pastor should read the following passage.

God is our refuge and strength, a very present help in trouble. Therefore will not we fear, though the earth be removed, and though the mountains be carried into the midst of the sea; though the waters thereof roar and be troubled, though the mountains shake with the swelling thereof. There is a river, the streams whereof shall make glad the city of God, the holy place of the tabernacle of the most High. God is in the midst of her; she shall not be moved: God shall help her and that right early. The heathen raged, the kingdoms were moved: he uttered his voice, the earth melted. The Lord of hosts is with us; the God of Jacob is our refuge. Come, behold the works of the Lord, what desolations he hath made in the earth. He maketh wars to cease unto the end of the earth; he breaketh the bow and cutteth the spear in sunder; he burneth the chariot in the fire. Be still and know that I am God: I will be exalted among the heathen, I will be exalted in the earth. The Lord of hosts is with us; the God of Jacob is our refuge. (Psalm 46:1–11)

Service for a victim of tragedy

In those difficult cases where murder, suicide, or unexpected, sudden death has occurred, the pastor must use extra tact and discretion in all that he does or says. The task to be performed is to offer comfort and spiritual resources to those who remain. The facts and circumstances of death cannot be changed. In no case is the pastor called upon or required to offer explanations or to evaluate guilt or innocence in the situation at hand. He must recognize the extreme grief in the lives of people brought on by unusually distressing circumstances and try to meet their needs in positive and constructive ways.

Song

Scripture: Psalm 23

Song

Quiet organ music during the message

Funeral Message: "Insoluble Problems versus Indisputable Help"

Read: Romans 8:18–39

Suffering, perplexity, and heartaches are real and painful realities in all of our lives. In the early verses of this passage, Paul pictures the groanings of the universe about us. Things are not always right with us no matter how much we may want them to be. In 1 Corinthians 15:19 Paul wrote: "If in this life only we have hope in Christ, we are of all men most miserable."

There are times when trouble seems a more frequent visitor to the life of a Christian than to any other. While our hearts are unhappy and our minds are confused about all that has happened, we must not lose sight of the promise, "For I reckon that the sufferings of this present time are not worthy to be compared with the glory which shall be revealed to us" (Romans 8:18).

I. Help for a Time of Deep Personal Need (Romans 8: 26–27)

    A. The Spirit of God, "the one called to our side," stands with us to help in our times of weakness.

        1. Your many friends are with you to help as they are able.

        2. Where human help cannot reach, God's Spirit is ready to help us in the inner man where we hurt most.

    B. God's Spirit is our helper in prayer.

        1. We are not wise enough to know what to ask.

        2. Grief and feelings are too deep to be expressed in words.

    3. *The Holy Spirit is able to translate an unutterable sign as prayer before the throne of grace.*

II. *Assurance for a Time of Doubt (Romans 8:28)*

    A. *We are given assurance of a master plan for life (Romans 8:28).*

    B. *God has a goal for us—"to be conformed to the image of his Son" (Romans 8:29; 1 John 3:2).*

    C. *We have assurance of His love regardless of what our problems may be (Romans 8:31–37).*

    D. *We have the assurance provided by our personal security in Christ (Romans 8:38–39).*

The psalmist has promised that the Good Shepherd will go with us through all the valleys which have dark shadows. Not only that, but He will stand with us in a real and personal way in the difficult days of readjustment ahead.

Thou wilt guide me with thy counsel, and afterward receive me to glory. Whom have I in heaven but thee? And there is none upon earth that I desire besides thee. My flesh and my heart faileth; but God is the strength of my heart and my portion forever. (Psalm 73:24–26)

Prayer

Move to the place of interment. When the family is seated at the grave site, the pastor should read Psalm 40:1–3 and 2 Corinthians 1:3–4.

Benediction

Service for a Christian in adult years

Prelude

Song or quiet organ music

Scripture Reading:

When thou passest through the waters, I will be with thee; and through the rivers, they shall not overflow thee: when thou walkest through the fire, thou shalt not be burned; neither shall the flame kindle upon thee. (Isaiah 43:2)

Behold what manner of love the Father hath bestowed upon us, that we should be called the sons of God: therefore the world knoweth us not because it knew him not. Beloved now are we the sons of God, and it doth not yet appear what we shall be: but we know that, when he shall appear, we shall be like him; for we shall see him as he is. (1 John 3 : 1–2)

Prayer
Song or organ music
Funeral Message: "Please Be Reminded"
There are many parts of our Christian faith that we know quite well. In a time of stress, a lack of knowledge is not our problem. The real need is to take a moment to remember where our help is. Isaiah wrote about this help:

Hast thou not known? hast thou not heard, that the everlasting God, the Lord, the Creator of the ends of the earth, fainteth not, neither is weary? There is no searching of his understanding. He giveth power to the faint; and to them that have no might he increaseth strength. Even the youths shall faint and be weary, and the young men shall utterly fall: But they that wait upon the Lord shall renew their strength: they shall mount up with wings as eagles; they shall run and not be weary; and they shall walk and not faint. (Isaiah 40 : 28–31)

The questions in this passage are rhetorical. The answers are obvious. Yes, we have known, and yes, we have heard of God's sufficient strength for His people. We only need to be reminded.
Please be reminded of the brevity of life:

The days of our years are threescore years and ten; and if by reason of strength they be fourscore years, yet is their strength labor and sorrow; for it is soon cut off, and we fly away. Who knoweth the power of thine anger? even according to thy fear, so is thy wrath. So teach us to number our days, that we may apply our hearts unto wisdom. Return, O Lord, how long? and let it repent thee concerning thy servants. O satisfy us early with thy mercy; that we may rejoice and be glad all our days. Make us glad according to the days wherein thou hast afflicted us, and the years wherein we have seen evil. Let thy work appear unto thy servants, and thy glory unto their children. And let the beauty of the Lord our God be upon us: and establish thou the work of our hands upon us; yea, the work of our hands establish thou it. (Psalm 90 : 10–17)

Please be reminded of the destination of a Christian life:

. . . *Blessed are the dead which die in the Lord from henceforth: Yea, saith the Spirit, that they may rest from their labors; and their works do follow them. (Revelation 14:13)*

And I saw a new heaven and a new earth: for the first heaven and the first earth were passed away; and there was no more sea. And I John saw the holy city, new Jerusalem, coming down from God out of heaven, prepared as a bride adorned for her husband. And I heard a great voice out of heaven saying, Behold, the tabernacle of God is with men, and he will dwell with them, and they shall be his people, and God himself shall be with them, and be their God. And God shall wipe away all tears from their eyes; and there shall be no more death, neither sorrow, nor crying, neither shall there be any more pain: for the former things are passed away. And he that sat upon the throne said, Behold, I make all things new. And he said unto me, write, for these words are true and faithful. (Revelation 21:1–5)

Please be reminded of the reward of a Christian life:

For I am now ready to be offered, and the time of my departure is at hand. I have fought a good fight, I have finished my course, I have kept the faith: Henceforth there is laid up for me a crown of righteousness, which the Lord, the righteous judge, shall give me at that day: and not to me only, but unto all them also that love his appearing. (2 Timothy 4:6–8)

It is not as though we do not know these things. We do know that everlasting life through faith in Jesus Christ bears great dividends in time and eternity. Our daily prayer in the months ahead should be, "Lord, help us to remember, lest we forget."

Move to the place of interment.
Read: 1 Corinthians 15:50–58
Benediction

The Memorial Service

There may be occasion when a memorial service is desirable, when the body of the deceased is not present for some good reason. This author has conducted such services when the body was lost at sea, and on another occasion when the body had been donated to scientific research following death. Such a service should follow the general outline of a funeral service without, of course, immediate reference to a body. The service should be planned as a tribute to the deceased and as a service of comfort to survivors.

The Pastor's Ministry after the Funeral

At the first news of a death, friends and family congregate to offer sympathy and help of every type. There are frequently almost too many people around for the family to have any privacy or to get any rest. After the funeral, however, the group disperses rapidly. The house is empty and quiet within a matter of hours. This may be the time when a pastor is needed most. He should stop by for a visit soon after the funeral—within a day or two—and see what help, comfort, or counsel may be necessary. The sensitive, caring pastor will continue in whatever ways possible to minister to those in grief until a measure of readjustment and emotional stability has been realized.

Let the pastor remember that many things he does may be forgotten by his people, but they will always love him for being with them in the shadows of grief.

CHAPTER X

The Church Ordinances

Few doctrines have created more controversy than those related to baptism and the Lord's Supper. Each denomination has its own views, and even within a given denomination there is not always total agreement. Since there have been so many treatises written on these two subjects, this author will make no attempt at a theological study. Such is not the purpose of this work.

As stated in the introduction, the writer has been a lifelong Southern Baptist. This, of necessity, makes clear his view on the lack of saving efficacy of the ordinances of the church. In his judgment the New Testament does not validate a sacerdotal theology at this point. Neither the Lord's Supper nor baptism has saving power, but each is a testimony of the believer's faith, which has made salvation his through the grace of Jesus Christ.

The Meaning and Purpose of Baptism

Numerous works have been written on the origin and meaning of the word *baptism*. For the purpose of this work the definition of the ordinance in *The Baptist Faith and Mes-*

sage: A Statement Adopted by the Southern Baptist Convention is
sufficient. It says:

> Christian baptism is the immersion of a believer in water in the
> name of the Father, the Son, and the Holy Spirit. It is an act of
> obedience symbolizing the believer's faith in a crucified, buried,
> and risen Savior, the believer's death to sin, the burial of the old
> life, and the resurrection to walk in newness of life in Christ
> Jesus.

Baptism is a testimony to faith in the final resurrection of
the dead. Being a church ordinance, it is prerequisite to
the privileges of church membership and to the Lord's
Supper.

Doctrinal misunderstandings and problems

To say that others have not always subscribed to or appreciated the view stated above is a gross understatement.
Because the word *baptize* has not been really translated but
only transliterated in most versions of Scripture the problem of misunderstanding is compounded. With a proper
translation of the word itself many questions as to the
mode of baptism could be answered. Historically, Baptists
have been regarded as narrow-minded and bigoted on this
matter, but most have continued to hold to what they believe is the scriptural teaching on the subject. Even under
heavy criticism the local church and pastor should maintain this distinction of doctrine with Christian love and
goodwill toward all.

Facilities and assistance for the ordinance

Most churches in recent years have built baptistries into
their buildings with the capability of controlling water
temperature. This, of course, adds to the worshipful atmosphere when the ordinance is observed, as well as to the
comfort and dignity of the occasion. In his early days in
the ministry, the writer found it very difficult to maintain

ministerial poise and dignity while wading out into a river in subfreezing weather with no protection other than regular clothing. If he had ever been tempted to compromise a bit on the mode of baptism, that would have been the time. These are better days, however, and even those churches who do not have facilities are usually able to use those of a sister congregation.

If possible, the church should purchase baptismal robes for the candidates. This can prevent embarrassment because of the fact that ordinary clothing frequently becomes transparent when wet. If robes are not available the pastor should instruct the candidates to wear materials that will not be so thin as to cause problems of immodesty when they are immersed in water.

There should be an active baptism committee composed of several couples. As a man and his wife work together, they can give personal help to new converts—ladies and men—so that they are given maximum assistance in preparation and follow-up. The couple can also make sure that the comfort and privacy of each candidate is assured.

The man should take responsibility for the cleanliness and proper filling of the pool with water at a comfortable temperature. The wife should be sure that the robes are ready and that proper instructions about towels and dry clothing are distributed. When the ordinance is concluded the couple in charge should take care of cleanup and help the candidates in every way possible. To have good friends on a committee, who function thoughtfully and efficiently, can be of great help to the pastor and of service and value to the people who are baptized into the fellowship of the church.

The baptismal service

When all parties are dressed and ready for the service, the pastor should meet with them for a time of instruction.

The thoughtful pastor will remember that, while this may be a frequent observance for him, it is a once-in-a-lifetime experience for the candidates. Some may be afraid, but all will be nervous and apprehensive. Words of assurance and guidance will be appreciated. Using one of the candidates to help him, the pastor should do a practice exercise for the group so that all may see the proper posture, the position of the hands, the protection of the nostrils, the hinging point for the backward motion, and the recovery procedure. The pastor who takes the time to explain not only the message in baptism but the physical process as well will consistently have more confident and relaxed subjects for the ordinance.

Some pastors prefer to baptize many people in one service and thus have the ordinance infrequently. The writer has baptized every Sunday evening for years. This frequent observance does two things: first, it highlights the individual in a better way, and second, it keeps evangelism before the congregation on a weekly basis.

Usually, the ordinance was observed at the beginning of the Sunday evening service in the following way:

1. The choir enters the choir loft and sings "Trust and Obey," or some other appropriate song, to prepare for the ordinance.

2. The pastor enters the baptistry and reads or quotes appropriate scripture (Matthew 3:13–17, Mark 1:9–11, Luke 3:21–22, Romans 6:3–10).

3. The candidates are baptized.

4. The pastor leads a prayer asking God's blessings on the candidates and the church fellowship into which they have been baptized.

5. The minister of music continues with the service until the pastor can change and return to the sanctuary.

The baptismal service should be brief, simple, scriptural, reverent, and dignified. It is an experience of worship which will be remembered throughout life by those involved as new converts.

The Meaning and Purpose of the Lord's Supper

The Lord's Supper has been a sacred and meaningful experience for Christians around the world. The importance of this ordinance as a memorial of the Master's death was set forth by the Master himself. The definition of this ordinance is also taken from the *Baptist Faith and Message:*

> The Lord's Supper is a symbolic act of obedience whereby members of the church, through partaking of the bread and fruit of the vine, memorialize the death of the Redeemer and anticipate His second coming.

The way this ordinance is observed depends upon the pastor and the local congregation. Some observe it at the end of a regular service not especially related to the ordinance. The judgment of this author is that such a solemn and significant memorial deserves more attention. Consequently, he builds the entire service around the Lord's Supper. The music, Scripture, prayers, and sermon are all designed to move the service to its climax in the reverent sharing of the broken bread and the cup.

Preparation for the Lord's Supper

Anything that is done well requires thought and preparation. First, the service itself should be carefully planned. The memory of the Lord's death should not be merely "tacked on" to the end of something else. In addition to planning the order of worship and the sermon, the pastor should be sure that a responsible committee of the church or the deacon group takes responsibility for the preparation of the elements—the bread and the cup.

Another important part of the preparation is to make sure that each deacon knows where he is to serve, the sequence of events of the service, and the way he is expected to work in conjunction with the pastor, his fellow deacons, and the congregation. If a man moves at the wrong time or is in the wrong place, he is embarrassed, the church becomes uneasy, and the service itself loses some of its effect. The people love this ordinance and want to see it well done.

Well in advance of such a service, the pastor can mimeograph a sheet with positions numbered on a drawing. At the time of the service the sheets are given out to each deacon with a numbered position assigned for each man. This determines the way he enters the auditorium, the aisles in which he is to serve, and the section of pews for which he has responsibility. Thus, with sheet in hand on which he has circled his number, the deacon need feel no uncertainty about his role in the service. A sample of the assignment sheet follows:

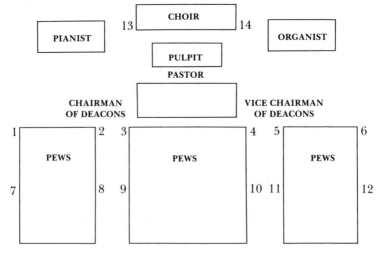

The time and frequency of the ordinance

The frequency with which the church observes the Lord's Supper will depend upon the individual church, its constitution, and its pastor. Some observe it annually, most seem to observe it quarterly, but others may prefer a monthly or even a weekly schedule. In the churches where the author has served, the Lord's Supper has been observed once each quarter. The time has alternated between the morning and evening services; for instance, in the first and third quarters the ordinance has been held in the morning service, and in the second and fourth quarters it was done in the evening. The desires and needs of the individual church should govern the time and frequency of observance.

CHAPTER XI

Policies and Programs for Effective Ministry

The church can do what it plans to do. The wise pastor will help his church to do adequate planning and programming for ministry. The apostles discovered long ago that the preacher cannot carry the whole load. Because of recognized human limitations, appropriate long-term planning must be done if the church is to function smoothly and effectively. Some of this foundational work should have been done in organizing the church, but, if this was not the case, remedial steps should be taken to establish order and system in the programming of God's work.

There are some essentials for an effective church program. If the basics are in good order, the details of the program are not difficult to work out.

Policy Making

The development of church policy is absolutely essential. This is the planning and writing down of approaches to be taken when problems or needs arise or when they are anticipated. In a sense, policies are statements of attitude. If they are to be useful, policies must be developed in ad-

174

vance and recorded for use when given situations arise. Policies drawn up after the fact are of little use in effective programming.

Churches should develop and maintain a statement of policy and publish it at appropriate times in church newsletters or other publications directed to the membership. If there are no stated policies, too much time is spent establishing responsibility and accountability.

Policy may be drawn up in a variety of ways, but to be properly maintained and published some basic "operating documents" are needed.

Church constitution

The church constitution is in a very real sense a statement of policy. Each church will draw up its own document as it determines the need. Some congregations have attempted to spell out every detail of operation while others have drawn up rather simple, general guidelines to be supplemented with policy additions as needed. This writer subscribes to the latter view. A sample constitution is included as a possible guide.

CHURCH CONSTITUTION

ARTICLE I
Identification

This congregation is incorporated as the _____ Baptist Church. The office and principal place of business shall be in the city of _____

ARTICLE II
Purpose

The purpose of this organization shall be to worship the Almighty God according to the teaching of the Holy

Bible, to sustain the ordinances and doctrines and to practice the precepts and examples of the church of our Lord Jesus Christ as set forth in the New Testament, to preach and propagate among all people the Gospel of God's salvation by personal faith in Jesus Christ, the Savior and Lord.

ARTICLE III
Polity and Doctrine

The government of this church shall be vested solely in the body of the believers who compose it as an autonomous group. It shall be subject to the control of no other ecclesiastical body, but shall recognize and sustain the obligations of mutual counsel and cooperation which are common among Baptist churches.

The church may adopt its own standards and qualifications and various auxiliaries, organizations, and committees, as it may deem just and proper, consistent, however, with the principles and standards as reflected by the Scriptures.

Every member of the church who holds an office in any phase of church life and activity shall be responsible to the church and will hold the office only by the will of the church.

As far as may be consistent with the principles and teaching of the Bible, this church shall cooperate with and have representation in the denominational causes sponsored by Southern Baptists including the Southern Baptist Convention, state convention, and city association, and other affiliated auxiliaries and causes of Baptist churches of the city, state, nation, and world. Messengers or representatives as may be allowed this church at any such convention, meeting, or council shall be elected by the church at any of the regular meetings of the church for worship or monthly conference. Messengers or representatives shall represent the church and shall enjoy privileges afforded them at such conventions or religious meetings. The pastor at all times represents the church at such conventions or religious meetings, but speaks authoritatively for the congregation only by vote of the church. It is a part of the responsibility of the pastor to represent this church in the promotion of Christ's Kingdom at all such meetings.

This church accepts the Scriptures as its sole authority on doctrine, and in matters of faith and practice. It shall subscribe to articles of faith and a church covenant as recognized by the Southern Baptist Convention.

ARTICLE IV
Reception and Dismissal of Members

Upon approval of the Church, applicants may be received or accepted by:

1. *Faith.* Any person publicly confessing personal faith in the Lord Jesus Christ, giving evidence of a regenerate heart, and adopting the views of faith and practice held by the church, after baptism shall be admitted into the membership of the Church.

2. *Statement.* Those who have been baptized upon profession of faith and previously accepted into the membership of a Baptist church of like faith and order, but who, because of loss of records or similarly unavoidable circumstance have no regular letter of dismissal, shall be received into membership.

3. *Letter.* Members from Baptist churches of like faith and order may be received into membership by letter of recommendation from such churches.

4. *Restoration.* Any member whose name has been erased from the church roll or who has been excluded from church membership, may be restored by request upon confession of any error committed or by giving sat-

isfactory evidence to the church of having maintained a Christian character.

The policy of this church shall be to remove names of members from the church roll and dismiss those persons from church fellowship only in the following manner:

1. *Death.*

2. *Letter.* Letters of recommendation for any member who is in good standing with the church shall be granted by vote of the church to any Baptist church of like faith and order upon proper request for letter from said church. It will be the policy of this church to issue letters of recommendation only to Baptist churches of like faith and order.

3. *Exclusion*:

In case a member be guilty of conduct unbecoming to a Christian so that the church and the name of Christ are brought into disrepute, it will be the responsibility of the membership committee to confer with such person in accordance with New Testament teaching in the hope of restoring that one. If he will not hear these brethren, it will be their responsibility to report his attitude to the church and if he will not hear the church, the name of the member in question shall be removed from the church membership rolls, if a majority of the members present at any regular business meeting of the church votes to exclude him.

In case any member joins another denomination, the church will exclude such a person from its membership.

ARTICLE V
Divine Worship

Meetings for divine worship shall be on the Lord's day, morning and evening, on Wednesday evening, and on such other occasions as may from time to time be selected.

The ordinances of the Lord's Supper and of baptism shall be observed at a worship service with such frequency as the church determines. The pastor shall administer the ordinances except in cases specially authorized by the church.

ARTICLE VI
Business Meetings

The church shall hold a regular business meeting on the Wednesday after the second Sunday of each month for the purpose of hearing reports and considering such matters of business as may properly claim attention. Special business meetings may be called by the pastor, the deacons, or by vote of the church. Business meetings may be adjourned to meet at any designated time.

The pastor shall preside at all business meetings of the church; in the event of his absence, the chairman of deacons or a designated substitute shall preside. Regular business meetings shall consist of a presentation of the minutes of the preceding regular business meeting and all intervening special business meetings, a report from the treasurer, reports from all committees and organizations whose reports may be properly scheduled, old business, and new business. Special business meetings shall consist of matters indicated in the call. *Robert's Rules of Order* shall normally be followed at business meetings.

ARTICLE VII
Financial Matters

The financial needs of this church, its organizations, and causes fostered by it, shall be supported by tithes and gifts of money which shall be paid into and disbursed from the church treasury. The church treasurer shall be custodian of all church funds. All disbursements of monies from the treasury shall be made only on authority of the church.

For the sake of efficiency, the church shall operate on a budget determined, adopted, and subscribed by the church. Extraordinary disbursements and proposals for raising special funds must be authorized by the church.

No debt, commitment, or other obligation shall be created except by specific authority of the church.

All property, both real and personal, all monies, all equities, and the like shall be held and controlled by the church.

All persons handling funds of the church shall keep books of account of all funds received into and disbursed from the treasury; shall deposit such funds as soon as possible after receipt in the name of the church in a bank subject to state and national supervision and approved by the church; shall be under corporate surety bond payable to the church in such amounts as the church shall determine; shall submit all books, records, and support documents for audit at such times as the church shall direct.

ARTICLE VIII
Officers

All officers shall be members of this church. The scriptural officers of this church shall be the pastor and deacons. Its organizational officers shall be the clerk, treasurer, trustees, librarian, director of the Sunday school, director of the church training program, director of the Women's Missionary Union, director of the Brotherhood, and others as the church may require from time to time, with such assistants as may be required, whose number, manner of election, terms of office, duties of office, and compensation (if any) shall be determined by the church.

At the expiration of any term of office, that office shall be vacant until filled by the church.

As its needs may require, the church shall create salaried positions on the church staff for the efficient operation of its program.

Certain special functions of this church shall be performed through standing committees and special committees, each with definite duties and limitations of authority as the church shall authorize.

ARTICLE IX
Church Policies

The church shall adopt policies to give practical effect to this constitution, which shall be in every particular subject to and in harmony with the letter and intent of this constitution.

ARTICLE X
Changes and Amendments

Proposed amendments or changes shall be read in a regular business meeting one month prior to being voted on. The day it is read, the proposed amendments or changes and date of vote on same shall be posted on a bulletin board in a prominent place in the church building and shall remain there until voted on.

This constitution can be changed or amended by a two-thirds vote of members present at a church business meeting.

This constitution adopted by the church in regular business meeting held on _____(date) shall supersede all prior resolutions, precedents and actions of the church not in harmony with its provision.

Financial policy statement

In addition to the church constitution, the church needs a policy statement on the use of funds for necessary purchases to operate the program.

PURCHASING POLICY

All requests for expenditure of church funds must be made on a materials and services requisition. The requisition must be prepared as an original and two copies and submitted by the proper organizational head for approval by the finance committee. After the requisition is approved, the original is forwarded to the treasurer. The first copy is returned to the person initiating the request and the second copy is retained by the finance committee.

The person initiating the request will return the first copy to the church office within seven days, together with evidence of purchase (sales ticket or cash register tape). If items are charged, then they will verify receipt of material by indicating the date received and the quantity on the first copy and return it to the office. Damages or other information should be noted on the first copy.

Church organizational or committee heads will approve only expenditures associated with their activities. In order to assist the finance committee in giving its final approval to all requests for expenditures, and to keep the staff informed of the activities and needs of the church, each department or committee head will submit his request to the assigned staff member.

Pastor	Min. of Ed.	Min. of Music/Youth
Missions Committee	Sunday School	Music Committee
Planning Committee	Training Union	Flower Committee
Personnel Committee	W.M.U.	Recreation Committee

Weekday School Committee	R.A. Committee	Youth Committee
Finance Committee	Kitchen Committee	Usher Committee
Ordinance Committee	Nursery Committee	
Publicity Committee	Library Committee	
	Maintenance Committee	

No church department head or committee chairman may spend more than one-sixth of his designated annual budget funds, not to exceed $50, in any one month without the approval of the finance committee (except Sunday school and church training literature). Any proposed expenditure committing the church for more than $50 must first be approved by the finance committee, regardless of the one-sixth limitation on general expenditures listed above.

All charged purchases made at the Baptist Book Store or other designated Southern Baptist agency, and office supplies, regardless of where purchased, will be made through the church office controlled by the minister of education or his designated representative in his absence.

All requests for expenditure as described above will be prepared on the materials and services requisition and approved by the appropriate party.

Property policy statement

A statement on the use of church property and facilities is needed. This will be stated in light of the size of the facilities and in line with the organizations and number of people involved. A sample may be as follows:

Policy on use of church buildings and equipment
_____Baptist Church.

Purpose: **These properties are for worship, evangelism, study of God's**

Word, training in Christian character, and developing in every area a mature, well-rounded Christian life. All use of church property must be related to this purpose.

Conduct: People using church property must keep in mind that it is dedicated to God. Social activities must be confined to social areas and all other rooms used for the purpose provided. Employees, members, and guests are requested not to drink beverages or eat during Sunday school, worship, church training or any other such function (except in the nurseries). All are requested to refrain from the use of tobacco inside the church buildings or near entrances. Alcoholic beverages are prohibited on church premises.

Outside Groups: Due to the busy schedule of our own activities, our buildings cannot be used by outside groups unless the group activity is endorsed by the deacons and approved by the church in business session. Permission must be requested by members of our church through the church office. Any group given permission must conform to the general church policy.

Arranging Meetings:	Members are to schedule all meetings of any organization of church through the church office as far in advance as possible and are to endeavor to avoid conflicts. Room assignments will be made by the church office with convenience and economy in mind as to air conditioning. Each group will be responsible for arranging or having arranged the area for use and for returning all properties to their proper place after use.
Keys:	Only members of the church staff and other authorized persons should have keys. When such a person cannot be present to open and close the buildings a definite understanding should be made as to who should do it.
Electric Lights:	Organizational officers are to see that all lights and room heaters are turned off when rooms are not in use.
Nursery:	Requests for having the nursery open should be made through a member of the nursery committee, preferably the chairman. All requirements of this committee must be complied with.
Kitchen and Dining Area:	Permission to use this area must be cleared through the church office. No meals are to be pre-

pared or served except those in connection with church-related functions. Coffee is to be served only for scheduled functions. Any group using the kitchen is responsible for cleaning it or having the cleaning done.

Storage Areas: Each group is urged to use only the space provided for it and is asked not to borrow from others without permission.

Heating and Air Conditioning: Only designated individuals should operate the controls or thermostats on major units.

Room Accessories: Always contact the church office before attaching anything to the walls. Teaching aids may be attached to the tack strip or picture rail at the workers' discretion. Room assignments will be made each fall in cooperation with all organizations. No area is the exclusive domain of any particular group.

Signs and Posters: All must be checked by the church office before being put on the main bulletin board. Bulletin board space will be assigned. All outdated material must be removed.

Borrowing Church Property: Borrowing church property is discouraged. With only two exceptions all properties are to remain at the church. Library books may be checked out by the procedure recommended by the library committee. A small number of folding chairs can be borrowed for church functions in homes but they must be requested through the church office and checked out and in at regular office hours.

Musical Instruments: Permission to use them must be granted by the music director, pastor, or music committee if they are for any unscheduled event.

Church committee statement

A document spelling out the duties of various church committees is helpful. In his last pastorate, the writer led in the compilation of such a document. The sources are varied and mixed. More than fifty different documents were consulted in the process of drawing up these job descriptions.

CHURCH COMMITTEES

Definition: A church committee is "a small group of individuals appointed or elected to perform certain tasks that cannot be done as efficiently by the entire church membership or by one of the educational organizations."
Purposes:
1. To provide information which will assist the congregation in reaching final decisions.
2. To provide, through creative thought and thorough

discussion, more effective ways for carrying on the work of the church.

3. To provide the opportunity to make good use of the knowledge and abilities of the persons best qualified in particular fields of interest.

4. To provide opportunity for Christian maturity by sharing the work of the church; to involve the congregation in carrying out the assigned duties of the church.

GUIDING PRINCIPLES

1. Committee work should be determined on the basis of need.

2. The number of committees should be determined on the basis of well-defined areas of work to be done.

3. The duties of committees should be clearly defined and well publicized.

4. The number of persons placed on a committee should be no greater than is needed to do the job.

5. Individuals should be placed on committees where they can both learn and serve best.

6. Committee members should be provided with opportunities for training.

7. Committees should meet with some degree of regularity.

8. Committees should make periodic reports to the church. Such reports shall be furnished to the church staff for duplication by the Wednesday preceding the regular deacons' meeting.

9. A plan of supervision of church committee work should be provided.

10. The rotation of members of committees should be carried out where rotation is specified.

GENERAL RECOMMENDATIONS

Committees in our church shall be of two general types: standing and special. A *standing committee* shall be one whose responsibilities are more or less continuous throughout the year. A *special committee* shall be one that is needed for a particular task for a limited time.

All standing committees functioning for the entire church shall be recognized as church committees. They shall be elected by the church and shall be responsible to the church. Special committees may be appointed by the pastor or elected by the church as the church desires.

Because of the close relationship between the work of some committees and the responsibilities of the deacons, it is recommended that the chairmen of the following committees shall be deacons: finance, insurance, and properties.

The personnel of all standing committees (except the committee on committees) shall be recommended to the church by the committee on committees. The same shall be true of special committees when requested by the church. The chairmen of committees shall be recommended also by the committee on committees at the time when the committees are recommended. New personnel for standing committees shall be elected not later than the January church business conference and shall serve for the calendar year.

In the event of a vacancy on a committee, the committee on committees shall recommend to the church someone to fill the unexpired term. This will be done at the beginning of the year or at any time during the year as the committee on committees thinks best.

All committees shall have three or more members, as is recommended to the church by the committee on committees.

After a maximum of three years, members of a committee shall rotate off the committee and may be re-elected at the discretion of the church.

Ex-officio members of committees shall have all of the privileges of other members, except the right of voting.

The committee on committees shall be nominated by the nominating committee and elected by the church no later than the December business meeting.

Committees authorized to spend church funds shall do so within the financial plan adopted by the church.

AUDIO-VISUAL COMMITTEE

MEMBERSHIP: three members. The director of audio-visual education will be the ex-officio member.

TERM OF OFFICE: three years on a rotating basis.

RESPONSIBILITIES:

1. Provide a medium of communication to prevent overlapping and duplication in the use of audio-visuals by leaders of organizations.
2. Work closely with the director of audio-visual education in these areas:
   (a) decisions concerning the purchase of equipment, including materials to be used by more than one group;
   (b) recommendations to the budget committee for an annual audio-visual budget;
   (c) recommendations related to proper building facilities for audio-visual presentations;
   (d) assistance in repair and maintenance of equipment presently owned by the church;
   (e) assistance in the physical handling of equip-

ment and the proper usage of this equipment when needed.

3. Work with the church staff in the maintenance, use, and purchase of sound equipment for the church facilities.
4. Assist in recording of worship services for distribution to shut-ins. Help set up equipment and return it to the proper storage area following services.
5. Be alert to new opportunities of teaching through audio-visuals and assist in promoting the use of these materials throughout the program of the church.

BAPTISM COMMITTEE

MEMBERSHIP: eight members.
TERM OF OFFICE: three years on a rotating basis.
RESPONSIBILITIES:

1. Make baptism a meaningful testimony to the dual design of immersion, demonstrating the resurrection of Christ, and the death of the believer to the old life and resurrection to the new life through faith.
2. Study the baptismal facilities and recommend needed improvement.
3. Arrange for maintenance of baptistry and dressing rooms.
4. Arrange for cleaning and storage of baptismal robes, towels, and other articles.
5. Arrange for baptistry to be filled.
6. Assist in preparing candidates for baptism.
7. Assist the pastor in the service of baptism.
8. Assist the candidate before and after the service.

BUS COMMITTEE

MEMBERSHIP: six members.
TERM OF OFFICE: three years on a rotating basis.
RESPONSIBILITIES:
To formulate the necessary policies and administer the operation, care, and use of the church bus.

CHURCH COUNCIL

MEMBERSHIP: the regular members of the council, unless otherwise determined by vote of the church, shall be the pastor, members of the church staff, Sunday school director, church training director, W.M.U. director, R.A. director, chairman of deacons, and librarian.
TERM OF OFFICE: one year.
RESPONSIBILITIES:

1. Coordinate the activities of all units of the church and develop wholehearted cooperation from the membership regarding the adopted programs.
2. Suggest objectives and church goals.
3. Review program plans recommended by church officers, organizations, and committees.
4. Recommend to the deacons or congregation the use of leadership, calendar time, and other resources according to program priorities. Recommendations agreed upon by the council, calling for action not already provided for, shall be referred to the deacons and the church for approval or disapproval.
5. Evaluate program achievements in terms of church goals and objectives.

COMMITTEE ON COMMITTEES

MEMBERSHIP: five members.
TERM OF OFFICE: one year. A new and different committee is to be elected annually.

RESPONSIBILITIES:

1. Nominate to the church annually, in harmony with established policies, members to all committees elected by the church except where the method of selection is otherwise specifically stated in the policy description of the committee.
2. Nominate one member of each committee as committee chairman.
3. Stimulate prompt and complete action by all committees.
4. Initiate training of committee personnel and see that all committees elected by the church have a job description and understand their duties.
5. Nominate the initial three members of the church nominating committee at the appropriate time.
6. Coordinate with the nominating committee, the missions committee, and other organizational leadership to best advance the total church program, enlist as many church members in service as possible, and minimize the number of persons requested to serve in multiple capacities.
7. Work with the pastor and church staff in developing and recommending required changes in church committee policy, organization, structure, and responsibilities.

FINANCE COMMITTEE

MEMBERSHIP: six members.
TERM OF OFFICE: three years on a rotating basis, unless specifically elected to fill an unexpired term.
RESPONSIBILITIES:

1. Supervise the church's financial activities and the administration of the approved budget.

2. Meet prior to the monthly business meeting to study the treasurer's report.
3. Review the approved budget every quarter and recommend adjustments regarding income and new requirements to the deacons and the church as needed.
4. See that the appropriate financial records are kept and that these records and adopted procedures are audited annually.

FLOWER COMMITTEE

MEMBERSHIP: six members.
TERM OF OFFICE: three years on a rotating basis.
RESPONSIBILITIES:
1. Secure and arrange flowers for use in church auditorium.
2. Work with appropriate committees to provide flowers for special church functions.
3. Dispose of flowers and clean and care for floral equipment and supplies.
4. Supervise the care of permanent plants in the church buildings.
5. Handle requests for floral arrangements given as memorials.
6. Assist and advise in selection, placement, and care of outside plants and shrubs.

FOOD SERVICES COMMITTEE

MEMBERSHIP: six members. The church hostess shall serve as an ex-officio member.
TERM OF OFFICE: three years on a rotating basis.

RESPONSIBILITIES:

1. Formulate and recommend to the church policies outlining the proper use of the food service facilities. Included in these recommendations should be information concerning kitchen personnel, cost of meals, reservations, accounting and handling of income and expenses, use of the kitchen by groups other than church groups, sanitation, types of food service, and the general supervision of food preparation in areas other than the church kitchen.

2. Communicate all policies and procedures to the kitchen staff, church leaders, and the church.

3. Evaluate and report to the church, as is appropriate, the services rendered by the kitchen in terms of church program needs.

4. Prepare a yearly financial budget for the operation of meal service equipment and submit it to the budget planning committee.

5. Assist the church hostess in an advisory capacity as is required.

6. Recommend food handling procedures to assure compliance with the city (or county) board of health.

7. Periodically spot-check the food services operation to assure compliance with established operating procedures.

8. Assist in the employment of church hostess and kitchen workers by interviewing applicants if needed and outlining duties of all paid kitchen personnel. This would be subject to the action of the church personnel committee and approval of the church if necessary.

INSURANCE COMMITTEE

MEMBERSHIP: three members.
TERM OF OFFICE: three years on a rotating basis.
RESPONSIBILITIES:

1. Recommend to the budget committee allocation for adequate insurance coverage in every area of the church life.
2. Report to deacons, trustees, and the entire church from time to time concerning insurance coverage.
3. Work in cooperation with the properties committee in regard to fire extinguishers, and with the maintenance supervisor and janitors in regard to the kind of care of the building that will minimize fire hazards.
4. Study, plan, and recommend a suitable insurance program to protect the church against liability to persons injured on the church property or at any church function, on or off of the church property.
5. Work jointly with church bus committee to provide adequate insurance for regular and special trips.
6. Be alerted to any accidents that occur on the church grounds or in the church buildings or to any injuries sustained by employees of the church while on duty.
7. Have at least one annual meeting for the specific purpose of reevaluating the insurance program.

LIBRARY STAFF

MEMBERSHIP: three members. The director of library services is an ex-officio member.
TERM OF OFFICE: three years on a rotating basis.

RESPONSIBILITIES:

1. Maintain an adequate church library.
2. Work under the leadership of the church-elected director of library services to review books, assist in processing books, and carry out church library policies and procedures.
3. See that the library is equipped and properly housed.
4. See that the library is organized, with the books properly arranged and the hours clearly announced and kept.
5. Promote the use of the library.
6. Assist in the preparation and administration of the library budget.
7. Help keep the library in good repair and in proper order.
8. Assist with the custody and care of all audio-visual equipment, records, recordings, and filmstrips owned by the church.
9. Study and read leadership materials to become more knowledgeable of current library opportunities.

MISSIONS COMMITTEE

MEMBERSHIP: six members from the sponsoring church and three from each mission. Those from the sponsoring church shall be recommended by the committee on committees and elected by the church.

TERM OF OFFICE: three years on a rotating basis with two new members from the sponsoring church and one from each mission being elected each year.

RESPONSIBILITIES:

1. Survey and suggest to the church areas for the possible location of new missions.

2. Work closely with the executive secretary-treasurer and missions committee of the local association.

3. Foster good relations between the mission and church.

4. Recommend to the church the amount of money to be spent from its own funds in support of the mission or chapel. This amount should be credited each month to a special ledger account in the books of the church treasurer under the name of the mission or chapel. The church treasurer or a financial secretary from the sponsoring church will pay salaries and expenses pertaining to the mission from funds credited to the mission account.

5. Work with the mission pastor and the sponsoring church pastor to prepare the proposed budget for the mission, presenting it to the mission for acceptance and then to the sponsoring church for adoption.

6. Serve as a pulpit committee seeking God's leader for the mission. Whenever the missions committee recommends a man, he then should preach before the mission. After recommendation from the mission, the sponsoring church should issue a call to the individual. He is therefore to be called by the church, with the knowledge and approval of the mission. All other officers of the mission will be nominated by the mission group and elected upon the missions committee's recommendation by the sponsoring church.

7. See that the mission does not in any way obligate the sponsoring church or the local association without the express written permission of those organizations.

8. Guide the mission to remain in mission status until it becomes numerically and financially strong enough to be self-sustaining in a full-time program and has enough leaders from its own ranks enlisted to take care of its organized work. When the missions committee deems it proper, they shall recommend to the sponsoring church that the mission be organized into a church.

MUSIC COMMITTEE

MEMBERSHIP: six members.
TERM OF OFFICE: three years on a rotating basis.
RESPONSIBILITIES:

1. Be responsible to the church for the overall music program, equipment, and instruments.
2. Work with the minister of music, choir directors, organist, pianist, choirs, and others as needed to determine plans, procedures, and programs.
3. See that there are adequate musical instruments and that they are in tune.
4. Recommend hymnals and special music materials for the choir.
5. Take the lead in all music training efforts.
6. Work to improve the general standards of music for the church.
7. Supervise the use and care of music properties.
8. Prepare and administer, in consultation with the minister of music, the music budget on the basis of the projected needs of the music staff.

NOMINATING COMMITTEE

MEMBERSHIP: a committee of three shall be nominated by the committee on committees and elected by the church at the appropriate time. The committee of three elected by the church shall then nominate the directors of Sunday school, church training, Women's Missionary Union, and Royal Ambassadors. When elected by the church, these four shall complete the committee of seven responsible for the nomination of all church organizational officers and teachers, including nominees for vacancies that occur during terms of office. The nominating committee is not responsible for nominating the deacons or church committee members other than the committee on committees.

TERM OF OFFICE: one year.

RESPONSIBILITIES:

1. Lead in the staffing of all church-elected leadership positions filled by volunteers.

2. Select, interview, and enlist church program organization leaders and general officers. Program organization leaders are the Sunday school director, church training director, Woman's Missionary Union Director, and Royal Ambassador leader. General church officers are the moderator, clerk, treasurer, and trustees.

3. Approve volunteer workers before they are invited to serve in church-elected leadership positions. The program organization leaders and committee chairman will be enlisting workers to serve in leadership positions. The workers should be approved by the nominating committee before the program leaders or committee chairman enlist them.

4. Distribute church leadership according to priority needs. Leadership is like any other resource in a church. It needs to be budgeted. Leaders should be placed where their talents can best be used to move the church toward the accomplishment of its mission.

5. Help church leaders to discover and enlist qualified persons to fill church-elected positions of leadership in their respective organizations. The nominating committee should be a source from which the program leaders get assistance in discovering potential workers. The nominating committee should encourage leaders to enlist the workers they will guide. However, the committee should be ready to give any assistance that may be needed.

6. Present volunteer workers to the church for election. The nominating committee is responsible for nominating workers to the church for official election.

7. The nominating committee shall nominate the members of the committee on committees at the appropriate time.

8. The nominating committee shall be responsible for coordinating with the committee on committees, the missions committee, and other organizational leadership to best advance the total church program, enlist as many church members in service as possible and minimize the number of persons requested to serve in multiple capacities.

NURSERY COMMITTEE

MEMBERSHIP: six members.
TERM OF OFFICE: three years on a rotating basis.
RESPONSIBILITIES:

1. Work in close cooperation with the nursery coordinator, paid nursery personnel supervisor, and division director of Sunday school.

2. Assist in coordinating the church's nursery activities and helping the nursery parents and workers to

work together so as to correlate home and church teaching efforts for the greater effectiveness of each.

3. Become familiar with recommended nursery procedures.

4. Formulate and recommend nursery policies for church adoption including the review, evaluation and revision, as necessary, of the nursery activities.

5. Inform church members of nursery policies.

6. Develop and request a budget for operations and supplies.

7. Recommend purchase, construction, and remodeling of nursery equipment and facilities as needed.

8. Make recommendations to the property committee through the minister of education concerning the care and cleanliness of the rooms.

9. Help department workers enlist church members to assist the regular workers in the nurseries.

10. See that the nursery is open and staffed for all church services and special meetings, working with the weekday and Sunday nursery coordinators.

11. Assist in the employment of paid nursery workers by interviewing and making recommendations to the church if necessary.

12. Recommend needed policy changes, equipment, or personnel to the staff member who is responsible for this area of work.

13. Strengthen home-church relationships through meetings, visitation, appropriate literature, and publicity.

14. Work with the proper church leaders in the selecting, enlisting, training, and supervision of any paid workers that are necessary.

PERSONNEL COMMITTEE

MEMBERSHIP: three members.
TERM OF OFFICE: three years on a rotating basis.
RESPONSIBILITIES:

1. Meet upon call by the chairman or the pastor.
2. Work with the pastor in all matters pertaining to employees and staff members (except the pastor) and present salary recommendations of all employees and staff members (except the pastor) to the finance committee.
3. Work with pastor to fill any vacancies on the paid church administrative staff or corps of employees and make recommendations to the deacons of the church. (In the case of the ministerial staff, approval must be given by the entire church upon recommendation of the personnel committee. The pastor is recommended by a special pulpit committee.)
4. Establish, maintain on a current basis, and administer the policies for the staff and employees regarding duties, vacations, sick leave, and benefits, and also set the working hours of all employees.
5. Research the needs for additional personnel. In expanding the staff or corps of employees to include personnel not already provided for in the current operating budget, it will be necessary for the committee to bring this recommendation to the deacons for approval and through them to the church for authorization.
6. Terminate the services of any employee or staff member, except the pastor, if it is in the interest of the work of the church (with the approval of the deacons).

PROPERTIES COMMITTEE

MEMBERSHIP: six members.
TERM OF OFFICE: three years on a rotating basis.
RESPONSIBILITIES:

1. Maintain the buildings and the grounds, and recommend adaptation and remodeling as the church's needs arise.
2. Supervise general building upkeep, including the janitorial services, minor repair, and the redecoration of present buildings.
3. Lead in the beautification and care of all grounds owned by the church, including the parking area.
4. Supervise all grounds maintenance such as mowing, edging, trimming, and weeding.
5. Secure maintenance of safe conditions in all buildings and on surrounding grounds.
6. Inspect and inventory church properties, establishing an inventory and service record of all equipment.
7. Maintain current instructions for the operation and maintenance of all equipment.
8. Recommend to the personnel committee the employment, training, and supervision of maintenance personnel; define the duties of and instruct such personnel.
9. Develop and initiate scheduled cleaning procedures and standards concerning floor care, painting, kitchen, rest rooms, and other facilities, and provisions for necessary equipment and supplies.
10. Develop and initiate a program of preventive maintenance, including safety measures and accident and fire protection in church buildings, grounds, parking

areas, dwellings owned by the church, and all other church property.

11. Request and administer maintenance, furniture, and equipment budgets to take care of expected needs.

12. Continuously review and project present and future needs and make recommendations for special or large repair needs, equipment, and other property needs. Supervise the performance of required work after church approval.

13. Take over upkeep of any new building and cooperate with the building committee, who will make the proper contacts to obtain corrections in the guarantee period.

14. Cooperate with the insurance committee to provide proper insurance coverage on all church properties.

PUBLICITY COMMITTEE

MEMBERSHIP: six members.
TERM OF OFFICE: three years on a rotating basis.
RESPONSIBILITIES:

1. Help give publicity to every cause in the total church program.

2. Arrange and plan any paid advertising for the church program.

3. Prepare and submit news stories to the local paper concerning the church program.

4. Supervise and plan all publications of the church.

TELLERS COMMITTEE

MEMBERSHIP: twelve members.
TERM OF OFFICE: one year.

RESPONSIBILITIES:

1. Take responsibility for counting the monies received by the church. At least two of the committee shall be present at all times when the money is counted and prepared for deposit.
2. Take care of deliveries to the bank for deposit.

USHERS COMMITTEE

MEMBERSHIP: a minimum of three.
TERM OF OFFICE: one year.
RESPONSIBILITIES:

1. Be responsible to the church for the general conduct, seating arrangements, ventilation, and order in all worship services.
2. Greet people as they enter and leave the church, seat people at the proper time, and provide bulletins, and other materials at the time of seating.
3. Arrange for the best possible seating of the congregation for all the worship services.
4. Adjust and adapt heat and ventilation to the needs of the congregation.
5. Be ready and available at all times during the regular worship services to meet any emergencies which may arise.
6. Receive the offering at each regular church service, or any special service at which collection is received.
7. Be attentive to the needs of the congregation and the pastor at all times. Help prevent interruptions and distractions.
8. Be responsible for handing out visitors' cards and other needed services as required.

WEEKDAY SCHOOL COMMITTEE

MEMBERSHIP: three members.
TERM OF OFFICE: one year.
RESPONSIBILITIES:

1. Work closely with the pastor to secure applications for nursery school workers and recommend to the church persons for employment.
2. Advertise the nursery school and promote registration.
3. Make monthly arrangements for receiving tuition.
4. Advise workers on policies of school operation.
5. Purchase and maintain equipment in accordance with church policy.

YOUTH COMMITTEE

MEMBERSHIP: three members nominated by committee on committees plus one adult worker from each youth department of the Sunday school, one choir parent from each youth choir, and the director of youth activities.
TERM OF OFFICE: one year.
RESPONSIBILITIES:

1. Provide regulations for church approval on the use of the church facilities and supervise enforcement thereof.
2. Prepare a yearly financial budget for youth activities and supervise expenditures of funds.
3. Provide necessary facilities for all youth activities as can be provided through budgeted funds.
4. Supervise and provide chaperones for all youth functions.

5. **Promote and publicize the youth activity program of the church.**

6. **Counsel with the minister of youth on activities related to the youth program.**

Personnel policy statement

In the event the church has more than one paid staff worker, some general policies on staff-church relations are necessary. Such a statement should be tailored to fit each individual church and may need review and modification as the staff grows. A sample statement of such personnel policies and procedures follows:

PERSONNEL POLICIES AND PROCEDURES

1. **Employment: Unless specifically stated, employment by the church is not a contract. When it is considered in the best interest of the church, employment and compensation can be terminated with or without a stated cause, and with or without notice, at any time, by the employee or the church. Release must be in compliance with the church constitutional requirements.**

2. **Employee Absence:**
   (a) **Absences due to death in the immediate family. In the case of the death of a member of the immediate family, the employee is paid for the absence from scheduled work for a period not to exceed one week. Definite arrangements in such matters shall be made with the pastor or personnel committee.**
   (b) **Absence due to death of a relative other than the immediate family. In the case of the death of a relative other than the immediate family, the employee is paid for the day of burial plus two additional days of travel, if that much time is**

needed. If the deceased relative lived in the home of the employee at the time of death, the policy for death in the immediate family will apply.

(c) Absences for jury and witness duty. An employee is paid for the time absent on jury or witness duty. Any payments received from the government for such services are to be retained by the employee. If the employee's services as a juror or witness are not required for the entire day, he is expected to report to the church for the remainder of the day. He is also expected to report for work on any regularly scheduled work day when court is closed for a holiday not recognized by the church.

(d) Absences for personal business. It is occasionally necessary for an employee to be absent from work briefly for personal reasons. Such absences may be arranged by securing the approval of the pastor. Absences of longer than one day need the approval of the personnel committee. Excessive absences are discouraged, and when such absences are not arranged in advance by the employee, reduction in pay may result.

(e) Absences of extended leave. Should the occasion arise when a leave of absence is requested by a member of the church staff or corps of employees due to personal business, extended illness, illness in the family, or some other reason, such leaves will be formally approved by the pastor and personnel committee.

3. Personal Illness: Illness requiring absence from regularly assigned duties should be reported to the pastor no later than 8:00 A.M. on the first day of absence. In reporting, please give the best possible in-

formation concerning the date of expected return to service.

4. **Illness Benefits:** Regular employees of the church who are ill receive illness benefits within any 365-day period as follows:

   (a) After the first year of employment, employees with up to two years of continuous service receive full pay for each day of absence up to a maximum of three weeks.

   (b) Employees with from two to five years of continuous service receive full pay for each day of absence up to a maximum of eight weeks.

   (c) After the fifth year, one additional week will be allowed for each additional year of service up to a maximum of twelve weeks. After the maximum illness benefits have been paid, any vacation earned may be applied to cover additional illness. However, after the maximum illness benefits have been paid, payment of any earned vacation allowance will be paid only on the employee's request.

5. **Employees Absent on Church Business:** Persons who represent the church at workshops, conferences, or retreats will schedule such absences from the office with the pastor. If reimbursement for travel or other necessary expenses is expected, approval by the personnel committee is required in advance and claim should be made with substantial evidence to support all requests for reimbursement.

6. **Holidays:** All employees of the church are to receive pay for church-recognized holidays. These holidays are New Year's Day, Independence Day, Labor Day, Thanksgiving Day, and Christmas Day. (Christmas Eve afternoon is also considered a holi-

day if it falls on a working day.) In the event one of these holidays falls on Sunday, the offices will normally be closed the following Monday; if a holiday falls during the vacation period of an employee, he will be given another day. The program of the church frequently necessitates a skeleton organization working on these holidays. When it is necessary for an employee to work on a holiday, however, the pastor or personnel committee should arrange for time off immediately following the holiday.

7. Office Hours: The offices of the church are open Monday through Friday from 8 A.M. to 5 P.M.

8. Overtime: Most employees are employed on the basis of the job to be done. Though specific hours may be stated as office hours, other special work time may be occasionally necessary. An effort will be made to keep extra hours work to a minimum, but no employee should feel imposed upon when asked to work additional hours within a given day. In the event employees are covered by the wage-hour law, arrangements will be made so that other time can be taken off so that the total time will not exceed forty hours within a week.

9. Vacations: Those employees subject to a vacation will be entitled to two weeks of vacation with pay at the end of the first full year of employment. Those employees considered eligible for vacation are the pastor, minister of education, minister of music, and the secretaries. All employees will work with the pastor in coordinating vacations to eliminate conflicts.

10. Salary Adjustments: Salary increases are based on merit and job responsibilities. Once each year, the work progress and salaries of the minister of music,

minister of education, and the church secretaries shall be reviewed by the personnel committee in consultation with the pastor. If any adjustments in salary are deemed advisable, they shall be recommended to the finance committee in time for them to review the suggestions and refer them to the budget planning committee.

11. Retirement: Age 65 shall be considered the normal retirement age. However, any employee, upon reaching age 65, may, upon review and approval of the personnel committee, be retained on a year-to-year basis.

12. Severance Allowance Eligibility: A regular employee released from the payroll for reasons other than proven dishonesty, proven immorality, or conduct prejudicial to the best interest of the church is eligible to receive a severance allowance based upon his length of continued service. The purpose of this severance allowance is to provide financial assistance to released employees while they are seeking other employment. Payments of severance allowance are one-sixth of a week's pay for each two months of service to a total not to exceed one month. Employees who resign are not ordinarily paid a severance allowance. They receive pay up through the last day worked and for any vacation earned.

13. Space Allocation for Staff and Employees: When assigning office space to personnel, careful consideration is to be given to working conditions, flow of work, and overall layout of available office area. All personnel should understand that office space cannot be assigned to anyone permanently. In the interest of all, adjustments in space must be made as the

need arises. Authority to allocate office space to various persons is a function of the pastor and personnel committee.

14. Parking: It is expected that all employees will observe standard parking procedures at all times. Park in such a manner as to occupy one parking lane and observe restricted areas as the curb marking and other signs may indicate.

15. Coffee Break: Coffee breaks should be observed with great discretion regarding the length of time involved. No person should feel that a given time is reserved exclusively for this use. Refreshments should not be brought into work offices.

16. Gifts: Each employee is asked to use the greatest discretion in the matter of gifts to be given to other employees. Courtesy and friendship is by no means discouraged. Solicitations of contributions among staff members to purchase gifts for anyone for any occasion is discouraged.

17. Handling of Money: Employees should be extremely sensitive to the fact that careless or improper handling of church receipts brings quick and severe criticism. The finance committee is officially responsible for the receiving and proper accounting for the funds of the church. Employees should be most diligent in channeling of receipts properly to the person responsible for receiving them.

18. Money and Valuables in Desks: No money or other valuables, either personal or belonging to the church, should be left in desks in the office. If one has money or valuables which belong to the church, turn them in to the business office before the end of the business day on which they are received.

19. Loans and Endorsements: Employees are asked, as a

matter of policy, not to make loans to or endorse security loans for other employees, or for any other person.

20. Physical Examination: All potential employees who work professionally in the kitchen and nursery areas shall take a physical examination, at church expense, before being employed and at least once annually thereafter.

21. Relationship of Personnel Committee to the Staff: The personnel committee shall function through the pastor, or an alternate in the case of absence. No other employee shall have any relationship with the personnel committee, or any member thereof, regarding personnel matters.

Planning

Planning is the deliberate process of developing the appropriate course of action to accomplish a stated objective. Planning must be consistent with policy and should reflect conditions that are known or anticipated to exist at a given point in time.

The pastor should lead his church in both short- and long-term planning. Short term planning may be done with the staff, church council, deacons, or appropriate existing committees of the church. Such matters as the calendar of activities for the new year would come under this classification. Long-term planning may be done with the above groups or with a special long-range planning committee. Long-range planning may include something like an anticipated building several years in the future.[1] Both types of planning are necessary for intelligent and consistent programming and budgeting.

Programming

Programming is the means of accomplishing the work planned. When planning has been done according to policy, the program should follow through with a detailed and time-phased approach. Programs are the immediate and systematic steps to the realization of goals previously set.

The church council, under the leadership of the pastor, should lead in programming. The council should be made up of the Sunday school director, director of church training, W.M.U. director, president of the Baptist men's group, chairman of the deacons, the chairmen of strategic program-related committees, the librarian, nursery coordinator, church hostess, and other support personnel. Church staff members should attend as consultants and information sources.

In the planning and programming done by the church council, that body serves as an advisory and correlating group. The council should help to set goals and objectives and develop ways and means for reaching those goals. This group should study and correlate all proposals made by its individual members. Another major function is the development of a church calendar for the year.

If the program is to be time-phased the council should give attention to necessary sequences of events in order to avoid panic actions when time has become short. Any tentative schedule is subject to alteration and revision, but the following monthly priorities may be of help to keep the program moving on schedule.

1. January: emphasis on Bible study.
2. February: prepare for spring revival services. Elect the church nominating committee.

3. March: Elect the directors of organizations and add them to the nominating committee.
4. March through April: spring revival services.
5. April: train the church council members and begin planning with the church council for the church year to begin in October.
6. May through June: begin organizational planning.
7. June: staff level prebudget planning.
8. June or July: Vacation Bible School.
9. August: elect organizational leaders and the budget planning committee.
10. September: train leadership and plan the budget.
11. October: launch the program; adopt and promote the budget.
12. November: conclude the budget promotion; promote mission offering.
13. December: concentrate on fellowship and worship.

Programming should precede budgeting and give guidance in budget development. For both to be effective, control must be maintained at all times. Since the budget and its controls are to be discussed in the following chapter, perhaps a brief word on program control will be sufficient at this point.

Controlling is the process by which responsible leaders determine whether work accomplished or anticipated conforms to policies, plans, and programs previously developed. Evaluation is an important part of controlling. When evaluation has been done, those in responsible leadership positions can determine what steps to take in correcting deficiencies or discrepancies.

In program control the church council should be the group responsible. They should monitor all facets of the program, report to the council each month, and make corrections or additions to the program as needed.

Helps available in programming

A wealth of material and help is available to the pastor who wants to lead his church in an effective program. Each state convention provides pamphlets and personnel to give guidance in all phases of the work. A letter of inquiry will usually bring an abundance of material to the pastor's desk. It is important for the pastor to remember that he is not alone in the work. There are resource people who can and will help at the associational, state, and national levels.

Church Administration magazine is "must" reading if a pastor is to stay current. In addition to this, help is available in state papers, periodicals for organizations, bulletins from fellow pastors, training books for organizations, and, last but not least, from other churches whose programs are meeting with success.

Selectivity in programming

The sensitive pastor will be highly selective in his recommendations on programming for the local church. He will be careful with his church and honest with himself as he leads. Certain motives can bring trouble to the church and grief to the pastor. Some problem-causing motives in church programming are the desire to surpass other churches for the sake of prestige and notoriety, the setting up and striving for statistical goals only for the sake of breaking previous records, the promotion of irrelevant programs to court denominational favor, and the refusal to cooperate with others merely to show independence. Such motives must be shunned. The pastor and his leaders must learn what is needed in the local church and tailor a program to meet those needs. One wise leader said that all suggested programs are to be treated "cafeteria style." By that he meant that you should take what fits your need and leave the rest.

CHAPTER XII

Budgeting for Effective Ministry

After policies have been made and programs have been drawn up, the church must have some financial plan by which to work as it meets its program goals. The budget is a plan and commitment to underwrite the stated objectives. The pastor must teach his people that the budget is a means to an end. When church budgeting is considered in its correct context, it becomes a "costing out" of those programs previously adopted by the church.

The Program and the Budget

Should the budget be tailored to the program or should the program be tailored to the budget? This is the age-old question that always comes up in one form or another. Differences of opinion are found in most churches on this issue. This author subscribes to the idea that the needs of the community and congregation should receive first consideration. When the needs have been identified and a program has been planned to meet those needs, then the budget should be worked out.

The program must be in mind before wise and accurate

budgeting can be done. Many questions must be answered. What building and equipment adjustments are there to be made? What salary changes are needed? Will staff additions come during the budget period? Will an enlarged program demand new facilities and materials? Will a mission present new financial responsibilities? Will nursery or day school expenses be different on the basis of an expanded Sunday school? What has inflation done to buying power? What cost of living raises are necessary? How many merit raises need to be budgeted? The questions are numerous and the answers are not always easy. When the program is well designed, however, the finances can usually be found. Good budgeting procedures must be preceded by sound, aggressive program planning.

Planning the Budget

Who should plan the church budget? The answer varies from church to church, but the best answer is that those who know what is needed to carry on the program should have a voice in preparing the budget. The pastor and church staff should serve as resource persons for a committee made up of the following: the Sunday school director, church training director, W.M.U. director, Baptist Men's representative (president or R.A. director), chairman of the deacons, chairman of the finance committee, chairman of the youth committee, chairman of the property committee, and one member at large. Such a group will be able to anticipate needs better than any other. When such leaders have input at the budget planning stage, they are better able to live with the results.

When should the budget be planned? Many churches are operating on a January to December fiscal year. When this is the case, the pastor and staff should do some prebudget planning.

In June, the pastor should request the paid staff members to share anticipated budget needs in writing. In July, he should do some research on salaries, allowances, and fringe benefits in a number of churches of size comparable to his own. This information should be shared in writing with the personnel committee. By August, the budget planning committee should have been elected by the church. Individual folders for each member should be prepared. Each folder should include a copy of the current budget, a five-year budget comparison showing what has been done in each category during the five-year period, statistics showing amount budgeted, expenditures in each category for the year to date, and a blank to be filled in with a figure for the coming year.

The budget planning committee should meet, organize, and be given an orientation session. Detailed budget suggestions developed in prebudget research by the staff and others should be shared by the appropriate persons in subsequent meetings.

Throughout September, budget planning committee meetings should be scheduled as often as is necessary to hear all requests and make final decisions. The proposed budget should be shared with the deacons and the church finance committee in October. After study by these groups, a joint recommendation by the budget planning committee, the finance committee, and the deacons should be presented to the church at an announced meeting. By October or early November the church should adopt the budget and begin promotion immediately in order to conclude the campaign before Thanksgiving. (A number of good promotional programs may be secured from Southern Baptist Convention Stewardship Services, 127 Ninth Ave., N., Nashville, Tenn. 37203.)

In each church there will be a different set of needs to be faced by the budget planning committee, and no set form will satisfy every situation. The author shares a form for a worksheet which may be altered to suit the local church and its program. Each committee member should have a copy in a working folder.

Budget Planning Worksheet 19_____

_____Church

Missions:	Last Year	Proposed for Next Year

Missions:	Last Year	Proposed for Next Year

Missions:	Last Year	Proposed for Next Year
Cooperative Program	_____	_____
Associational Missions	_____	_____
Local Mission	_____	_____
Special Missions:	_____	_____
Weekday Ministry	_____	_____
Bus Ministry	_____	_____
Personnel	_____	_____
Seaman's Mission	_____	_____
Other	_____	_____

Administration:

Salary—Pastor	_____	_____
Salary—Minister of Education	_____	_____
Salary—Minister of Music	_____	_____
Salary—Minister of Youth	_____	_____
Secretarial Salaries	_____	_____

Housing Allowances   _____   _____
Utilities   _____   _____
Automobile Expenses   _____   _____
Retirement and
   Social Security   _____   _____
Health Insurance   _____   _____
Group Life Insurance   _____   _____
Convention Expense   _____   _____
Pulpit Supply   _____   _____
   Total   _____   _____

Education and
Organizations:
Sunday School   _____   _____
   Literature   _____   _____
   Supplies   _____   _____
   Activities and
   Promotion   _____   _____
   Vacation Bible School   _____   _____
Church Training   _____   _____
   Literature   _____   _____
   Supplies   _____   _____
   Activities and
   Promotion   _____   _____
Woman's Missionary Union   _____   _____
   Literature   _____   _____
   Supplies   _____   _____
   Activities and
   Promotion   _____   _____
Library   _____   _____
Visual Aids
   New Equipment   _____   _____
   Maintenance   _____   _____
   Film Rental and
   Purchase   _____   _____

Equipment and
   Furnishings   _____   _____
Workshops, Conventions,
   and Assemblies   _____   _____
Study Course and'
   Training Activities   _____   _____
   Total   _____   _____

Music:

Instrumentalists   _____   _____
Supplies   _____   _____
Music Library   _____   _____
Music Literature   _____   _____
Graded Choir Materials
   and Activities   _____   _____
Equipment Maintenance   _____   _____
Choir Tour   _____   _____
Music Promotion   _____   _____
   Total   _____   _____

Youth:

Mission Tour and
   Activities   _____   _____
Youth Retreats   _____   _____
Banquets   _____   _____
Social Activities   _____   _____
Athletic Program   _____   _____
Recreation   _____   _____
Puppet Ministry   _____   _____
Drama   _____   _____
   Total   _____   _____

Service Ministry:
Office Supplies   _____   _____

Office Equipment	———	———
Equipment Maintenance	———	———
Publicity	———	———
Postage	———	———
Annual Budget Expense	———	———
State Paper Subscriptions	———	———
Nursery Salaries	———	———
Nursery Supplies	———	———
Salary—Hostess	———	———
Revival Expense	———	———
Flowers	———	———
Ordinance Expense	———	———
Church-wide Activities	———	———
Church Bus Expense	———	———
Total	———	———

Buildings and Equipment:

Salary—Custodian	———	———
Maintenance Personnel	———	———
Insurance	———	———
Utilities	———	———
Janitorial Supplies	———	———
Repairs and Maintenance of Buildings	———	———
Repairs and Maintenance of Equipment	———	———
New Equipment	———	———
Maintenance of Grounds	———	———
Total	———	———

Debt Retirement:

Mortgage Loan Service	———	———
Monthly Notes	———	———

Capital Expenditures:

Reserve for Development	_____	_____
Site Improvement	_____	_____
Purchase of Major Equipment	_____	_____
Total	_____	_____
Total Budget	_____	_____
Needed per week	_____	_____

Budget Administration

Guidelines for proper budget administration should be spelled out in the church constitution or policy statement. Usually a church-elected finance committee is charged with the responsibility of handling and disbursing funds within the budget parameters or income. Procedures are also suggested in financial policy statements.

If possible the finance committee should organize itself into at least three functioning subgroups. The *budget promotion subcommittee* should keep the church aware of budget giving, goals, and needs throughout the year. The *audit and control subcommittee* should monitor purchase orders or requisitions submitted, keep expenditures in line with income, initial purchase orders as approval for expenditures is granted, and supervise the preparation of monthly written reports to the church. If possible, this group should either conduct or sponsor an annual audit of the church financial records. The *disbursement subcommittee* should check approved purchase orders and pay for such purchases with countersigned checks. All church checks should be signed by two members of the finance committee. Paid staff members should be protected from unnecessary criticism and pressure by being freed from check signing authority and responsibility.

The purchase order or requisition system should be established by the finance committee with church approval. This writer asked the finance committee of a church he pastored to grant a blanket authorization not to exceed fifty dollars to each member of the ministerial staff. This was sufficient for small purchases if needed. No expenditure over fifty dollars could be made by anyone without the approval of at least three members of the finance committee. Those responsible for approving purchase orders checked the appropriate folder in the church office on Wednesday evening and on Sunday. No request had to wait longer than three days for disposition. In this way the finance committee was always aware of both needs and resources. In no case should such a committee become arbitrary or dictatorial but should always operate in line with the church's directions.

Advantages of Good Budgeting

Good budgeting is good discipline for a church and its staff. One of the chief benefits of the budgeting procedure is that it encourages responsible leadership into an early consideration of the policies, planning, and programming necessary for an intelligent budget. When the church leaders have required themselves to look to the future, they find that thorough budget planning becomes much easier. As the program is developed the budget is outlined accordingly.

Responsible budget planning requires an adequate and meaningful organization. Those who take part in the total life of the church should have opportunity for input to the budget plans through their designated representatives on the budget planning committee. Those who have shared in identifying and establishing goals and objectives will be most effective in determining what is needed to realize what has been planned.

The budgeting process demands realism. It requires that the things talked about be set down in cold figures. In the planning and programming phases many thoughts, ambitions, and dreams are exchanged. Thoughts begin to take shape and become tangible in the budgeting process. While budgeting is not intended to thwart or discourage program planning, it does give it a dimension of reality and feasibility. Real cooperation and coordination are called for when the budget is being set down.

The control phase of budgeting forces a periodic and critical analysis of expenditures and accomplishments. An honest look at what is being done with God's money is never out of order. The very fact that a church pursues sound budgetary practices is of interest to creditors. It is a point favoring loans or other financial assistance on the part of the business community.

Problems in Church Budgeting

No plan is better than the people who work it. The whole process of budgeting in the church can be a bane or a boon depending upon the attitudes of those who lead in its planning and administration. Budgeting may not be a pleasant or profitable experience if those involved do not understand its principles, or if the program to be under-written is not accepted as valid and worthwhile. In some cases church leaders may approach budget planning without any clear concepts of what is needed in the program. The organizational structure and related authority must merit respect, and the accounting system must command confidence or serious problems may be the result.

Finally, those who are responsible for the administration of the budget must analyze results and correct discrepancies and deficiencies without becoming bogged down in needless details. Most of the problems in budgeting are due to wrong attitudes, insufficient information, or a lack of basic confidence in what is being done.

The Budget as a Tool

The budget is nothing more than a working tool. It is an informal estimate or projection of anticipated program costs, and can be only as good as the experience and assumptions upon which it is based. This operational tool is valid at the time of approval if it has been planned well, but it must remain flexible and subject to amendment if circumstances change.

Another limitation of the budget is that it puts nothing into effect in its own power. The program underwritten will not just "happen" because it is in the budget. The vote of the congregation assures nothing but authority and intended support. Programs may be financed by the budget, but they must be implemented by active people.

The budget does not take the place of administration. It is a tool for effective administration and is to be used in conjunction with human and physical resources available to the leadership of the church in carrying on a program with spiritual purpose and impact.

CHAPTER XIII

The Pastor and the Church Staff

When does a church need a staff? This is a big and troublesome question. Few churches question their need for a pastor, but many have problems in moving beyond that point. In fact, a vast majority of churches have no paid staff other than the pastor and perhaps a custodian, and they have no legitimate needs in this area.

Church Identity and Staff Need

In "no staff" churches needs are limited by the small number of people in the congregation. In such organizations the expectations are also not extreme, and the members have learned to do many things for themselves. With the organization of necessary committees, the careful planning of work to get the most done with the least amount of lost motion, and perhaps a part-time, volunteer secretary, the pastor can do an effective job in administration and ministry.

To do the job without the advantage of paid help in a small church the pastor must exercise personal discipline and plan his time. Several suggestions might be of help.

1. Establish certain times to do administrative work.
2. Organize work by making a list of things to be done each day.
3. Utilize the telephone when possible. This saves time and expense in running errands, finding information, and ordering materials.
4. Prepare a place at the church for intrachurch communications. A tray, file folder, or pigeon hole for each leader or committee can save time. Simply train the people to check for notes, materials, or messages in their assigned places.
5. Prepare simple forms or note pads for written communications.
6. Ask responsible individuals to give assistance in running errands or picking up materials for the church.

Pastors frequently find their own time to be more effective as they broaden the base of participation among volunteers in the small church situation.

Another group of churches may fall into an "in between" category. These congregations are too large for the pastor to carry all the load, but yet they are too small to afford one or more full-time staff persons. The suggestions listed for the small church fit the "in between" church and may be used effectively, but additional help beyond the volunteer type is necessary.

When the congregation is convinced that more help is needed, the pastor should ask that a personnel committee be elected. After this has been done the pastor and the new committee should have some working meetings to write policies (see Chapter X), determine needs, study resources, and plan strategies in looking for the people needed.

After the working sessions have been held, the policies should be recommended to the church and the positions to be filled should be established by vote of the people. Following these steps the pastor should investigate possible persons to be suggested to the committee for subsequent interviews.

Many churches of this type find it convenient and more feasible to seek out individuals who can work part time for the church while attending school or being employed elsewhere as their major vocations. If this is the course decided upon, several suggestions might be helpful.

1. Do not advertise that a search for an employee is being conducted. There may be unwanted applications for the position.

2. Be sure to select quality people. Only those with the highest moral and spiritual qualifications should be sought. This may cause some delay in filling the position, but it should be remembered that while good people are difficult to find, workers of poor quality are even harder to move when they are once established in a job.

3. Have a clear understanding about the amount of time a part-time worker will be able to devote to the church. Some jobs of this type have evolved into full-time work on part-time pay. This is unfair and usually leads to problems.

4. Establish some time for a weekly staff meeting when the part-time workers can be present.

5. The pastor must give assistance in planning and scheduling the work of his part-time help in order to make his own work and time fill in whatever gaps might be left.

When the church is of such size that one or more full-time staff persons are needed, many of the suggestions listed above may be applicable. However, at such time as the church needs ministers and secretaries or others whose full time is to be utilized, additional care is needed. This is an important move and thoughtful attention and prayer must be devoted to the task in order to prevent wrong decisions and choices. The multiple staff member church can find itself greatly helped or hurt by the very process of preparation and selection. The pastor's ministry and the church's effectiveness may be enhanced or jeopardized by the addition of others to the staff.

Church and Pastoral Preparedness

Concepts are important in the work of the church. How does the church look upon the acquisition of other workers? This question is not difficult to answer if the pastor is firmly established as the selfless, dedicated undershepherd of the flock. If he has "paid his rent" with the people through his own ministry, they will love and respect him enough to follow his leadership when staff members are needed. In such a position of esteem the pastor is both honored and challenged. The people depend upon him, and he must not lead them into costly and destructive mistakes.

The wise pastor will make it his job to see to it that the church is prepared before staff members are employed. By thoughtful study in conjunction with church leadership he should help to establish the need for each staff position. A part of such studies should be the consideration of whether a part-time or a full-time job is involved. As the time approaches when actual job descriptions are written or seriously discussed in detail, a thorough understanding must be developed within the congregation about what a person in such a position can be reasonably expected to do. The people must not get the impression that the addition of one more paid worker will be a cure-all for all church needs and problems.

234 THE PASTOR AND THE CHURCH STAFF

Another factor in preparing the church for another worker is the determination of the financial ability and willingness of the church. An adequate salary accompanied by appropriate allowances and fringe benefits is one of many essentials in such a process. These matters must be thought through at least in broad outline before an individual is sought.

Not only should the pastor help the church to be prepared but he must be ready for the coming of another person to work at his side. The man who has never been responsible for anyone but himself may be in for some real adjustments emotionally and administratively, and in his personal work habits.

Emotionally, the pastor must be mature and secure enough that he does not feel threatened by or become jealous of the staff worker. He must be able to let the people rejoice in every success of the new worker, and he must also be ready to accept criticism that may come to him personally if the staff colleague does not perform up to the expectations of some people in the church. The mature pastor is frequently called upon to absorb the unpleasant and reflect the pleasant to the fellow worker. This may not seem fair, but is frequently the way it is. Let the pastor remember that any praise directed to the staff is a credit to him also, and any blame going to them is partially his responsibility.

Administratively, the pastor must be prepared to give the time and attention necessary to make the staff a smoothly functioning unit. One indispensable ingredient in this area is the weekly staff meeting. There is no way for a staff to be effective in its work and harmonious in its relationships unless the pastor invests this time each week.

This writer established a firm rule that the staff meeting was to be at 9 A.M. every Monday. Apart from illness or absence from the city, no staff member was excused. The meeting opened with a devotional led by one of the staff members, followed by the sharing of prayer concerns and a time of prayer. Next came the calendar review for the week at hand; on the last Monday of the month a projection of the major items for the coming month was discussed. Conflicts, scheduling problems, and sharing of staff involvement in various activities could be taken care of at this period. After the calendar and program considerations were discussed, items of special interest to the entire staff were given attention. When all matters of a general nature had been handled, the secretaries and other administrative workers returned to their duties. The pastor and the ministerial staff took a short break for coffee and then returned to do program planning and to share burdens, problems, victories, and joys. At such times the atmosphere was always relaxed and informal. These meetings proved to be some of the most pleasant and profitable times this writer ever spent in the work of a local church. Such can be the experience of any pastor who is willing to make himself available administratively.

Not only must the pastor be prepared emotionally and administratively, he must also be prepared to set the right work example. The pastor who believes that the coming of additional staff members reduces his job has not had experience with a multiple staff church situation. As the church grows and adds new workers, the work of the under-shepherd increases. He must not only meet with the staff collectively in staff meetings, but he must also be available to each of them for periodic working conferences. Those who are assistants can go just so far in their individual tasks before they need some time with their leader to validate, confirm, or redirect them in the work. The pastor must be willing and available to give such assistance, and he must also set the pace in his personal work schedule. When he was in the pastorate, the writer asked each man on the ministerial staff to set a visitation goal. Ordinarily, each staff member took ten prospects per week to be visited, and the pastor took twenty. The staff that can see the pastor out in front as the pacesetter knows that the leader is truly leading and not just pushing.

The pastor who prepares himself and his church for the employment of staff workers is wise, and he finds himself, the staff, and the congregation happier because of his wisdom and care.

Staff Qualifications

The pastor should lead his church to seek the best people who can be found for staff positions. It is a well-known fact that weak leadership is one of the most expensive things that a church can have. In a day when other professionals are forced to meet increasingly high standards, people are not likely to be impressed with unqualified and incompetent people in church leadership positions.

Education is something that is expected in all professional positions. There may have been a time when the pastor in some church situations felt little pressure about a college and seminary education because the educational level in the church was not high. In recent times, however, even the smallest rural churches may have several college graduates or master's degrees within the congregation. The pastor who does not have an education may find himself in a difficult position unless he has worked hard to compensate for this lack by study through a rigorous program of self-improvement.

The staff member must be trained in like manner. Most churches that are large enough to require several staff members can require high standards, and they do. The church worker must not only have college and seminary training, but also must have achieved a fair level of competence in his job. Churches have learned to tell when a man holds a degree and when he is truly educated.

Another qualification is dedication. Those who lead churches must demonstrate the love and fervent spirit they talk about. To talk about selfless service and hard work for Christ and then not show it in one's actions and work tends to create a credibility gap in the minds of the church members. For the sake of the Lord the staff member should have a desire to do the best possible job at each task that he faces.

There is an essential difference in the work of a called minister and that of other people. The church must always be in large measure a labor of love. The staff position is more than a nine to five job or a way to make a living. To be sure, a living is involved, but the task of caring for souls must have a much higher motivation or it will not succeed. A willingness to work hard because of a deep love for God and people is the most important qualification for a good staff member.

General and Specific Job Descriptions

There are two schools of thought on staff job descriptions. Some pastors are of the opinion that each position should carry with it a detailed job description with nothing left out. Many sincere efforts have been made to realize this goal, and many have resulted in frustration. Some, however, have done creditable jobs and strong, effective staff organizations have resulted. One of the most complete helps at this point has been written by Robert A. Young and is entitled *The Development of a Church Manual of Administrative Policies*. Any pastor would do well to purchase a copy and have it available for ready reference.

This writer has studied a variety of job descriptions for various positions and found some deficiency in each. How does one pinpoint and describe every detail of a job that calls for working with people? There are simply too many variables to make this possible.

For many years in different types of church situations he grappled with the problem and in the process came out with a simple three-point job description for all who work for the church. It presupposes *high quality, God-called*, and *willingly dedicated* people, and requires them to *love the Lord, love His people, and work accordingly*. Many have said that it is too simplistic and will not work. The truth is that when people work because they love the Lord and His people, they spend more hours and do a better job than they will for any other reasons. With the right kind of people and the highest possible motivation of love, the work goes well, and people are happier in their work at the church.

Staff Relations

Many churches have experienced serious problems in the church fellowship because staff members could not get along with each other. This is sad, and it is also unnecessary. The pastor should help the staff to practice some of the basics of the teachings of Christ on interpersonal relationships. He gave guidelines that will work if they are put to work. They are simple, brief, and practical. Anyone can understand them, and most staff members will profit greatly by their use.

Jesus taught us, as the basic rule of relationships, to treat the fellow worker as we would want him to treat us. He also taught us to talk about personal conflict with the ones involved and not with others. He impressed upon us that we should be more forgiving and less critical of each other. There are those who say this does not work. How do they know unless they have given His ideas an honest try?

There are some for whom vaccines do not work—those who have not tried them.

The staff that loves Christ, the church, and each other is a happy group. When the leaders lead in matters like love, understanding, forgiveness, longsuffering, and Christian grace, the church senses the difference Christ can make and begins to grow in His likeness.

CHAPTER XIV

The Pastor and His Deacons

Happy is the pastor who has a good relationship with his deacons. Unfortunately, however, this is not always the case. Both offices were intended by the Lord to enhance the growth and fellowship of His church, and when the relationship is good this goal can be accomplished. When the two do not work together, both suffer and the church is not strengthened.

Acquaintance with the Deacons

When a pastor moves to a new church, he should make it his business to get to know his deacons on a personal basis. This will take time and careful, tactful work, but it is well worth all the effort expended. As they come to know and understand each other they are better able to function harmoniously. During that critical first year in the church the wise pastor should learn some of the following:

1. The deacon's age and tenure in the local church and community are important. The man who has lived in the same rural community for 50 years and has served as a deacon in the same small church for 25 of

those years has deep roots and strong influence. His word will carry more weight with the people than the word of a pastor who has only been in the church for six months.

2. The background of a particular deacon is important if the pastor is to understand him and communicate effectively. If this man has been a pillar of the church and is loved and respected by the people, there are reasons for his prominence. Find out what those reasons are.

3. The deacon's experience with pastors in that church or in other churches is important to an understanding of the way he views all pastors. If his experience has not been good, the new pastor will need to work harder to "live down" any bad images of preachers the deacon may harbor in his mind. The author found in one pastorate that most of the deacons had had an unpleasant experience with two previous pastors. The atmosphere was cool toward preachers when the author arrived on the scene. So deep were the wounds that it took a two-year rebuilding process to establish pastoral credibility with the deacons. This had to be done before much work could be accomplished, but once it was done things went smoothly.

4. Factors peculiar to a given community can be of real importance to pastor and deacon relations. How do most of the deacons earn their livelihood? Are they farmers, shift workers, day laborers, small business men, corporate executives, or traveling men? The way a man works will have much to do with his involvement in the church. A trucker cannot be at church visitation if he has a truck broken down in the middle of the highway seventy-five miles from home one hour before visitation is to begin.

Other factors peculiar to a given community may have to do with the deacon's family ties among the church members. In those situations where the people are related to each other the pastor needs to know the nature and the strength of those family relationships. If an elderly deacon has two sons, a son-in-law, and two nephews also serving as deacons, the pastor must know this and become a friend to all if he is to work with any of them. Such deacons may quarrel among themselves, but the pastor must never take sides with one against another.

5. The educational and cultural level of each deacon is a matter of great importance. This has much to do with the way a man thinks and acts in the church. The man with a good education is usually more progressive in his outlook on church affairs.

6. The home life of the deacon will have much bearing on his attitude at church. If his wife and children respect and support him, he is likely to be secure and effective in his work as a deacon. The deacon's stability and reliability in the leadership role will be greatly affected by what he faces in his family when he returns home.

7. The pastor also needs to know the prevailing attitude of the deacons toward themselves. Some have traditionally viewed themselves as a board of directors with the power to hire and fire preachers. Others have rightly seen themselves as fellow ministers and servants of the church. Whatever their self-image may be the pastor must know it and be prepared to work accordingly. He must also remember that while erroneous ideas can be altered, it takes time, patience, and understanding.

Attitudes of Pastors and Deacons

"Deacons are not the pastor's enemies. We want to be his friends." These words were spoken by a deacon of many years of experience in several different churches. When asked what he thought young preachers should be taught about pastor-deacon relations, this wise deacon lifted his fists to a boxing position and then gradually lowered them. With this dramatic gesture he said, "Tell young preachers not to come at their deacons with their guard up. We don't want to fight; we want to help."

There may be exceptions to what this deacon said, but this writer feels that most deacons feel exactly as he did. The pastor makes a mistake when he lets one or two negative personalities convince him that deacons are all bad.

The wise pastor may do well to form a personal checklist on his own attitude toward those who have been elected by the church to serve with him on a volunteer basis without salary. As he looks at his relationship to his deacons the pastor might ask himself some questions.

Have I tried to learn as much as possible about each of my deacons? Have I really gotten to know each man personally? In the give and take process of deliberation and discussion, do I make an honest effort to avoid the polarization of positions and personalities? Am I mature enough to recognize the difference between principle and procedure? Which of the two (principles or procedures) is negotiable and which is nonnegotiable? Am I secure enough not to take procedural differences personally? Can I look at differences of opinion objectively without feeling threatened to the point that I regard those who differ as my enemies? Do I practice what I preach about loving those who are not always very lovable?

Paul wrote to Timothy, "Pay close attention to yourself

and to your teaching; persevere in these things; for as you do this you will insure salvation both for yourself and for those who hear you" (1 Timothy 4:16 NASV). This is good advice to pastors and deacons in their attitudes toward each other.

Qualifications of Deacons

The office of deacon arose in a time of need in the life of the New Testament church. The number of believers had grown to the point that the needs could no longer be met by the apostles. Luke gives some of the earliest qualifications as well as the history of this important office of the church:

> Now at this time while the disciples were increasing in number, a complaint arose on the part of the Hellenistic Jews against the native Hebrews, because their widows were being overlooked in the daily serving of food. And the twelve summoned the congregation of the disciples and said, "It is not desirable for us to neglect the word of God in order to serve tables. But select from among you, *brethren*, seven *men of good reputation, full of the Spirit* and of *wisdom*, whom we may put in charge of this task. But we will devote ourselves to prayer, and to the ministry of the Word." (Acts 6:1–4 NASV)

The specific qualifications mentioned in this passage have to do with a man's standing among his peers, his ongoing relationship to God, and his genuine wisdom in relating to others, described in detail by James: "But the wisdom from above is first pure, then peaceable, gentle, reasonable, full of mercy, and good fruits, unwavering, without hypocrisy" (James 3:17).

Paul gives the most complete list of qualifications for the deacon in writing to Timothy:

> Deacons likewise must be men of dignity, not double-tongued, or addicted to much wine or fond of sordid gain, but holding to the

mystery of the faith with a clear conscience. And let those also first be tested; then let them serve as deacons if they are beyond reproach. Women must likewise be dignified, not malicious gossips, but temperate, faithful in all things. Let the deacons be husbands of only one wife, and good managers of their children and their own households. For those who have served well as deacons obtain for themselves a high standing and great confidence in the faith that is in Christ Jesus. (1 Timothy 3:8–13 NASV)

This list treats such standards as personality and decorum, integrity, influence in the community, stewardship, doctrinal soundness, proven reliability, impeccable morals, marital faithfulness, careful execution of fatherhood and home leadership, and marriage to a wife of the same characteristics.

Nomination and Election of Deacons

There are many ideas and systems used in the nomination and election of deacons. Perhaps the best system this writer found calls for the names of all the men of the church membership to be published on a nomination sheet. At the bottom of that sheet a number of blanks are provided for the membership to write in their nominations. On the Sunday when the nomination forms are distributed to all members of the church, the pastor should preach a sermon on the qualifications of the deacon. Each person is asked to make his nominations a matter of prayer, family discussion (for the benefit of children who are members), and thoughtful selection and is instructed to turn the list in to a ballot box at the church on the following Sunday.

When all nominations are in, the deacons (or an appropriate committee) tabulate the ballots in order of congregational preference. A special committee should then meet with the pastor to discuss the results. If confidential information should make it unwise to consider a man on the list, the pastor should share the fact that he has such information, but he should not break a confidence placed in him by divulging the nature of the information. At this same conference the committee should be informed as to whether the nominees are all tithers. This writer believes that a man must first be faithful in his stewardship before he is considered as a deacon.

When the committee has this basic information in hand, it should divide itself into teams of two and begin calling on the men, in order, beginning with the one receiving the highest number of nominations and working down the list until the required number have been interviewed and accepted. At each interview the team should talk to both the deacon prospect and his wife. The scriptural qualifications should be read and discussed, and the man should be asked if he meets the qualifications and if he is willing to serve.

After the list of needed candidates is complete, the committee should submit it to the church for formal election for a specified period of service. Many churches have a rotation plan for deacon service with the term of office lasting three or four years before the deacon is rotated to an inactive status for a minimum of one year. After the year has elapsed he is then eligible for nomination again. Some churches elect deacons for life and do not use a rotation plan.

Ordination and Installation of Deacons

When the church chooses men to serve as deacons, a service of ordination and installation is in order. This seemed to be the pattern set by the New Testament church at Jerusalem. When the apostles had made their recommendations concerning those who were to be selected, the church acted in the following manner:

> And the statement found approval with the whole congregation; and they chose Stephen, a man full of faith and of the Holy Spirit, and Philip, Prachorus, Nicanor, Timon, Parmenas and Nicolas, a proselyte from Antioch. And *these they brought before the apostles; and after praying, they laid their hands on them.* And the word of God kept on spreading; and the number of disciples continued to increase greatly in Jerusalem, and a great many of the priests were becoming obedient to the faith. (Acts 6:5–7)

In modern times the process of ordination may be a bit more elaborate in form, but its substance is essentially the same. After the deacons have been formally elected by the church, the pastor should call together an ordination council and organize it for the purpose of examining those needing ordination. The council may be composed of the pastor and ordained deacons plus any ordained ministers he may choose to invite. Only those who are ordained should participate. They should elect a chairman and a secretary before the examination begins. Questions on the qualifications set forth in the Scripture and on such matters as the church, the candidate's views on the Scripture, baptism, the deacon's duties, cooperation within the church, the church's cooperation with the denomination, and other necessary issues may be asked. When the examination is concluded the chairman should entertain a motion that the church authorize the council to proceed with ordination.

The service of ordination should be scheduled and announced in advance in order to allow those involved sufficient time to invite their families and friends to attend. At the hour of service the candidates for ordination and their wives should be seated on the front pew nearest the pulpit. The pastor should preside over an appropriately designed order of service. A suggested format is as follows:

Service of Ordination

Prelude	Organist
Call to Worship: "Rise Up O Men of God"	Choir
Invocation	Vice-Chairman of Deacons
Hymn: "Serve The Lord With Gladness"	
Hymn: "I'll Go Where You Want Me to Go"	
Report and Recommendation of the Council	Secretary
Charge to the Church	Pastor
Charge to the New Deacons	Chairman of Deacons
Hymn	
Offertory	Organist
Special Music	Choir
Ordination Sermon	Pastor
Laying on of Hands	All Ordained Men
Ordination Prayer	Senior Deacon
Invitation	
Benediction	

Fellowship period honoring the new deacons

The above order of worship is one of many which may be used. It does contain the essential elements for such a service. Obviously it may be changed to suit the desires of those involved.

If there are deacons to be installed who have been previously ordained, a time of recognition for these men and their wives should be included in the service. They should sit together on the pew immediately behind those to be ordained, and they should be asked to stand in the line to be greeted by the membership at the close of the service.

Deacon Orientation

Immediately after new deacons have been ordained and installed, the pastor should plan a special orientation period for them. An appropriate book such as *The Baptist Deacon* by Dr. Robert Naylor or *The Ministry of the Deacon* should be studied. Not only should he know what the Scriptural qualifications are, but he should also be well informed on church expectations. Some of these may be listed as follows:

I. The deacon should provide an example in Christian living for others in the church.
 1. His personal conduct must be above reproach.
 2. His language should be clean.
 3. His home life should be exemplary.
 4. His attitude must be positive and helpful.
 5. His stewardship must be unquestioned.

II. The deacon should serve the church to the best of his ability.
 1. He should attend all worship services unless providentially hindered.
 2. He should be an active witness for his Lord.
 3. He should give support to the total church program both in attitude and actions.
 4. He should attend all deacons' meetings unless providentially hindered.
 5. He should share in the church visitation ministry.
 6. He should stand ready to assist the pastor in any way possible.

The nature of the church program, the personality and desires of the pastor, and other factors may serve to modify this list, but these are the basic areas of responsibility.

Communication with the Deacons

How does a pastor communicate the necessary details of the church program to men who only meet once a month? This is a key problem in pastor-deacon relations. There is a tendency on the part of pastors to assume that the deacons should already know all that is going on in the church. This is seldom a valid assumption. No matter how dedicated a deacon may be he still has to spend most of his time at work. He cannot be at the church every day in order to keep up with what is going on. He wants to know, and he needs to know, but how can he stay informed?

This writer has always subscribed to the idea that deacons and churches function better when maximum information is available to them at all times. Churches make intelligent and sound decisions if they have sufficient data on which to base those decisions. At the point of informing the membership the deacon can be an invaluable resource person, provided he has the necessary facts available to him in an easily accessible form. It is great when the pastor can say to the congregation in its business session, "If you need further information or details, ask a deacon, and he can help you." In order to do this with confidence, the pastor and staff must help the deacon before he can be effective in helping the membership. Some type of tool for keeping the deacon up to date is necessary.

"The Deacon's Notebook" is the tool devised by the author to help his deacons to be knowledgeable about the details of the church program without having to remember all of it. In order to set up this system the pastor should purchase enough 8½ by 11 three-ring notebooks to supply one for each deacon, each ministerial staff member, and himself. With these notebooks he should buy enough index tabs to supply each notebook with thirteen sections (one general section and one section for each month from January through December). The notebooks should be worked up initially and kept up monthly by the church secretary. All notebooks should be kept in the church office on a shelf easily accessible to the deacon. Each should be labeled with the deacon's name on the spine of the notebook. The only time the books should leave the office is for the deacons' meetings. Duplicate copies of the materials included may be provided for the deacon's use at home if desired, but the notebook itself should remain at the church so that it can be kept current for his easy reference while at the church. After all, this is where he faces most of the questions that come from the members.

The Deacon's Notebook should have the following materials included for his information:

General Section in the front of the book:

1. A list of all active deacons should begin the book, with each man's address, home and work phone numbers, and place of employment carefully recorded. Each man's wife's given name should be listed in parentheses following his name, and, if desired, autobiographical sketches may also be included.
2. A list of all inactive deacons with the same information as above
3. A copy of the church constitution
4. Copies of church policy statements
5. A copy of the current church budget
6. A list of all church committees
7. Other general information items necessary for the local church

Monthly Sections for January through December

1. Minutes of last deacons' meeting
2. Minutes of last church business meeting
3. Financial report for the previous month
4. Committee recommendations if the deacons are to be asked to join in recommending to the church
5. Pastoral suggestions for the consideration of the deacons
6. Agenda for the meeting
7. Paper for personal notes and observations

The notebooks should be prepared by the secretary before each meeting of the deacons and carried to the meeting place by the chairman or the secretary of the deacons.

At the end of each year all dated materials should be taken out of the notebooks and made available to the deacons in manila envelopes. The binder may be used for a number of years before replacement is necessary. Usually, the notebook is given to the deacon at the end of his period of service and a new one is begun for his replacement.

The Pastor's Homework

"People have a tendency to be down on what they are not up on." Such were the words of a wise country preacher. Before the pastor comes before his deacons with a suggestion he must "do his homework." Proposals that are ill-conceived or hastily prepared seldom meet with a favorable response. The pastor must take time to think through his ideas, gather adequate data or documentation, and try them out with key deacon leadership before he comes before the group. The wise pastor will be aware of the "opinion leaders" among the deacons (see Chapter III). If the item at hand is of great importance, he might find it worthwhile to visit with each man who has such influence to gain the advantage of their views before his presentation. To be adequately prepared is always a good investment of time and effort.

The Deacons' Meeting and Beyond

The deacons should never consider themselves as a board of directors. They are really ministerial consultants and coworkers. Dedicated laymen can be of invaluable aid to a pastor and church staff if they regard themselves as fellow servants to the church. The deacons' meeting should be permeated with love and mutual confidence. Each man is there to help, and no man should be there to rule. Let the pastor and the deacons always remember that authority should reside in the church—not in the deacons or the pastor. They are there to help and give guidance. Final decisions should be made by the church.

When the deacons have considered a matter to go to the church, they should go with their recommendations as one voice. Full and free discussion should take place in the deacons' meeting, but when the body speaks all should cooperate. The church should never be confronted with a majority and minority report from its servants. The deacons and the pastor should go to the place of prayer until they can come to the church as one voice.

When the church has made its decision, the pastor and the deacons should move forward harmoniously in the implementation of the will of the congregation. The ministry of the church is enhanced by a unity of spirit and purpose among its leaders.

CHAPTER XV

The Pastor's Public Relations

What is public relations? Many have equated public relations with slick Madison Avenue advertising and sales campaigns. This is not the approach most pastors want to take to the ministry, so they avoid the term and its principles like a plague. Some pastors have gone to the opposite extreme with such statements as "I don't care what people think of me as long as they hear what I have to say." Of course, either extreme is inappropriate and should be avoided by the sincere undershepherd of God's church. There is, however, a strong middle ground where knowledgeable work is possible and needful.

Church and Pastoral Public Relations Defined

Public relations for a church and its pastor is the knowledgeable sharing of ideas and programs in such ways as to secure favorable response from those persons who need them. The pastor will recognize that he has more than one public to whom he must relate if his work is to go smoothly and people are to benefit spiritually from his ministry.

The pastor must be able to discern the interests of people and familiarize himself with their attitudes. As he does this, he must then present the policies and programs of the church in such ways as to gain voluntary acceptance by a majority of those involved. Once he has presented the program and found it acceptable he must implement the work to the best interest of those whom he serves. The task of a pastor in church public relations is to merit the good will of a maximum number of different people in order to persuade them to make decisions and take actions which will be in their own spiritual interest.

The Publics Identified

There are two basic publics with which the pastor must work. The internal public is that group of people who are directly related to the church in some way. The external public is the larger segment of the community not holding membership in the church or any of its organizations. Both publics have numerous subdivisions which must be recognized and understood if the pastor is to work with them effectively.

Again, a number of questions might be of help as a minister attempts to identify the various publics with whom he is to work. Who lives here? How many people live here? What is the distribution of the population according to age, sex, ethnic background, educational, and economic status? How long has the average resident lived here? How fast are they moving in and out? These and many other factors will tell a pastor who is there; how they function; and what can reasonably be expected. The undershepherd who is wise will want to know the people before he proposes a program of work.

A Positive Approach to Public Relations

The pastor must earn the public's support of his programs. In order to do this he must project a program of quality work and place a premium on the understanding and willing acceptance of his proposals by the public. To many people in the community who need its ministry the most the church often appears to be negative, stern, and forbidding. Some churches have given the impression of being quarrelsome and contentious. If such negative impressions of the local church are found to exist, extra efforts must be put forth not only to erase the bad image but to replace it with one that is more wholesome.

The basic message of the church is to show those in the community the positive, life-giving power that comes to the individual from Jesus Christ. This message cannot be communicated in a vacuum. As others view the church members they gain their first and perhaps most permanent impressions of the Christian faith. Those who are believers must share verbally and demonstrate in their own lives what Christ can do for the person, his family, and his community.

To make the gospel and the church attractive the pastor must lead his people to make the name of the church synonymous with friendly service to the community. The genuine courtesy and compassionate concern—the "second mile" attitude in helping others—speaks louder than all the sermons one can preach. Recently, this writer was a guest in a suburban church in a southern city. As he accompanied the pastor in visitation, they went into the home of a family with eight children, all of whom were less than nine years of age! The home was clean, and the mother had a fine disposition and great love for her family, but it was quite obvious that she was extremely fatigued. The pastor asked her how she would respond to a "mother's day out" program, in which the church nursery would be open, with competent workers, to care for her preschool-aged children one day per week in order to give her a chance to shop, go to the beauty parlor or a movie, or just enjoy some free time. The young woman's response was almost ecstatic: "That would be great!" She found it hard to believe that the church could really care about her personal need for a few hours rest or diversion each week. To have a good relationship with people the church must become an institution that cares about people every day, not just on Sunday.

A Pastor's Personal Public Relations

The man who serves as a pastor lives in a glass house and is constantly before the critical gaze of other people. The option of the pastor is not whether he will be criticized, but by whom and for what reasons. The nature of his position says that criticism is bound to come, and there are times when it hurts and times when it can help. He should never invite adverse criticism, but when it comes he must not let it defeat him. The minister who learns to accept it with good grace, and even to laugh at himself occasionally, will be far ahead of the game.

While some comments of a negative nature are the lot of every man of God, there are some ways to minimize major criticisms. The pastor must make sure that he is a man whose integrity is beyond question in the minds of his people. He must be scrupulously honest and sincere. His standards must be high, his speech clean and considerate, and his judgment and common sense should be good. The use of the pulpit must be always in the best interest of the people; it must never be used to lambast a certain segment while others sit in confused and hurt silence.

Many pastors' problems in churches and communities are in part self-induced. There are several points to consider for pastors who want good relations with their publics.

1. Don't starve your own soul. The pastor gives out all of the time. If he does not reserve some time for taking in fresh spiritual food, he will become dry and ineffective spiritually.

2. Don't sponsor any person, program, or idea without a thorough investigation of possible short-term and long-term consequences. Remember your church is closely identified with you in the community. You are there as their minister, not as a crusader for special causes or persons.

3. Don't make indiscriminate recommendations. In the minds of others you are closely identified with any cause or person you recommend. If that which receives your stamp of approval should not turn out well, your reputation and relationships may be damaged.

4. Don't get involved in politics. The pastor is there to be the friend of all people regardless of their political persuasion. He should speak out against evil and for good dealing with spiritual principles and values, not with personalities. You should vote your own convictions, but you should never allow your pulpit to become a platform for the endorsement of any party or candidate.

5. Don't try to run the church in an autocratic manner. The church belongs to the Lord and His people, not to the pastor. The man who gets the idea that he

alone is capable of making intelligent decisions is headed for trouble.

6. Don't abuse your credit. Good credit is a great asset for a pastor, but he must not allow himself to use it so much that he cannot pay his bills when they are due. If a problem arises and prompt payment is impossible, talk to the creditor and ask for additional time.

7. Don't become overly familiar with members of the opposite sex. Be sure to take adequate precautions against circumstances that appear questionable.

The pastor should understand what community norms are. This will vary greatly in different parts of the country, but the preacher who deliberately defies reasonable expectations may find his relationships with the people less than he would like. His personal habits in driving his automobile, dress, conversation, and even his use of leisure time can be enhancing or damaging to his influence with other people.

Public Relations on Sunday Morning

The pastor has a responsibility for the image of the church when new people arrive on the scene on Sunday. No visitation program will be successful in attracting people on a sustained basis if they encounter an atmosphere that is unattractive at the church on the occasion of their first visit.

The appearance of the church buildings and facilities can have a bearing on whether new people find it inviting. The pastor should lead and encourage the people of the church to maintain all buildings, equipment, and grounds in the best possible fashion. Cleanliness and neatness make a church attractive. Buildings do not need to be lavish or expensive to be in good condition. If they are freshly painted and well maintained, with a neat appearance both inside and out, newcomers get the impression that both the pastor and the people take pride in their church.

Any items that might pose a hazard to the safety of the people should receive attention. Such things as broken steps, rough or irregular sidewalks, loose stair treads, or slippery floors should be corrected, not only for the safety of people but as a protection for the church. In an era when lawsuits are proliferating, the church is also subject to court action if anyone is hurt on its premises due to negligence. The safety of those who attend must always be high on the list of priorities for both the pastor and the people.

The church must also have strong pastoral leadership if it is to present itself as a friendly church. The lack of friendliness at a church may well be the most frequently heard criticism of some pastors and congregations. The pastor can take constructive steps to reduce or eliminate such adverse comments.

1. Set up a registration desk where new families can be registered for Sunday school all at one place. Have one or more efficient volunteers who are familiar with the forms to give assistance.

2. Have some hosts or hostesses nearby to take the new family members to their respective departments. Begin with the youngest child, allowing the parents to see where each is placed, and work up to the adults. The host or hostess should quietly ask a friendly member of each department to step out and into the hall and meet the new arrivals. That member should then take responsibility for making the visitor acquainted and comfortable with the department or class.

3. The pastor should enlist one or two men to watch for late arrivals for Sunday school or early arrivals for worship services. Such persons should receive a warm greeting, an order of worship, and any desired assistance in finding a place.
4. Ushers should be carefully selected and trained. The church usher can be one of the greatest public relations assets a church can have. He should be schooled in how to greet people and make them feel welcome.
5. One or more persons should assume the responsibility for keeping the building properly heated or cooled and ventilated.
6. The pastor should be sure that the church nursery is properly staffed and in a clean, orderly condition for each service. A nursery coordinator should be elected by the church to take primary responsibility for this vital area and its workers.
7. In addition to all physical facilities being in good condition, the pastor should be sure that the order of service, the music, and the sermon are in the best possible form.

The attentive concern for details on the part of the pastor can have a positive effect on the church people. If the pastor cares, the people will care, and newcomers are attracted to a caring church.

Internal Promotions

The pastor must become a student of human nature and interpersonal communications. Those who sell toothpaste, cereals, or soft drinks are always in the process of learning what it takes to attract attention and stimulate people to action. The local minister must discipline himself to learn methods of reaching his own church and community with a message concerning the programs he espouses.

The use of well-located and well-maintained inside bulletin boards, attractive outside signs, quality mailouts, appropriate personal letters, telephone calls and other such media can help a pastor get his message to the people. After several years of promoting the church budget through regular mailouts and church paper articles, one pastor decided on a visual presentation. An amateur photographer gave assistance in making good slides on the various ministries of the church which were underwritten by the budget. A radio personality assisted with the preparation of a script for narration and a very attractive presentation was made in a Sunday morning service. The budget came to life in human terms as never before, and the promotion was a real success. The aggressive pastor does not need huge amounts of money to do a creditable job in promotions. A little ingenuity, some imagination, and a genuine concern for people can accomplish much.

The Pastor and the Media

When media publicity is mentioned, pastors may have horrible visions of monstrous advertising budgets that are not within their means. For this reason many make few attempts at communicating outside the realm of their own church paper. The real fact is that much valuable advertising can be done with little or no budget for such matters.

Most local newspapers are willing to print church news events if they are written up correctly. If the local church is to have a guest speaker for a special event, the pastor could have as many as three news articles in the paper without spending any money. He could write an advance story telling of the event and the speaker to be published a week before the event; a second story should be written for publication the day before the event using pictures, names of local people giving assistance, and prominent quotes from the personality who is to speak; a third story following the event could be written reporting what happened and what was said. Remember, people like to see their names and those of friends in print. Newspaper people know this and will welcome copy that is brought to them containing such information if it is well written.

Other articles could be written about church anniversaries, buildings, special programs, dedications, and local church leaders. For those events of a major nature the pastor should send the press a special invitation to attend. The reports of newsworthy happenings in a local church can be worth much in their advertising value. Such things can serve well to keep the ministry of the congregation before the eye of the public.

When the church spends money for media advertising, the pastor should enlist help to see that the materials are properly laid out and attractive. Advertising that is poorly done may do more harm than good among people who are accustomed to seeing a high degree of professionalism in commercial advertising. God deserves better than a second-rate effort in publishing news about His church.

If radio or television advertising is done, the assistance of the appropriate professionals at the station should be sought. It is to the best interest of the church and the station to assure that the money spent is well invested. All such electronic publicity requires skilled persons if the product is to be of high quality.

The pastor should read, study, ask questions, watch others and in every possible way learn all he can to put his church before the public with quality in the presentation. The institution for which Christ gave Himself deserves to go to the public with materials that merit acceptance.

CHAPTER XVI

Finally, Brethren

To write comprehensively about the work of the pastor is like trying to discuss "the universe and other things." Clearly, it is an important task because each man and each church has personality which becomes an integral part of ministry. No one can presume to give complete counsel to such diversity. If some helpful guidance has been gained from the pragmatics of this work, however, the author is sufficiently rewarded. Obviously, most of the material has been written with the seminary student or beginner in ministry in mind.

In these closing pages the attitude of the pastor comes into final focus. How does he feel about the task God has called him to perform? What are his sentiments toward the church people with whom he must work? Happy is the minister who learns how to maintain a cooperative frame of mind. People may not be all that he might wish, but the man who learns to work with them instead of against them is destined for success and real joy in his ministry. No one is strong or wise enough to be a successful "loner" in God's work. He needs people and people need him. He may not love their actions and attitudes, but a pastor must learn to love people in a deep and real way. Those who are leaders in the local church may not always share the under-shepherd's views, but his love and understanding can help to bring about a synthesis which will be mutually reward-ing to both pastor and congregation.

Domination versus Subjugation

There are some pastors who take an autocratic ap-proach to ministry. The entire church operation must re-volve around them, and no one else is allowed to share in the decision-making process. When the personality of the pastor is strong, it may seem that this system is not only working but actually is more efficient than the traditional plan where the group is more involved. A man with a dy-namic, aggressive approach to leadership can make things happen. This cuts down on lost time and energy in the various meetings necessary for a negotiated church pro-gram. At first, a strong autocracy may seem to recommend itself, but in the long run it frequently falls apart with dev-astating consequences.

Several factors should be considered as a pastor con-templates the possibility of a "one-man show." In most cases there is more personal insecurity than strength in-volved. The "strong man" image is often a smoke screen to conceal a very insecure personality. When this is the case, the weakness inevitably begins to surface, and when it does, both the pastor and the church are in deep trouble.

No one man is strong enough to be a church by himself. He needs other people and they need him. When the spir-itual and emotional well-being of a large group is in-volved, there are crippling and dangerous limitations to a single point of view imposed by any one person. Con-sensus of opinion may take time and work, but it is worth the price.

The resources of a large number of people are necessary for the good health of a church. The pastor who does his work without the input of others is carrying out the pastor's program. The man who enlists the help of the group in the decision-making process is carrying out the church's program.

The other extreme in church leadership is the pastor who shows no personal strength at all in his leadership. He fears opposition or difference of opinion to the point that he allows himself to be dominated completely by others. His ministry can become nothing more than that of a church errand boy. A minister thus subjugated by his own weaknesses and by the strengths of others loses respect and cannot do an adequate job as the church leader.

The spiritual nature of the task in church leadership demands a pastor and a people who can work together for the best interests of Christ's kingdom among men. It is only as they develop a spirit of sharing that they can really demonstrate the difference that their faith has made in their lives.

The Singular Nature of the Pastor's Position

There is no other job in the world that is like that of a pastor. He is on call seven days a week and may be needed at any hour of the day or night. He must be many things to many people, and he must be prepared to do a good job at every task. He must lead a large organization whose workers are largely volunteers. Christian persuasion is his only legitimate tool. He has no will or power to coerce anyone, yet everyone expects him to get the job done.

People come to him on a personal basis to talk about their problems, seek counsel and guidance, and to find a sympathetic friend who will not betray a confidence. Matters that are so sensitive that they could ruin individual lives or homes are frequently discussed with the pastor. He carries burdens and problems that are not his own, but he is expected to keep them to himself and tell no one.

The pastor will find himself moving from the counseling room where he has dealt with the problems of one person to the study where he must prepare to speak to many without letting the former color the latter. The extremes of emotional experiences will take their toll. This writer has found himself performing an informal wedding on Saturday morning, conducting a funeral in the afternoon, and moving back to the church for a formal wedding the same evening. Such is the life of a pastor; it is sometimes exhausting but never boring.

The Ebb and Flow of Popularity

As in the case of a football coach, the pastor may be a hero one moment and a bum the next. When one works with human nature and spiritual values at the same time, he may find himself with a difficult combination in some cases.

There will be occasions when the pastor simply cannot do some of the things people request. At other times he will find that he was expected to meet needs that he knew nothing about. On still other occasions he will be at the right place at the right time and able to meet expectations in a satisfactory way. When things are going well, the people are usually happy; if they do not go well the pastor is often the one who receives the blame.

Personal popularity for the pastor can ebb and flow like the tides of the ocean. It is never fixed and permanent. When he is riding a crest of popular approval, let him be prepared for that time when the tide will run low and personal acclaim will be strongly silent. On the other hand, when he seems stranded alone on the beach with no one left on his side but God, let him not lose heart, for a better day is coming. Paul's encouragement can help at such times:

> And let us not lose heart in doing good, for in due time we shall reap if we do not grow weary. So then, while we have opportunity, let us do good to all men, and especially to those who are of the household of the faith. (Galatians 6:9–10 NASV)

The most helpful thing a pastor can have in both good times and bad is the certain knowledge that he is where God has placed him trying to do what God called him to do. He may not always have the approval of men, but he can always be sure of God's approval if he remains faithful.

The High Call and Lowly Tasks

The call of God is an unforgettable experience. It is the highest honor that can come to a human, but it is also the greatest challenge wherever it may lead. To become the pastor of a great city church with a large and affluent membership is a challenge. To become the shepherd of a small, rural church made up of poor, uneducated people is a challenge. God measures His servants by their obedience and faithfulness, not by worldly standards of success. Some of the tasks to which He assigns His ministers may not be spectacular at all:

> Then the King will say to those on His right, come you who are blessed of my Father, inherit the kingdom prepared for you from the foundation of the world. For I was hungry, and you gave me something to eat; I was thirsty, and you gave me drink; I was a stranger, and you invited me in; naked, and you clothed me; I was in prison, and you came to me. Then the righteous will answer Him saying, Lord, when did we see You hungry, and feed You, or thirsty, and give You drink? And when did we see You a stranger, and invite You in, or naked, and clothe You? And when

did we see You sick, or in prison, and come to You? And the King
will answer and say to them, Truly I say to you, to the extent that
you did it to one of these brothers of mine, even the least of them,
you did it to me. (Matthew 25:34–40 NASV)

The place of service may be great or small, and the task
may be lowly, but the call is high and the man of God must
be faithful in things both few and many in number. The
supreme test for the minister is his faithfulness—not his
worldly success.

Loneliness in the Crowd

The pastor lives among people all his life. He is never
completely free from the demands and expectations of the
public. He speaks to crowds, visits with families, and counsels with individuals. His working hours are filled with
human needs and even his dreams may be of the church
members. In spite of his role as a public figure, there are
times when a pastor may be a lonely man in the midst of
the masses. He marches to the beat of a different drum-
mer, and he is not always understood. His stand on issues
may separate him from others temporarily or permanently. There may even come those times when family and
friends do not agree with him, but even in his loneliness he
knows he is not alone. There is that calm and commanding
Friend who says, "For I am the Lord your God who up-
holds your right hand, who says to you, Do not fear, I will
help you" (Isaiah 41:13 NASV).

The Coming Crown

For the faithful pastor the way may be difficult; people
may not be appreciative; the work may be hard; and the
hours may be long, but he always knows that his reward is

certain. The Word of God makes this crystal clear through the work of one who had paid the price in his service to the churches:

> I have fought the good fight, I have finished the course, I have kept the faith; in the future there is laid up for me the crown of righteousness, which the Lord, the righteous judge, will award to me on that day: and not only to me, but also to all who have loved His appearing. (2 Timothy 4:7–8 NASV)

With the assurance of His constant, abiding presence and strength, the pastor continues his faithful work among the people. Under the mandate and tutelage of the Great Shepherd of the sheep the undershepherd works earnestly. His is the task of ". . . equipping the saints for the work of service, to the building up of the body of Christ." The work is now; the crown comes later!

Appendixes

APPENDIX A

Sermon Work Sheet

Sermon Work Sheet _____ Target Date _____

Scripture _____

Theme: _____ Title: _____

Objective: _____

Proposition: _____

Exegetical Notes: _____

_____

Introduction:

_____

Tentative Outlines: #1 | #2

_____

Final Basic Outline: | Illustrations:

_____

Conclusion:

APPENDIX B

Course of Sermons from Acts

1. "Onward, the Gospel"   1:1-5
2. "Religion: Exclusive or Inclusive?"   1:6-7
3. "When and Where"   1:8
4. "Challenge to Action"   1:9-14
5. "Pentecost"   2:1-13
6. "Prayer, Power, and Preaching"   2:14-42
7. "Christian Fellowship"   2:43-47
8. "Such As I Have"   3:1-10
9. "Jealousy"   4:1-4
10. "No Other Name"   4:8-12
11. "Challenge to Critics"   4:13-22
12. "Prayer for Courage"   4:23-31
13. "The Grace of Generosity"   4:32-37
14. "Deception Detected"   5:1-11
15. "Designating Deacons"   6:1-8
16. "Facing Facts"   7
17. "Souls in the Desert"   8:26-39
18. "God Gets a Leader"   9:1-22
19. "Sight, Sighings, Success"   10:19-21
20. "Christians Trying Christians"   11:1-18
21. "Answered Prayer Knocks at the   12:1-16
    Door"
22. "Missions and Missionaries"   13:1-3
23. "Caution to Preachers (or   14:8-18
    Leaders)"
24. "Church Problems"   15:1-11
25. "Open and Closed Door Policies   16:1-13
    of God"
26. "Pearls before Swine"   17:22-32

273

27. "Insufficient Knowledge"   18:24–28
28. "The Plight of False Prophets"   19:13–20
29. "Worthy Example"   20:28–35
30. "Beginning of the End"   21:26–40
31. "The Defence of the Despised"   22
32. "Conspiracy Confounded"   23
33. "The Tragedy of Procrastination"   24:24–27
34. "A Fruitless Search"   25
35. "Challenge to Cowards"   26:24–32
36. "Storm at Sea"   27
37. "Why the Bonds?"   28

Series on Old Testament Personalities

1. "As Able As Abel" (Abel)
2. "Dare to Be Different" (Noah)
3. "Venture into the Unknown" (Abraham)
4. "The Faith of an Ordinary Man" (Isaac)
5. "Overcoming the Past" (Jacob)
6. "The Victory of Virtue" (Joseph)
7. "Man of Mountains" (Moses)
8. "Wilful Waste—Woeful Want" (Samson)
9. "Honest Confession" (David)
10. "The Impatience of Job" (Job)
11. "The Prince of Prophets" (Isaiah)
12. "The Preacher with a Broken Heart" (Hosea)

Series on New Testament Personalities

1. "When It's Best to Be Second" (John the Baptist)
2. "The Contribution of the Inconspicuous" (Andrew)
3. "How to Grow Strong through Weakness" (Peter)
4. "How to Live and How to Die" (Stephen)

5. "How to Be a Dynamic Layman" (Philip)
6. "Born Out of Season" (Paul)
7. "The Man with the Last Word" (John)
8. "The First and the Last" (Jesus)

Series on Great Prayers of the Bible

1. "Great Intercession" Genesis 18:20–33
2. "But Now, Forgive" Exodus 32:30–35
3. "A Mother's Prayer" 1 Samuel 1:10–13
4. "Prayer of Repentance" Psalm 51
5. "Prayer of the Forgiven" Psalm 32
6. "Prayer of Dedication" 1 Kings 8:22–53
7. "Power In Answer To Prayer" 1 Kings 18:37–39
8. "Prayer for Life" 2 Kings 20:1–11
9. "The Model for Prayer" Matthew 6:9–13
10. "A Prayer for Christians" John 17:1–26
11. "The Lonely Prayer Meeting" Matthew 26:36–46
12. "The Final Prayer" Revelation 22:20–21

Course of Sermons from the Life of Christ

EARLY LIFE:

1. "The Narrators" Luke 1:1–4
2. "Before Anything—Jesus" John 1:1–18
3. "Announcing a Double Miracle" Luke 1:5–38
4. "Life with a Purpose" Luke 1:76–80
5. "A Strange Message" Matthew 1:18–25
6. "The Fullness of Time" Galatians 4:4–5
7. "The Dedicated Life" Luke 2:40–52

MIRACLES:

8. "The Beginning of Miracles" John 2:1–11
9. "Help for Weak Faith" John 4:46–54

10. "Rewards of an Active Faith" Luke 5:1–11
11. "Help for the Helpless" Mark 4:35–41
12. "Life Made Over" Luke 8:26–39
13. "The Touch of His Hand" Mark 5:35–43
14. "The Helping Hands" Mark 2:1–12
15. "Miracle by the Way" Mark 5:25–34
16. "Doing the Unthinkable" Mark 1:40–45
17. "Unusual Faith" Luke 7:1–10
18. "Strength for the Weak" John 5:1–16
19. "A Marvelous Walk" John 6:14–21

PARABLES:

20. "What It Means to Be Lost" Luke 15:1–24
21. "The Gospel and You" Matthew 13:1–9; 18–23
22. "Day of Judgment" Matthew 13:24–30
23. "A Lot from a Little" Matthew 13:31–32
24. "To Be Desired" Matthew 13:44–50
25. "The Barren Tree" Luke 13:6–10

ISSUES OF LIFE:

26. "More Than Life" Mark 8:31–37
27. "Take Your Stand!" Mark 8:38–9:1
28. "Gleams of Glory" Luke 9:28–36
29. "How to Be Outstanding" Mark 9:33–37
30. "The Necessity of Forgiveness" Matthew 18:15–35
31. "Don't Look Back" Luke 9:57–62
32. "The Light of Life" John 8:12
33. "Causes of Illness" John 9:1–12
34. "Check on Your Religion" John 9:23–41
35. "The Good Shepherd" John 10:1–21
36. "Slavery or Freedom" John 8:31–38
37. "A Rich Pauper" Luke 12:13–21
38. "Avoid Embarrassment" Luke 14:7–11
39. "Just Passing Through" John 4:31–37

AROUND THE CROSS:

APPENDIX C

A Course of Sermons from the Gospel of John

1. "The Word of God"   1:1–5
2. "A Man from God"   1:6–7
3. "Abundant Grace"   1:10–18
4. "Religion or Christ?"   1:29
5. "One to One"   1:40–42
6. "The Contribution of the   1:40–42
   Inconspicuous"
7. "Prelude to Glory"   1:43–51
8. "The Zeal of Thine House"   2:13–17
9. "Fickle versus Faithful Men"   2:23–25
10. "The New Birth"   3:1–7
11. "The Standard of Faith"   3:14–15
12. "God's Gift"   3:16
13. "The Compact Gospel"   3:16–17
14. "The Hope of the World"   3:17
15. "Plus and Minus"   3:30, 36
16. "Spiritual Satisfaction"   4:1–26
17. "Help for Weak Faith"   4:46–54
18. "Like Father, Like Son"   5:17–35
19. "To Prove a Disciple"   6:1–14
20. "Be Not Afraid"   6:15–21
21. "A Marvelous Walk"   6:14–21
22. "If Any Man Will Do His Will" 7:17
23. "The Light and the Truth"   8:12–32
24. "Author of Liberty"   8:32–36
25. "God's Glory"   8:54–59
26. "A Time to Work"   9:1–7
27. "Check on Your Religion"   9:23–41
28. "Do You Believe?"   9:35–38

APPENDIX D

Quarterly Planning Form

PREACHING SCHEDULE   QUARTER   YEAR

Date	Subject Sunday Morning	Text	Subject Sunday Evening	Text	Subject Wednesday Evening	Text

APPENDIX E

Concentrated Study of Ephesians

"So Send I You" (Ephesians 1:1)

The highest place that a man can occupy is that of the personal emissary of the Eternal King. Paul repeatedly introduces himself in the market place of the world as the delegated spokesman of the Savior.

    I. Called forth: out of sin, out of oppressive legalism, out of ancestral pride, and out of self-defeating struggle

    II. Sent out: with a message of grace, with a scandalous gospel, with a word of encouragement, and with a promise of hope

    III. Gathered in: to a daily death, to a fresh dedication, to a strong inner compulsion, and to the throne of glory

"The Highest Call" (Ephesians 1:1a)

Paul always looked upon his conversion and call as the signal events of his life.

    I. The called: Paul (see Acts, Philippians 3:4–14, and Galatians for a history of this call experience)

    II. The office: apostle (study the meaning and history of the word, and the impact of apostles on the world; see also outlines on Ephesians 4:11)

    III. The Authority: by the will of God

"The Unique Situation" (Ephesians 1:1b)

How many unique (difficult) situations do you know? What makes them unusual? How many churches are there without serious problems?

   I. Less than ideal: the situation at Ephesus (see the setting at Ephesus for the worship of Diana and also at Colosse)

  II. More than minimum: trace the results of this in Ephesus by the end of the second century

 III. Sufficient Savior in Christ Jesus: our Lord does not seek the ideal situation, nor should we

"Best Wishes" (Ephesians 1:2)

When did you last receive a card from a friend or loved one wishing for you the best? Do you remember the warm glow? If it were from someone of stature you may have kept it to remind you of a valued friendship.

   I. Grace to you: provided from above

  II. Peace to you: infused regardless of problems

 III. Signed: God our Father and the Lord Jesus Christ

"In the Heavenlies" (Ephesians 1:3)

The work of the Father in redemption is presented in verses 3 through 6. The entire passage takes the form of a doxology, for without the initiatory action of his love there would be no redemption.

   I. Provider: "blessed be the God and Father of our Lord Jesus Christ"

  II. Provision: "every spiritual blessing"

 III. Province: "in the heavenlies"

 IV. Person: "in Christ" (Paul's favorite phrase) which refers to all the redemptive work—incarnation, death, and resurrection, ascension, and heavenly priesthood

"In Heavenly Places" (Ephesians 1:3–4)

The environs of the temple to Diana were filled with criminal elements, and the temple itself was populated by greedy priests, lewd prostitutes and selfish craftsmen. This was a far cry from anything heavenly, as was the seat of the true God.

   I. Praise: the meaning, the need, and the scarcity

  II. Power: spiritual power in a person—Christ

 III. Permanence: eternal purposes at work

 IV. Purpose: a marked contrast in character from the local religions

"Election" (Ephesians 1:4)

There are three votes in election—God votes for you, Satan votes against you, and you cast the deciding vote

   I. The fact of election: "He chose" does not mean that He saves or condemns in violation of man's will

  II. The objects of election: "us." God is sovereign but we are also free

 III. The realm of election: "in Him." The only way God could reach us was in Christ

 IV. The calendar of election: "before the foundations of the world"

  V. The purpose of election: "that we might be holy and blameless before him in love" (see Matthew 5:48)

"The Marked Man" (Ephesians 1:5)

The word translated as "foreordination" literally means to prehorizon, or to draw a circle about. The verbs in this passage are in direct sequence to those which have preceded. God has blessed us just as He chose us in love, having before drawn a circle about us.

   I. The arena of foreordination: "in love having foreordained"

  II. The goal of foreordination: "into sonship" by adoption

   III. The mode of foreordination: "Jesus Christ unto himself"

   IV. The reason for foreordination: "to the pleasure of his will"

"Difficult Doctrine" (Ephesians 1:5–6)

That which we worship challenges our best in devotion and thought. A God who is not greater than the base and crude about us is not worthy of our love.

   I. The actions of God: predestined

   II. The purpose of God: adoption

   III. The method of God: kind intention of His will

   IV. The reason of God: to the praise of the glory of His grace

   V. The generosity of God: fully bestowed on us in the Beloved

"In the Beloved" (Ephesians 1:7)

There is a chorus: "Christ is all I need, all that I ever need." The doxology in verse 6 leads us from the work of the Father in redemption to the work of the Son.

   I. Redemption: deliverance through his blood. It is hard to imagine the agony that God bore in the cross of Christ

   II. Forgiveness of our trespasses: it is hard to forgive when someone hurts you personally, but it is even harder to forgive when they hurt someone you love

   III. Riches of grace: we have forgiveness in proportion to the riches of God's grace

"What Have We Here?" (Ephesians 1:7–8)

In the worship of the "mother of all living"—Diana—thinking men found that which was not up to the standards of decency. What could be found in Christ?

I. His presence

II. His redemption: buying us back from ourselves

III. His forgiveness: the only remedy for the sin problem is Christ

IV. His riches of grace: as a Christian you always have something better than you had before. Life is never squandered but rather invested

"The Imponderables" (Ephesians 1:8–9)

I heard a young boy talking with pride about his uncle who is a professor of nuclear physics at Texas A&M. He said, "His thesis is *that* thick and you can't understand a word in it." There are some things past our understanding but they are still ours.

I. Imponderable grace abounded to us

II. Imponderable wisdom and understanding

III. Imponderable mystery of His will
   1. The vertical phase: God to man
   2. The horizontal phase: Jews versus Gentiles question solved in Christ
   3. Spiritual world gains insight to God's purpose through the church

"The Mystery of His Will" (Ephesians 1:9–10)

This is a study of the permissive will of God and the directive will of God. The world was prepared for His will in Christ. Those parts of the world related to you are being prepared for His will in your life.

I. His will unfolds: the mystery of His will

II. His will is good: according to His kind intention

III. His will is worked: administration suitable

IV. His will is complete in Christ: the summing up of all things in Christ

"The Fullness of Times" (Ephesians 1:10)

The word "dispensation" can mean stewardship or administration. The word "unto" means "with reference to" and stresses the designs of God in Christ's work.

    I. The fullness of times in the heavens
      1. Love seeks an object which responds
      2. Love is persistent
      3. Love and forgiveness
    II. The fullness of times on the earth
      1. Fullness may also mean the fitness—when the time was right
      2. All other administrations point to Christ

"The Inheritance" (Ephesians 1:11–12)

What is your lot in life? There was once a radio program called "The Missing Heirs." The idea was to find people who were entitled to an inheritance they knew nothing about. This is what God is doing. We are made an inheritance.

    I. The purpose of God: according to His purpose, God "set before himself" His intention to do something great for us
    II. The plan of God: He works all things according to counsel (plan), as architects work with plans and specifications
    III. The projections of God: plan of His will (wish). If God could have all that he wants of us, what would it be (verse 12)?

"Living in the 'Not Yet'" (Ephesians 1:12; Hebrews 2:8)

Maybe one of God's greatest mercies is that he does not always let us know what is ahead of us from day to day. The events of the morrow may be dreaded, but if we are in Christ the long-term goal is good.

I. There is a goal ("to the end"): We are not vaga-bonds, we are on the way to something great

II. We are involved: we should be involved in a great movement to change men, to redeem homes, to change the world

III. The goal is worthy: to the praise of His glory (see 1 John 3:2)

"What Has Happened to You?" (Ephesians 1:13)

When walking down the hall of a hospital you may see a young man with a broad grin coming out of the new fa-ther's waiting room headed toward the nearest pay phone. He has believed it and now he is on the way to share it. He has heard some good news.

I. What have you heard? There is a transition from "we" in verse 12 to "you" in verse 13. You like us have heard the word of truth. God's eternal verity is equated with the good news of Jesus Christ

II. What have you done? You have placed your faith in a person. This means you have trusted all to him, as the young father put the dearest things in his life into the hands of a doctor—his heart (wife) and his name (baby)

III. What is going on? Sealing by the Holy Spirit of promise: may be the locative case, describing where the believer is sealed—in the Holy Spirit, or it may be the instrumental case, telling by whom the be-liever is sealed. Sealing is putting upon an object an identifying and possessive mark, to be used for con-firming, securing, authenticating, or making par-ticular. The Holy Spirit puts God's branding iron on the individual to say, "This one belongs to me for time and eternity."

1. The seal is proof of God's ownership

    2. His presence is proof of our identity

    3. He brings God's standards to our attention and there accredits us as God's people

    4. As the royal seal of God He exercises authority over our lives

"The Great Transaction" (Ephesians 1:14)

There is a phrase "business as usual," which may mean that all is okay or that things are humdrum or boring. This verse speaks of business which is "unusual."

  I. Down payment: the Holy Spirit is God's earnest on a better day—the day of inheritance

  II. Paid in full: the redemption of God's cherished possession and glorification, paid in like kind to the down payment

  III. Joy of possession: unto the praise of His glory. God moves in completely—not partially

"Benefits of Believers" (Ephesians 1:15–19)

Paul prays for the believers that God may give to them all that God wants them to have. Too many of us lead lives of spiritual poverty when there is something better available.

  I. What are the benefits (1:17)?

    1. The source is the Father of glory, the glorious Father of majesty and of glory

    2. The spirit of wisdom, which is not the Holy Spirit, is the human spirit of wisdom, a gift from God in growth

    3. Revelation

    4. Full knowledge

  II. What are the results of the benefits (1:18–19)?

    1. Spiritual insight as the eye of the heart is enlightened

    2. Understanding of the hope of His calling

3. Understanding of the wealth of the glory of inheritance
4. Understanding of the greatness of His power
5. Understanding of the strength of His sufficiency

"The Mastery of the Master" (Ephesians 1:20–23)

The constructive power which God wants to release in the believer is the same power by which He raised Christ from the dead. Man has the power to induce death but only God has the power to master death.

I. Mastery over death (1:20)
II. Mastery over present and future worlds (1:21)
III. Mastery over circumstances (1:22a)
IV. Mastery in the church (1:22b–23)

Every team must have a "take charge" man who can command respect for the team. Christ is that one in the church.

"The Way It Used to Be" (Ephesians 2:1–3)

How many "before and after" pictures have you seen? The bad side is "before" and the good is "after." The spiritual condition of man before and after is the thrust of this passage.

I. Where Christ found you (2:1b)
   1. The meaning of the metaphor "death" is spiritual death
   2. The realm of death is trespasses and sin
II. What you were doing (2:2)
   1. Walking in the spirit of the age, according to the course of this world
   2. Living under the rule of Satan
III. What we were facing (2:3)
   1. The repugnance resulting from lives of lust and lostness

2. Children of wrath do things deserving God's awesome wrath

"You He did make alive" (2:1a).

"But God" (Ephesians 2:4–5)

How many stories have changed direction with the use of the adversative conjunction "but"? In our own right we had no life and no real future. By ourselves we were sunk, "but God" enters our scene redemptively through Christ.

 I. The adequacy of intervention: rich in mercy
1. The mystery of a righteous God's involvement with sinful men
2. The meaning of mercy
 II. The reason for intervention: the great love with which He loved us
1. Love has to be involved, as a father in his son's financial ruin
2. Love is effective and active
 III. The victory of intervention: it has made us alive together with Christ
1. The joy of rescue
2. The unbelievable status of the returning prodigal

"With Christ" (Ephesians 2:5)

It's great to travel in good company.

 I. Crucified with Christ (Galatians 2:20)
 II. Dead with Christ (Colossians 2:20)
 III. Buried with Christ (Romans 6:4)
 IV. Made alive with Christ (Ephesians 2:5)
 V. Raised with Christ (Colossians 3:1)
 VI. Suffering with Christ (Romans 8:17)

VII. Glorified with Christ (Romans 8:17)

VIII. Seated with Christ (Ephesians 2:6)

"On Top of the World" (Ephesians 2:6–7)

The state of the believer is a glorious state when compared to what he once was. I cannot complain about what I gave up to follow Christ. I had nothing and I was nobody.

I. Rejuvenation: He made us alive

II. Resurrection: He raised us up with Him

III. Resplendent reality: He made us to sit with Him in heavenly places

IV. Reason: that He might show the riches of His grace

"How to Be Saved" (Ephesians 2:8–9)

Paul is not saying that grace is the gift of God or that faith is the gift of God. Rather, he is saying that the entire process of "redemption by grace through faith" is God's gift. It does not have its source in man. Its source is in God.

I. What is grace? How many times does Paul use it and in what ways?

II. What is faith? Look to the examples of faith in the Bible and the definition in Hebrews 11

"God's Purpose in Us" (Ephesians 2:10)

Men are spending millions on strange-looking equipment in several areas. Some of it is to capture and utilize solar energy. Space scientists build and launch ludicrous-looking objects to circle the earth. God's choice product is not an accident, a personal overindulgence of divine emotion or a purposeless bulk. He has a purpose for each.

I. What: we are his workmanship, marked by Him as artists sign their own paintings

II. How: created in Christ Jesus (compare John 1:3 and Colossians 3:10)

III. Why: for good works

"No Hope" (Ephesians 2:11–12)

What a crushing blow it is to a family when a surgeon comes out and in the kindest words he can find says there is no hope. A few people have survived that sentence and lived for years.

I. The awful memory: "Remember . . . once" (2:11)

II. The awful condition: No hope without God (2:12b)

The awesome love of God is for awful sinners (Colossians 2:13).

"Power in the Blood" (Ephesians 2:13)

The court of the Gentiles was as far removed from the Holy of Holies as possible. The middle wall of partition was there. The offering of blood was far removed from them and ineffective under the old system.

I. Everything is different: "but now"

II. Everything is dependent on Jesus: "in Christ Jesus"

III. Everyone is important to Jesus: "ye that were once far off"

IV. Everyone can come in: be "made nigh"

V. Everyone is cleansed in the blood of Christ

"The Broken Wall" (Ephesians 2:14–16)

The Gentile was sinful and jealous. The Jew was proud and exclusive. One could go only so far in the temple. The other had gone just so far because of his vanity. Between them there was a wall and a conflict. Between them and God there was the common wall of sin.

I. Peace in a person (2:14)

II. Peace with a promise: the two—Jew and Gentile—will become one in Christ (2:15)

III. Peace through the performance (2:16)

For generations the conflict lingered. Christ made a solution real and feasible.

"Access to God" (Ephesians 2:17–19)

"You don't just walk up to the president and introduce yourself." These were the words of a preacher who attended a prayer breakfast and was intercepted by the secret service.

I. The invitation (2:17)
   1. The One came, inviting
   2. The invitation is to those far off (Gentiles) and to those near (Jews)

II. The introduction (2:18)
   1. The redemptive work of Christ
   2. The redemptive work of the Holy Spirit
   3. The redemptive work of the Father

III. The inclusion (2:19)
   1. No longer outsiders
   2. Citizens of heaven
   3. Members of the family

"Habitation of God" (Ephesians 2:20–22)

Paul changes from the analogy of a body to that of a building. His purpose is the same—to show that Jew and Gentile became one in Christ and that the new congregation or church thus formed is the dwelling of the Spirit of God.

I. The pillars (2:20)
   1. The ministry of apostles

2. The ministry of prophets
3. Christ as the foundation of both

II. The purpose (2:21)
1. Each group has a purpose
2. The purpose of union in Christ
3. The purpose of growth

III. The perfection: the people are God's dwelling place on earth (2:22; 1 Corinthians 3:16)

"The Prisoner" (Ephesians 3:1–2)

Ray Summers says, "It is an axiom of Christian history that God's plan is a man." In this chapter Paul discusses where he fits as a man in God's plan. God used unique ways to put his best man into the capital city of the world.

I. Prisoners for a cause (see Acts 21:15 through 28:31)

II. Prisoner with a cause (3:1b–2)

"The Mystery" (Ephesians 3:3–5)

The word *mystery* here does not mean something that is mysterious, but something discoverable only by revelation, which is hidden until the appropriate and appointed time for revealing it.

I. The mystery of Christ incarnate (1 Timothy 3:16)

II. The mystery of the church as His body (3:4–5)

III. The mystery of Christ's Indwelling (Colossians 1:27)

IV. The mystery of the church as the bride of Christ (5:32)

"Partakers of the Promise" (Ephesians 3:6–7)

The mystery spoken of earlier is in the radical change wrought by creating of a new entity—the church—and placing the Gentiles as coequals in it. This tremendous innovation of plan was revealed to Paul and committed to him as the distinctive responsibility of his ministry.

   I. Heirs together with God

  II. Members together of the body of Christ

 III. Sharers together of the promise

Paul's ministry (3:7) is not to preach that the blessings of God are to flow through the Jews to the Gentiles, but that they flow directly from the Head to the body, of which both groups are parts, and thus to the world.

"Less Than The Least" (Ephesians 3:8–9)

It is not until a man begins to stand in awe of God's mercy that he can begin to appropriate and appreciate it. Paul never got over the fact that a holy God could deal with him personally.

   I. Less than the least: the man (2:8a)
1. Chief of sinners
2. Born out of season
3. Persecuted the church
4. Continuing personal struggle (Romans 7)

  II. More than the most: the message (2:8b)
1. Grace was given to preach
2. The message was the unsearchable riches of Christ

 III. Better than the best: the fulfillment of God's best purpose (2:9)

"To the Intent" (Ephesians 3:10–11)

The church occupies the center of the stage in the eternal counsels of God. We have long-range planning committees in the church. *From eternity* God has centered his plans around the church.

I. The heavenly validation: the angels watch in wonder
II. The functional church: evangelism and missions
III. The continuing purpose: eternal, from eternity to eternity
IV. The supreme intention: Jesus is the bottom line for God

"Access in Confidence" (Ephesians 3:12–13)

If God is so intent on having a functional body of Christ—the church—that the heavens stand in wonder at it, He is then willing to invest of Himself in it to see it succeed.

I. Boldness in relationship: not brashness of the unrelated
II. Access in confidence: we may be sure of his sufficiency
III. Source of strength: is through our faith in Him
IV. Assurance of providence (3:13)

"The Fullness of God" (Ephesians 3:14–19)

Compare Paul's prayers in Ephesians 1 and 3. In the first he prays for knowledge, and in the second for experience. In the first he states that "God is light," in the second that "God is love." In the first prayer Paul asks for light concerning God's power and provisions for us, emphasizing the new man in heaven, in the presence of God and glory. In contrast, in the second he asks for love experienced by God's presence in us, concentrating on the new man on earth, with God's presence and glory in him.

I. Inward strengthening by the spirit (3:16)
II. The experience of the indwelling Christ (3:17)
III. The fullness of God (3:19)

"The Benediction" (Ephesians 3:20–21)

The first section ends as it began with another doxology. *Phrase is piled upon phrase* in an attempt to depict his ability with us.

I. Unlimited ability: able to do exceeding, abundantly, above
II. Unlimited generosity: above all we ask or think (see 1 Corinthians 2:9)
III. Unlimited power: power that works in us
IV. Unlimited glory (3:21)

With a benediction of praise to God, Paul prepares to embark on practical matters for a gloriously endowed church.

"The Worthy Walk" (Ephesians 4:1–3)

Through three chapters Paul has discussed the redemption of Christ for all men. Now he will show what this means when it is applied to the everyday life of the individual or the group.

I. The request (4:1)
    1. The high calling (Philippians 3:14)
    2. The holy calling (2 Timothy 1:9)
    3. The heavenly calling (Hebrews 3:1)
II. The requirement (4:2)
    1. Lowliness: humility
    2. Meekness: tamed power
    3. Longsufferance: patience with weakness of others
    4. Forbearance: love that sticks
III. The results (4:3)
    1. A disciplined effort and giving diligence

2. Guarding the unity of the Holy Spirit
3. Binding together in peace

"One for All and All for One" (Ephesians 4:4–6)

The unity in Christ comes into sharp focus in these verses. There is no favored people against all other nations. All believers are bound up in Christ on the same basis.

   I. One body: most New Testament passages refer to the church as local, but here it is the body of believers—the universal church

  II. One Spirit: Christ, the head; the church, the body; and the Spirit is the life and power of the church

 III. One hope: all have the same hope that is involved in being called out by God

 IV. One Lord: there are no divided loyalties, only one Lord and Master in Christ. Jesus taught that no man can serve two masters

  V. One faith: there is one and only one way by which man comes into a vital, saving relationship with God in Christ, and that is by way of faith or trust

 VI. One baptism: the inner experience of faith stands at the beginning of reality of man's relationship to Christ. The external act of baptism stands at the beginning of the external demonstration of that which one has experienced

VII. One God and Father of all: the single God and Father of Jesus is "over all, through all, and in all"

"According to Measure" (Ephesians 4:7–8)

There is strength, comfort, and reassurance in belonging to something great. When a naval fleet moves in unison an observer can look at ships as far as he can see and know that they are all parts of the whole. Yet each has a task and the resources to accomplish that task.

I. Gifts beyond measure: was the grace given
II. Gifts according to measure: according to the measure
III. Gifts from the victor: He led captivity captive

"The Descender and Ascender" (Ephesians 4:9–10)

There are three views on this passage: incarnation, that God became man and descended into the lower parts of earth; incarnation, death, burial, and resurrection; or that Christ went into hell and released the saints who had previously died and led them back to heaven. The second view of interpretation seems to harmonize best with the New Testament.

I. The Descender: to servanthood, to rejection, to crucifixion, and to death (see also Philippians 2:5–8)
II. The Ascender: He ascended from the grave into heaven and into spiritual power and wealth, from which he bestows gifts on the church (see also Philippians 2:9–12)

"Apostles" (Ephesians 4:11)

This is one of three catalogues of gifts given in the writings of Paul (see also 1 Corinthians 12:28–30 and Romans 12:6–8). The apostles were the trail blazers sent with the message of redemption to a pagan world.

I. The call of apostleship (Mark 1:17, 20 and 2:14; Luke 6:17)
II. The qualifications for apostles (Acts 1:21–22)
III. The last apostle (Acts 22:21)
IV. The credentials (Galatians 1:11–24)
V. The life of apostles (1 Corinthians 4:9–13)
VI. The tribute to apostles (Revelation 21:14)

"Prophets" (Ephesians 4:11)

The prophets were those who were spokesmen for God, giving evidence of speech under the direct movement of the Holy Spirit. In addition to the writing prophets, twenty-two others are referred to in Scripture as prophets. In the Christian church there are only five references to the prophet.

    I. Prophets to activate the church (Acts 11:27–30)

    II. Prophets to implement missions (Acts 12:1–3)

    III. Prophets to Lead in Orderly Worship (1 Corinthians 14:29–33)

"Evangelists" (Ephesians 4:11)

The evangelists were the ones whose responsibility it was to spread the good news. The work and the workers have fallen into disrepute. They should be known for the work that they perform in the name of Christ.

    I. Known for service rendered: the reputation of Philip as an evangelist is based on his work in mass evangelism (Acts 8:9–13) and personal evangelism (Acts 8:26–40; see also Acts 21:8)

    II. Known as a necessity in the Christian calling (2 Timothy 4:5) this office is not greatly mentioned except in terms of laymen as the examples. All Christians are expected to spread the good news (see Acts 6:5; 8:5, 26, 34; 21:8).

"Pastor" (Ephesians 4:11)

The word *pastor* was one which indicated the leadership of a group as a shepherd leads a flock. He was closely and constantly identified with a local group. The office is subject to perversion or exaltation.

I. The marks of perversion
  1. Insensitive and pleasure-loving (Isaiah 56:10–12)
  2. Negligent and divisive (Jeremiah 23:2)
  3. Erroneous (Jeremiah 50:6)
  4. Selfish (Ezekiel 34:2–3)
  5. Unloving (John 10:12)
II. The marks of exaltation
  1. Wise and gentle (Matthew 10:16)
  2. Selfless service (Matthew 20:26)
  3. Diligent in work (2 Corinthians 4:1–2; 6:1–10)
  4. Spiritually qualified (1 Timothy 3:17)
  5. Equipped (2 Timothy 3:16–17)

"Teachers" (Ephesians 4:11)

The words *pastor* and *teacher* are grouped as though this were one single office, and in many ways it is. However, there may be teachers who are not called to be pastors. The teacher is one who instructs, especially in doctrine.

  I. Christ as a teacher (Matthew 4:23; 5:1–2; 7:29)
 II. Paul as a teacher (Acts 11:26; 15:35; 18:11; 28:31)
III. The gift of teaching: In one of his catalogues, Paul ranks teaching third, after apostles and prophets

"The Purpose of It All" (Ephesians 4:12)

All the gifts of functional ministry look to one end, and that is the building up of the body of Christ. These are not offices with honor or self-interest to be enjoyed. These are services to be employed for the one constructive purpose of building, increasing, or making to grow the body of Christ.

  I. Leadership given (4:11)
 II. Development for ministry anticipated (4:12a)

III. Growth of the church expected (4:12b)

The leadership has as its purpose the preparation of the people for ministry.

"Till We Attain" (Ephesians 4:13)

Since our son was five years old he has walked up beside me to see how tall he is in comparison. Years have passed and he is steadily gaining, and it appears that he will equal or surpass me. As Christians we have a goal which we will never equal or surpass, but that goal is always worthy.

    I. Attainment in oneness (4:13a)

   II. Attainment in knowledge (4:13b)

  III. Attainment in maturity (4:13c)

The Christian or the church is measured in comparison to Jesus.

"No Longer Children" (Ephesians 4:14–15)

The great ambition of every child is to cease being a child. No one wants to be looked upon as a child. To say that one is acting like a child is not a compliment.

    I. Undesirable immaturity (4:14)

      1. A passing phase

      2. Unstable, tossed to and fro

      3. Gullible to the sleight of man

   II. Desirable maturity (4:15)

      1. Reliable

      2. Progressive

      3. Captivated

"The Growing Body" (Ephesians 4:16)

One of the great joys of the Christmas season one year was to see our six-month-old grandson, whom we had not seen since he was only one day old. We were amazed at how he had grown. That kind of growth is normal for a healthy child. It is regrettable that normal growth does not always occur in the church.

    I. The source for growth: Christ, the head (4:15b)
   II. The design for growth: body fitly framed and knit (4:16a)
 III. The process for growth: working of each part (4:16b)
 IV. The goal for growth: unto the building . . . in love (4:16c)

"The Ways of the World" (Ephesians 4:17–19)

Archaeologists have found ample evidence of the vilest sort of moral and social conditions in the first century. Images carved in stone depicting immorality were a part of everyday scenery. The first-century Christians were called upon to leave their old life-style but still had to walk in its market place. The challenge was great then and is great now.

   I. The ways of the world: empty minds and darkened thoughts alienated from life of God and ignorant of God; hard hearts devoted to lust and greed (4:17b–19)
  II. The ways of the witness (4:17a; Romans 12:1–2; 2 Corinthians 6:17–18; John 17:15–17)

"Renewed in the Spirit" (Ephesians 4:20–24)

The problem of being a new spiritual creation in Christ while remaining in the physical body and living among men is always with us (Romans 7:14–25). Because of this we need constant and ongoing renewal.

   I. Deliverance delineated (4:20–21)
  II. Departure from death (4:22)
 III. Dynamics of dedication (4:23–24)

"The Inseparables" (Ephesians 4:25)

There is an old cliché which says that we must either hang together or hang separately. As Christians we need each other. We have left the old life and those in it, and we cannot go back. No one of us can survive or be effective without the others. There is a sound formula for unity.

    I. The Disallowed: wherefore putting away falsehood (4:25a)

   II. The Desired: speak ye truth each one with his neighbor (4:25b)

 III. The Dedication: we are members one of another (4:25c)

"How to Handle Anger" (Ephesians 4:26–27)

The word *anger* has to do with righteous revolt against the evil that surrounds us. In the life of the Christian, righteous indignation is needed, but self-righteous fussing is not needed.

    I. Anger is real: be ye angry

   II. Anger can be controlled: sin not

 III. Anger can be terminated: let not the sun go down on your wrath

 IV. Anger can be dangerous: neither give place to the devil—"when the man starts playing God he begins to act like the devil" (Guinn)

"The Bible and the Modern State" (Ephesians 4:28)

There was a time when thieves were put behind bars and honest men remained free. Now, the honest men go home and get behind their burglar bars while thieves walk the streets. We live in a sick society where men refuse to take jobs because they can do better on welfare or unemployment. The Bible gives a formula that our government needs.

I. Steal no more: the motivation of an experience with Christ is best, but where this is lacking, strong deterrents should be provided
II. Let him labor: "the idle mind is the devil's workshop"
III. That he may have enough for himself and for those who cannot work

"Watch that Word" (Ephesians 4:29)

When I first got out of the Navy and started to preach I had to watch every word. My vocabulary had to be changed. While some may not have the problem of profanity, all must be careful with words. Good words may be used in harmful ways and they cannot be called back. Words of criticism, words of anger, and thoughtless words can hurt.

I. Hurtful words: let no corrupt speech proceed out of your mouth
II. Helpful words: such as is good for edifying as the need may be
III. Healthful words: that it may give grace to them that hear

"Don't Put Down a Friend" (Ephesians 4:30)

In all that we do or say as Christians we are involving a dear friend who wants the best for us. The Holy Spirit does not visit us when we are good and leave us when we are bad. He lives with us all the time. When we speak harshly or allow anger to get out of control, we hurt a friend.

I. The Spirit who cares (4:30a)
II. The Spirit who keeps (4:30b)

He is not a fickle but a constant friend. He brought us to
Jesus the first time. He is committed to bringing us home
to Jesus at the end.

"Imitators of God" (Ephesians 5:1–2)

If one wants to see and hear himself he should pay attention to his children. The tendency to imitate parents is especially strong in young children. The tendency may
strengthen or weaken with the passage of time depending
on the parent's worthiness.

   I. The right model for imitation: imitators of God
     (5:1a)

  II. The right reason for imitation: as beloved children
      (5:1b)

 III. The right guidelines for imitation (5:2)

The goal to be realized is imitation of our Father (1 John
3:2–3)

"The Inappropriates" (Ephesians 5:3–4)

George Goebel once came out with a funny line about
things not appropriate to the occasion. He said, "That's
about as inappropriate as a brown shoe at a tuxedo party."
There are some things which should not be found in the
lives of God's children.

  I. The Inappropriates (5:3–4a)
    1. Moral impurity: fornication and all uncleanness
    2. Greed: covetousness
    3. Dishonesty: filthiness
    4. Loose and shady humor: foolish talk and jesting

 II. The Appropriates (5:4b)
    1. That which becomes the set apart (5:3b)
    2. A grateful spirit

"The Unqualifieds" (Ephesians 5:5)

If one is to lay claim to an inheritance he must establish his identity as a member of the family. Paul says there are some attributes that clearly indicate who is and who is not part of God's family.

    I. The disinherited (5:5a)
   II. The heirs (1 Thessalonians 5:4–10; Romans 8:12–17)
 III. The inheritance (5:5b; 1 Peter 1:3–5)

"The Deceivers" (Ephesians 5:6)

Deception is a trademark of Satan. In the beginning his strategy was to make evil appear to be not so bad. He is still selling the same bill of goods to men today. The effort to give respectability to sin is everywhere in evidence.

    I. The agents of deception (5:6a)
   II. The strategy of deception (Isaiah 5:20–23)
 III. The judgment on deception (5:6b)

"The Unspeakables" (Ephesians 5:7–12)

There is no sin in being tempted. The sin comes when we hold on to temptation as a thing to be cherished. Paul says that Christians are to divorce themselves completely from the works of darkness and join themselves to the task of disciplined Christian living.

   I. The disapproved (5:11–12)
     1. Unfruitful works of darkness
     2. The unspeakable evils of society
  II. The approved (5:7–10)
     1. A new life-style (5:7–8)
     2. Goodness, righteousness, and truth are fruit of the light

"In the Spotlight" (Ephesians 5:13–14)

Whether light is a blessing or a curse depends upon the nature of one's activity. The criminal likes to operate in the dark and dreads the appearance of a police car's spotlight. Those who are working to rescue a trapped or lost person welcome the appearance of a light.

  I. The reproof of light (5:13)
 II. The restoration in light (5:14a)
III. The reassurance of light (5:14b)

"Redeem the Time" (Ephesians 5:15–16)

Time was—is past: Thou canst not it recall:
Time is—thou hast: employ the portion small.
Time future is not and may never be:
Time present is the only time for thee.

  I. Time for cautious living (5:15)
 II. Time as opportunity (5:16a)
III. Time for reclamation (5:16b)

"The Will of God" (Ephesians 5:17)

"When all else fails read the instructions." My oldest son and I thought we knew how to assemble the electric train I bought for my grandson. We failed. When we read the instructions we saw the wisdom of the maker of that train set. When we followed his design it all worked properly.

  I. The permissive will of God (5:17a)
 II. The directive will of God (5:17b)

"Filled with the Spirit" (Ephesians 5:18–21)

What about the morning after? As New Year's Eve approaches each year I have heard several radio commentaries on what to do about a hangover the morning after. Paul says that Christians have the best solution to the "morning after" problem. Be not filled with wine, but be filled with the Spirit.

    I. The command to be filled with the Spirit (5:18a)

    II. The joy of being filled with the Spirit (5:19–21)

    III. The results of being filled with the Spirit (Galatians 5:22–24)

       "The Way of a Wife" (Ephesians 5:22–24)

The pendulum of human opinion swings dizzily and erratically from one extreme to another. What we need most is not the mood of a moment but the ageless wisdom of a loving God for each member of the Christian family.

    I. The way of love and respect (5:23)

    II. The way of unselfish devotion (5:24)

The analogy of wife and church is the highest compliment possible to womanhood.

       "The Way of a Husband" (Ephesians 5:28–29)

One of the developments of our time is disturbing: the portrayal of the American male as a buffoon who is outsmarted by all those around him is sowing destructive seeds for the future. For the husband to be respected he must merit and expect respect.

    I. The way of self-giving love (5:25)

    II. The way of attentive devotion (5:28)

    III. The way of disciplined dedication (5:29–31)

Real love always cherishes the one it loves. It loves not in order to extract service, not to insure its own physical comfort and satisfaction, not for its own convenience, it cherishes the one it loves.

       "The Way of the Lord" (Ephesians 5:26–27)

The one who never enjoyed a home or an earthly family of his own still can teach us the principles upon which happy home life is built. Quality marriages can be fashioned only by quality people. The way of the Lord is quality.

I. The quality of His way of love (5:25)
II. The quality of His way of working (5:26)
III. The quality of His way of recognition (5:27)

The mystery of Christ and the church: the church is not yet perfect but He loves it (5:32).

"The Abiding Union" (Ephesians 5:31–33)

In a time of passing fads we are in need of some things that last. If people worked as hard at building marriages as some do at tearing them down, our divorce rate would be lower and our homes safer.

I. Abiding loyalty in union (5:31)
II. Abiding example of love at its best (5:32)
III. Abiding joy and stability (5:33)

Life has three dimensions—spiritual, emotional, and physical—and is like a three legged stool. It needs all three to be right.

"The Way for Children" (Ephesians 6:1–3)

If anyone ever owed a debt of gratitude to Christ it is women and children. He did more than anyone in history to give them the dignity of personhood. The Roman "patria potestas" gave fathers absolute power over their families. He could sell, enslave, or repudiate his children.

I. Obedience in the Lord (6:1)
II. Honor as a commandment (6:2)
III. Promise in godly relationships (6:3)

"The Way for Parents" (Ephesians 6:4)

Parents need to grow up! Children do not need you to be a "buddy" but a parent. They want to see us as adults—not as overaged kids trying to be as young and irresponsible as they are. Grow up! Your children will profit more from example than from criticism.

   I. Parents of provocation: provoke not to wrath brought on by the exasperation of parental inconsistency
  II. Parents of protection and provision: in the nurture and admonition of the Lord

"The Way for an Employee" (Ephesians 6:5–8)

The working man owes much to a faith whose Savior loves all men. In Christ all men have a new worth. There are few if any slaves left in our world, and that is primarily due to a concern for human dignity introduced by Jesus Christ.

   I. The Christian responsibility of a workman on the job: loyalty, cooperation, and devotion (6:5)
  II. The Christian motivation of a workman on the job: every piece of work ought to be good enough to show God (6:6–8)

"The Way for an Employer" (Ephesians 6:9)

The Christian employer must look at his employees as people and not as things.

   I. God's formula for good business
      1. Be not wasteful with God-given substance (Proverbs 12:27)
      2. A careful and arduous way of life (Proverbs 12:17)
      3. Clean and upright life-style (Proverbs 23:20)
  II. The businessman's formula for godliness
      1. A dedicated life: you are not your own, you are bought with a price
      2. A dedicated business: your success is not just in

what you gain, but in what you do with your
profits

3. A faithful steward and compassionate friend to
others (6:9)

"The Way to Be Strong" (Ephesians 6:10)

How can a man be strong in the face of so many problems?
There is temptation (James 1:14–15), basic selfishness
(James 4:3), an uncertain future (James 4:13–15), and
consistent inconsistency (James 4:17). Our problems are
so great that we cannot manage ourselves, much less in
our own strength guide others. In spite of all this there is a
way to be strong.

    I. The hope of strength: be made strong
   II. The assurance of strength: in the strength of his
      might

In the Navy I felt strength because I was part of something
great.

"The Arena of Conflict" (Ephesians 6:12)

In prison Paul doubtless heard his guards tell war stories
and stories of the gladiators in the Coliseum in Rome. He
seizes upon these experiences to talk about the Christian
life as a conflict with spiritual forces of evil.

    I. The nature of the struggle: "wrestling" is a hand-
      to-hand combat, as we are in a one-on-one con-
      frontation
   II. The nature of the opponent: not human but sa-
      tanic; Paul believes in a personal devil (Ephesians
      4:27, 6:11, 6:16)

"The Whole Armor" (Ephesians 6:13–17)

"What to wear?" A question asked by everyone every day.
"What to wear?" can be answered in some interesting and

sometimes amusing ways. It will depend upon the person, the occasion, the season, the resources, and the judgment of the individual.

   I. Spiritual occasions and reasons for dress (6:10–12)

  II. What to wear for the warfare at hand: Paul studied the battle dress of the soldier and gave each piece a spiritual equivalent (6:13–17)

"The Duty of the Winner" (Ephesians 6:18)

The result of the struggle is assured. In Christ we shall have victory. What shall be our attitude toward the struggle and toward the resulting victory? Shall we swagger and boast as did the Roman soldier? No, ours is to be a different disposition, like that of the lowly Nazarene who has given us the victory.

   I. The duty of prayer and supplication (6:18a)

  II. The duty of constancy in intercession (6:18b)

 III. The duty of watchfulness and perseverance (6:18c)

"The Ambassador in Bonds" (Ephesians 6:19–20)

From his prison cell Paul entreated the churches to pray for him. He was in the capital of the world with an opportunity to penetrate the household of Caesar and confront the seat of the empire. He needed courage and strength from God to be a good representative of Jesus as he wore his chains.

   I. The need for strong representation (6:19)

  II. The reason for representation (6:19b–20a)

 III. The challenge of representation (6:20b)

"The Second Chair" (Ephesians 6:21–22)

How many men have there been who helped great men to be great? We know and think much of Paul and his great feats of faith, but we pay little heed to those who paid so much of their lives in helping us to have a Paul who so greatly magnified Jesus.

    I. The beloved and faithful Tychichus (6:21a)

  II. The faithful detail man (6:21b)

 III. The personal emissary (6:22a)

 IV. The concerned friend of all (6:22b)

Without men and women in the "second chair" we could have no church.

"Gifts from God" (Ephesians 6:23–24)

The heart of a great soul has been felt throughout this great epistle. He has lifted us to the heights and instructed us in the best. His final word is a wish that the choicest gifts of God shall be ours.

    I. Peace in the family of God (6:23a)

  II. Love for and faith in God and each other (6:23b)

 III. God's love to those who love in sincerity (6:24)

Whether the church be in Ephesus in the first century or anywhere in the world today, the message fits.

APPENDIX F

APPLICATION FOR SCHEDULING WEDDING
Champion Forest Baptist Church
Houston, Texas 77066

Wedding date _____ Hour _____

Rehearsal date _____ Hour _____

Wedding cleared on church calendar: Date _____ By _____

Conference with Pastor, Date _____ Time _____

BRIDE ELECT	GROOM ELECT
Name _____	Name _____
Address _____	Address _____
Home phone _____	Home phone _____
Work phone _____	Work phone _____
Church membership _____	Church membership _____
_____	_____
Parents _____	Parents _____
Parents address _____	Parents address _____
_____	_____

Address after marriage _____

Minister _____ Organist _____

Vocalist _____ Florist _____

Photographer _____ Caterer _____

Degree of formality _____

Wedding to be held in: Sanctuary __ Or Pastor's office __

Is reception to be held at the church _____

If reception is to be held at other place, where? _____

Special features: _____

Anticipated number of guests _____

Bride's attendants (no.) _____

Groom's attendants (no.) _____ Ushers (no.) _____

(For Saturday weddings only)

Will flowers be left after wedding for use in sanctuary on Sunday morning? _____

YOUR WEDDING
CHAMPION FOREST BAPTIST CHURCH
12501 Champion Forest Drive
Houston, Texas 77066

Suggestions, Policies, Fees, and Regulations

Introduction

Marriage in the church is a religious ceremony, and all the elements of the service have significance. It is a holy time, the birth of a new family through the union of two individuals. You are urged to make thorough preparation, spiritual as well as temporal.

The members and staff of Champion Forest Baptist Church wish to extend every possible assistance to you in order that your wedding in the church will be a memorable experience.

Serious study and careful consideration have gone into the preparation of the church's wedding policies and regulations. They have been approved by the church and are a part of the standing policies of the church body. You are urged to read the following material carefully prior to making your final plans. We hope that it will be of great assistance to you.

MAKING THE RESERVATION

The date of the wedding should be set as soon as possible. Tentative dates may be set by telephone to the church office; however, it will be necessary for the bride and/or her mother to have a personal conference with the pastor before a date can be confirmed and entered on the church calendar. No dates should be announced until this conference is held.

Unless either the bride, the groom, or their parents or guardians are members of Champion Forest Baptist Church at the time the wedding is scheduled, the wedding is classified as one of nonmembers. No nonmember wedding can be scheduled earlier than sixty (60) days before the date desired, in order to permit members of the church to have preference of dates. Weddings may be scheduled on Saturdays. When possible we encourage weddings on Friday night. Cleaning of buildings and arrangement of furniture for Sunday worship is difficult following a Saturday night wedding.

It is the policy of the church not to schedule weddings on major holidays such as Christmas, New Years' Day, Thanksgiving Day, Labor Day, Easter Day, etc., as custodians are allowed freedom to enjoy the holidays as do others.

No evening weddings may be scheduled to begin later than 8:00 P.M. on weeknights or 7:30 P.M. on Saturdays.

FEES

For Members	Custodian Fee	$25.00*

(No charge is made to members for use of the facilities)

For Non Members	Custodian Fee	25.00*
	Use of Facilities	$100.00

	*Additional For	
	Reception	$10.00

Gratuity for minister and soloist is left to the discretion of the bride and groom. Organist's fee is to be discussed personally with the organist.

Payment of all fees for the use of the church facilities and the service of the custodian is required five (5) days in advance of the wedding.

REHEARSALS

The rehearsal should begin promptly at the time scheduled. A large number of people are involved and delays consume the time of everyone involved. Please insist that everyone be prompt.

1. The minister will be in charge of the rehearsal unless prior arrangements have been made.
2. Each rehearsal, unless otherwise agreed upon, will be the evening before the wedding.
3. Both sets of parents should be present for the rehearsal.
4. The ushers should be present for the rehearsal.
5. Deliver the marriage license to the minister at the rehearsal.

REGARDING DRESS AND VALUABLES

The bride is responsible for determining when or if wedding dresses are to be delivered to the church. She will plan to have some member of the wedding party to be responsible for receiving the dresses. The church will in no way be responsible for personal items such as dresses, wraps, purses, silver, and glassware brought to the church for use in a wedding or reception; nor will it be liable for such items if lost, stolen, or damaged.

MUSIC

A wedding is a service of divine worship in which two persons are joined together in holy wedlock. As soon as the date of the wedding is set by the minister and the bride, an appointment will be made by the bride, if the church's minister of music or church organist is to be involved, regarding the choice of music to be used, whether vocal or instrumental. They are familiar with the ceremony and the procedure under which music is sung and played. They are likewise prepared to discuss appropriate music with the bride. Since the couple to be married will wish their wedding music to be in the best taste, such a conference will be helpful to them in choosing or approving music appropriate for the solemnization of the marriage vows.

It is not necessary to use the minister of music as a soloist. However, the bride should still counsel with him concerning the service and appropriate music to be used.

TAKING OF PICTURES

The photographer may take pictures before or after the ceremony in any part of the building. However, no pictures can be taken in the sanctuary during the ceremony except time exposures. The photographer may take a picture of the bride and her father as they start down the aisle and the bride and groom as they leave. The wedding party may return to the church immediately following the ceremony for the pictures, if they desire. No pictures may be taken in the sanctuary following the reception. (The custodian must begin cleaning immediately following the ceremony and pictures.)

INSTRUCTIONS TO THE FLORIST

1. No furnishings may be moved without approval from the church office. The custodian will remove all furnishings customary for all weddings.
2. Nails, tacks, staples, pins or anything that will mar the woodwork and wall finishes must not be used.
3. All candles must be dripless. Polyethylene material must be used under candelabra to protect the carpets.
4. The florist should call church office 24 hours in advance of wedding to set a time for decorating. Decorations must be completed at least one hour before the ceremony.
5. The florist is expected to remove all decorations and equipment promptly following the ceremony.
6. The florist will be held responsible for any damage done by the decorations to the building or furniture, and is responsible for cleaning any wax from carpet or furniture.
7. Flowers, ferns, candles, or other decorative items are not allowed on the piano or organ console.
8. The church properties must be left in the condition in which they are found.
9. Air conditioning or heat will not be turned on longer than is necessary to cool or heat the sanctuary before the wedding.
10. Variations to the preceding policies must be approved by the Properties Committee. Any inquiries for deviations must be referred to chairman of the Properties Committee.

GENERAL

If you plan to have a child in your wedding, he or she should preferably be at least five years of age.

There will be no smoking within the church building. Alcoholic beverages are strictly prohibited at any time in or around the church.

If you have further questions, you may call the church office. Phone numbers of the organist and church staff members may be secured from the church office.

CHAMPION FOREST BAPTIST CHURCH
Houston, Texas 77066

STATE REGISTRATION REQUIREMENTS FOR MINISTERS

The following information was accurate at the time when it was obtained, in 1978, but it should be remembered that laws often change. The pastor should check for himself upon moving to another state.

State	Requirement for Registration to Perform Weddings (Yes or No)	For Further Information See:
Alabama	No	

Alaska	No	Alaska statutes 25. 05. 261, 271, 281, 291, 301, 311, 321
Arizona	No	Marriage License Division 101 West Jefferson Phoenix, Arizona 85003
Arkansas	Yes	Arkansas Statutes Annotated, 55-218
California	No	
Colorado	No	
Connecticut	No	General Statutes of Connecticut, Section 46-3
Delaware	Yes (out-of-state)	Rosalie O'Bara, Clerk of the Peace City/County Building 800 French Street Wilmington, Delaware 19801
Florida	No	Florida Statutes Section 741.07, 741.08
Georgia	No	
Hawaii	Yes	Research and Statistics Office Department of Health P.O. Box 3378 Honolulu, Hawaii 96801
Idaho and Illinois		No information available. Pastor should check with Secretary of State's office upon establishing residence.
Indiana	No	Indiana Legislative Council 302 State House Indianapolis, Indiana 46204
Iowa	No	
Kansas	Yes	Local Probate Office or

		Kansas Baptist Convention 1001 Gage Topeka, Kansas 66606
Kentucky	Yes	Kentucky Revised Statutes KRS 402.060
Louisiana	Yes	

Maine	Yes	Secretary of State
		Department of State
		Augusta, Maine 04333
		For funerals:
		Leo J. Murphy,
		Chairman
		State Board of Funeral
		    Service
		c/o Plummer Funeral Home
		16 Pleasant Street
		Augusta, Maine 04330
		or
		Department of Human
		    Services
		Augusta, Maine 04333

Maryland	No	Article 62, Section 3A(a)
Massachusetts		No information available. Pastor should check with Sec- retary of State's office upon establishing residence.
Michigan	No	
Minnesota	Yes	County Court House or Council of Churches 1671 Summit Avenue St. Paul, Minnesota 55105
Mississippi	No	County Chancery Clerk

Missouri	Yes	RSMo 451.100
		or
		Dr. Rheubin L. South
		Executive Director
		Missouri Baptist Convention
		400 East High Street
		Jefferson City, Missouri
		65101
Montana		
Nebraska	No	Nebraska Statutes 42-115
		or
		Allen J. Beerman
		Secretary of State
		Suite 2300; Capitol Bldg.
		Lincoln, Nebraska 68509
Nevada		No information available. Pastor should check with Secretary of State's office upon establishing residence.
New Hampshire	Yes	RSA 457:31–32
		or
		Secretary of State
		State House
		Concord, New Hampshire 03301
New Jersey	No	
New Mexico	No	New Mexico Statutes 57-1-2 and 57-1-3
New York		No information available. Pastor should check with Secretary of State's office upon establishing residence.

North Carolina	No	SBC; attn. Church Ministries 127 Ninth Avenue, North Nashville, Tennessee 37234
North Dakota	No	Section 14-03-09 North Dakota Century Code
Ohio	Yes	Secretary of State Columbus, Ohio 43216
Oklahoma	Yes	Oklahoma Statutes 43-7-8
Oregon	Yes	County Clerk
Pennsylvania	No	Secretary of the Commonwealth Department of State Harrisburg, Pennsylvania 17120
Rhode Island		No information available. Pastor should check with Secretary of State's office upon establishing residence.
South Carolina	No	
South Dakota	No	South Dakota Compiled Laws Chapter 25-1-30
Tennessee	No	Department of Insurance Division of Regulatory Boards 506 Capitol Hill Bldg. Nashville, Tennessee 37219
Texas	No	
Utah	No	Statutes of Utah 30-1-6
Vermont	Yes	VSA Section 5144

Virginia	No	Pastors must be "bonded by the court in which they conduct church services"— Larry Murphy, Sr. Executive Asst. to the Governor, Statute 26.04.050 Revised Code of Washington or City or County Clerk
West Virginia	Yes	State Code 48-1-12a
Wisconsin	Yes	Wisconsin Statutes Chapter 245.16–17
Wyoming	No	

Notes

Chapter II

1. H. E. Dana, *A Manual of Ecclesiology* (Kansas City, Kansas: Central Seminary Press, 1944), p. 26.
2. Charles E. Jefferson, *The Building of the Church* (New York: Macmillan Co., 1923), p. 23.
3. Ibid., p. 13.
4. Lyle E. Schaller, *Hey, That's Our Church* (Nashville: Abingdon Press, 1975).
5. Edgar N. Jackson, *A Psychology for Preaching* (Great Neck, New York: Channel Press, 1961), p. 45.
6. Matthew Simpson, *Lectures on Preaching* (New York: Phillips and Hunt, 1879), pp. 20–21.
7. Elton Trueblood, *The Incendiary Fellowship* (New York: Harper and Row, 1967), p. 45.

Chapter III

1. J. Daniel Bauman, *An Introduction to Contemporary Preaching* (Grand Rapids: Baker Book House, 1972).
2. Merrill R. Abbey, *Communications in Pulpit and Parish* (Philadelphia: Westminster Press, 1973).
3. Chester Pennington, *God Has a Communication Problem* (New York: Hawthorn Books, 1976).
4. George E. Sweazey, *Preaching the Good News* (Englewood Cliffs, N.J.: Prentice Hall, 1976).
5. W. Charles Redding, "The Organizational Communicator," *Business*

and Industrial Communication (New York: Harper and Row, 1964), p. 31.

6. G. W. Allport, *Handbook of Social Psychology*, ed. A. Murchison. (Worcester, Mass.: Clark University Press, 1937), p. 906.

7. Jon Eisenson, J. Auer, and J. Irwin, *The Psychology of Communication* (New York: Appleton-Century-Crofts, 1963), p. 232.

8. Ibid., p. 233.

9. Ibid., p. 234.

10. T. M. Higham, "Is 'Communications' a Sacred Cow," *Business and Industrial Communication*, p. 557.

11. Dorwin Cartwright, *Group Dynamics* (New York: Harper and Row, 1968), p. vii.

12. Paul F. Second and C. W. Backman, *Social Psychology* (New York: McGraw-Hill, 1964), p. 190.

13. Erwin P. Bettinghaus, *Persuasive Communication* (New York: Holt, Rinehart and Winston, 1968), p. 13.

14. John A. Broadus, *On the Preparation and Delivery of Sermons* (Nashville: Broadman Press, 1944), p. 2.

15. Carl I. Hovland, I. L. Janis, and H. H. Kelley, *Communication and Persuasion* (New Haven: Yale University Press, 1953).

16. Clyde E. Fant, *Preaching for Today* (New York: Harper and Row, 1975), p. 44.

Chapter V

1. J. Daniel Bauman, *An Introduction to Contemporary Preaching* (Grand Rapids: Baker Book House, 1972), p. 13.

2. *The Minister's Library, A Selected Bibliography*, is available from the Baptist Book Store, 3901 Gentilly Blvd., New Orleans, La., 70126.

Chapter XI

1. If a building program is a part of the long-range plan for a church, help should be sought from the Department of Church Architecture at the Baptist Sunday School Board of the Southern Baptist Convention (127 Ninth Ave., N., Nashville, Tenn. 37203). The pastor should order two documents to begin such a planning process: *The Church Building Survey and Planning Committee Guide*, and the *Church Building Committee Guide*. A pastor should acquaint himself with these materials and lead his committee in their use.

Suggested Reading for Pastors

The History of Preaching

Broadus, John A. *Lectures on the History of Preaching*. New York: A. C. Armstrong Co., 1876.

Brilioth, Yngve. *A Brief History of Preaching*. Philadelphia: Fortress Press, 1965.

Dargan, E. C. *A History of Preaching*. 2 vols. New York: A. C. Armstrong and Son, 1905.

Dodd, C. H. *The Apostolic Preaching and Its Developments*. New York: Harper Co., 1949.

Farrar, F. W. *Lives of the Fathers*. 2 vols. New York: Macmillan Co., 1889.

Garvie, Alfred E. *The Christian Preacher*. New York: Scribner's Sons, 1923.

Goodspeed, Edgar J. *A History of Early Christian Literature*. Chicago: University of Chicago Press, 1942.

Holland, Dewitte, ed. *Preaching in American History*. Nashville: Abingdon Press, 1969.

Jones, Edgar Dewitt. *The Royalty of the Pulpit*. New York: Harper Co., 1951.

Ker, John. *Lectures on the History of Preaching*. London: Hodder and Stoughton, 1888.

Kerr, Hugh Thomson. *Preaching in the Early Church*. New York: Fleming H. Revell Co., 1942.

Lake, Kirsopp. *The Apostolic Fathers*. Vol. 2. New York: Macmillan Co., 1912–1948.

Lindsay, Thomas. *The Church and the Ministry in the Early Centuries*. New York: Doran Co.

Neale, J. M. *Medieval Preachers and Medieval Preaching*. London: J. C. Mozley, 1856.

Pattison, T. H. *The History of Christian Preaching*. Philadelphia: American Baptist Publication Society, 1903.

Petry, Ray C. *No Uncertain Sound*. Philadelphia: Westminster Press, 1948.

Roberts, Alexander. "An Ancient Family," *The Ante Nicene Fathers*. Vol. 7. Grand Rapids: E. B. Eerdmans Publishing Co., 1950.

Stanfield, V. L. *Notes on the History of Preaching*. New Orleans: New Orleans Baptist Theological Seminary, 1963.

Thompson, E. T. *Changing Emphases in American Preaching*. Philadelphia: Westminster Press, 1943.

Tullock, John. *English Puritanism and Its Leaders*. Edinburgh: William Blackwood and Sons, 1861.

Turnbull, Ralph. *A History of Preaching*. New York: Sheldon, Lamport and Blakeman, 1956.

Wiersbe, Warren. *Walking with the Giants: A Minister's Guide to Good Reading and Great Preaching*. Grand Rapids: Baker Book House, 1976.

General

Bauman, J. Daniel. *An Introduction to Contemporary Preaching*. Grand Rapids: Baker Book House, 1972.

Baxter, Batsell B. *The Heart of the Yale Lectures*. New York: Macmillan Co., 1947.

Blackwood, Andrew W. *The Preparation of Sermons*. New York: Abingdon-Cokesbury Press, 1948.

Broadus, John. *On the Preparation and Delivery of Sermons*. New York: Harper and Brothers Co., 1944.

Brooks, Phillips. *Lectures on Preaching*. New York: E. P. Dutton and Co., 1877.

Brown, C. R. *The Art of Preaching*. New York: Macmillan Co., 1948.

Crum, Milton, Jr. *Manual on Preaching*. Valley Forge: Judson Press, 1977.

Dargan, E. C. *The Art of Preaching in the Light of Its History*. New York: Doran Co., 1922.

Davis, H. Grady. *Design for Preaching*. Philadelphia: Muhlenberg Press, 1958.

Erdahl, Lowell O. *Preaching for the People*. Nashville: Abingdon Press, 1976.

Forsyth, P. T. *Positive Preaching and the Modern Mind*. Grand Rapids: E. B. Eerdmans Publishing Co., 1964.

Horne, Chevis F. *Crisis in the Pulpit*. Grand Rapids: Baker Book House, 1975.

Jones, Ilion T. *Principles and Practice of Preaching*. New York: Abingdon Press, 1956.

Jowett, J. H. *The Preacher: His Life and Work*. London: Hodder and Stoughton.

Kennedy, Gerald. *His Word through Preaching*. New York: Harper Co., 1977.

Killinger, John. *The Centrality of Preaching in the Total Task of the Ministry*. Waco, Tex.: Word Books, 1969.

Kirkpatrick, Robert W. *The Creative Delivery of Sermons*. New York: Macmillan Co., 1944.

Mitchell, W. F. *English Pulpit Oratory from Andrewes to Tillotson*. New York: Macmillan Co., 1932.

Mounce, Robert. *The Essential Nature of New Testament Preaching*. Grand Rapids: E. B. Eerdmans Publishing Co., 1960.

Pattison, T. H. *The Making of the Sermon*. Philadelphia: American Baptist Publication Society, 1960.

Read, David H. C. *Sent from God*. Nashville: Abingdon Press, 1974.

Reu, J. M. *Homiletics*. Chicago: Wartburg Co., 1922.

Sangster, W. E. *The Craft of Sermon Construction*. London: Epworth Press, 1949.

Smyth, Charles. *The Art of Preaching*. New York: Macmillan Co., 1940.

Sweazey, George E. *Preaching the Good News*. Englewood Cliffs, N.J.: Prentice-Hall, Inc., 1976.

White, R.E.O. *A Guide to Preaching*. London: Pickering and Inglis, 1973.

Biblical Preaching

Berkhoff, L. *Principles of Biblical Interpretation*. Grand Rapids: Baker Book House, 1950.

Blackwood, A. W. *Expository Preaching for Today*. Nashville: Abingdon-Cokesbury Press, 1953.

Cox, James. *A Guide to Biblical Preaching*. Nashville: Abingdon Press, 1976.

Dodd, C. H. *The Bible Today*. New York: Macmillan Co., 1947.

Faw, Chalmer E. *A Guide to Biblical Preaching*. Nashville: Broadman Press, 1962.

Ford, D. W. C. *An Expository Preacher's Notebook*. London: Hodder and Stoughton, 1961.

Keck, Leander. *The Bible in the Pulpit*. Nashville: Abingdon Press, 1978.

Knott, Harold E. *How to Prepare an Expository Sermon*. Cincinnati: Standard Publishing Co., 1930.

Koller, Charles. *Expository Preaching without Notes*. Grand Rapids: Baker Book House, 1962.

Meyer, F. B. *Expository Preaching*. Grand Rapids: Baker Book House, 1974.

Miller, Donald. *Fire in Thy Mouth*. Nashville: Abingdon Press, 1954.

———. *The Way to Biblical Preaching*. New York: Abingdon Press, 1957.

Perry, Lloyd. *Biblical Sermon Guide*. Grand Rapids: Baker Book House, 1970.

Rad, Gerhard Von. *Biblical Interpretations in Preaching*. Nashville: Abingdon Press, 1977.

Ramm, Bernard L. *Hermeneutics*. Grand Rapids: Baker Book House, 1967.

Scherer, Paul. *The Word of God Sent*. New York: Harper and Row, 1965.

Skinner, Craig. *The Teaching Ministry of the Pulpit*. Grand Rapids: Baker Book House, 1973.

Smart, James D. *The Strange Silence of the Bible in the Church*. Philadelphia: Westminster Press, 1970.

Smith, Charles W. F. *Biblical Authority for Modern Preaching*. Philadelphia: Westminster Press, 1960.

Stevenson, Dwight. *In the Biblical Preacher's Workshop*. Nashville: Abingdon Press, 1967.

White, Douglas M. *The Excellence of Exposition*. Neptune, N.J.: Loizeaux Brothers, 1977.

Theology

Abbey, Merrill R. *Living Doctrine in a Vital Pulpit*. New York: Abingdon Press, 1964.

Barth, Karl. *The Preaching of the Gospel*. Philadelphia: Westminster Press, 1963.

Browne, R. E. C. *The Ministry of the Word*. London: SCM Press, 1958.

Clowney, Edmund. *Preaching and Biblical Theology*. Grand Rapids: E. B. Eerdmans Publishing Company, 1961.

Fant, Clyde. *Preaching for Today*. New York: Harper and Row, 1975.

Mitchell, Henry H. *The Recovery of Preaching*. New York: Harper and Row, 1977.

Ritschl, Dietrich. *A Theology of Proclamation*. Richmond: John Knox Press, 1960.

Stewart, James S. *A Faith to Proclaim*. New York: Scribner's Co., 1953.

Wedel, T. O. *The Pulpit Rediscovers Theology*. Greenwich, Conn.: Seabury Press, 1956.

Communication

Abbey, Merrill R. *Communication in Pulpit and Parish*. Philadelphia: Westminster Press, 1973.

_____. *Preaching to the Contemporary Mind*. New York: Abingdon Press, 1963.

Bois, J. Samuel. *The Art of Awareness: A Textbook on General Semantics*. Dubuque, Iowa: W. C. Brown Co., 1966.

Budd, Richard W.; Donohew, Lewis; and Thorp, Robert K. *Content Analysis of Communication*. New York: Macmillan Co., 1967.

Craddock, Fred B. *Overhearing the Gospel*. Nashville: Abingdon Press, 1978.

Emmert, Philip, and Brooks, William D., eds. *Methods of Research in Communication*. New York: Houghton Mifflin Co., 1970.

Flesch, Rudolph. *The Art of Plain Talk*. New York: Harper and Brothers, 1946.

Garrison, Webb B. *Creative Imagination in Preaching*. Nashville: Abingdon Press, 1960.

Howe, Reuel L. *The Miracle of Dialogue*. Greenwich, Conn.: Seabury Press, 1963.

Howes, Raymond F. *Historical Studies of Rhetoric and Rhetoricians*. Ithaca, N.Y.: Cornell University Press, 1961.

Jackson, Edgar N. *A Psychology for Preaching*. Great Neck, N.Y.: Channel Press, 1961.

Katz, Elihu, and Lazarsfeld, Paul F. *Personal Influence*. Glencoe, Ill.: Free Press, 1960.

Massey, James Earl. *The Sermon in Perspective: A Study of Communication in Charisma*. Grand Rapids: Baker Book House, 1976.

Pennington, Chester. *God Has a Communication Problem*. New York: Hawthorn Books, 1976

Stevenson, D. E., and Diehl, C. F. *Reaching People from the Pulpit*. New York: Harper Co., 1958.

Strunk, William, and White, E. B. *Elements of Style*. New York: Macmillan Co., 1959.

Pastoral Preaching

Asquith, Glenn. *Preaching According to Plan*. Valley Forge: Judson Press, 1968.

Blackwood, Andrew W. *Planning a Year's Pulpit Work*. Nashville: Abingdon-Cokesbury Press, 1942.

Gibson, George Miles. *Planned Preaching*. Philadelphia: Westminster Press, 1954.

Jackson, Edgar. *How to Preach to People's Needs*. New York: Abingdon Press, 1956.

Johnson, Howard A. *Preaching the Christian Year*. New York: Scribner Co., 1957.

Jordan, G. Ray. *Preaching during a Revolution*. Anderson, In.: Warner Press, 1962.

Kemp, Charles F. *Life Situation Preaching*. St. Louis: Bethany Press, 1956.

———. *Pastoral Preaching*. St. Louis: Bethany Press, 1963.

———. *The Preaching Pastor*. St. Louis: Bethany Press, 1966.

Luccock, Halford E. *In the Minister's Workshop*. Nashville: Abingdon-Cokesbury Press, 1944.

Pearce, J. Winston. *Planning Your Preaching*. Nashville: Broadman Press, 1967.

Worship

Abba, Raymond. *Principles of Christian Worship*. New York: Oxford University Press, 1957.

Allmen, J. J. Von. *Worship: Its Theology and Practice*. London: Lutterworth Press, 1965.

Davies, Horton. *Christian Worship*. New York: Abingdon Press, 1957.

Hahn, Ferdinand. *The Worship of the Early Church*. Philadelphia: Fortress Press, 1973.

Hardman, Oscar. *A History of Christian Worship*. London: University of London Press, 1937.

Herbert, A. S. *Worship in Ancient Israel*. Richmond: John Knox Press, 1959.

Oesterly, W. O. E. *The Jewish Background of the Christian Liturgy*. Gloucester, Mass.: P. Smith, 1965.

Pattison, T. Harwood. *Public Worship*. Philadelphia: American Baptist Publication Society, 1900.

White, James F. *Christian Worship in Transition*. Nashville: Abingdon Press, 1976.

Pastoral Work

Dale, Robert D. *Growing a Loving Church*. Nashville: Convention Press, 1974.

Dobbins, G. S. *The Churchbook*. Nashville: Broadman Press, 1951.

Faulkner, Brooks. *Getting on Top of Your Work*. Nashville: Convention Press, 1973.

Jefferson, Charles E. *The Building of the Church*. New York: Macmillan Co., 1913.

McBurney, Louis. *Every Pastor Needs a Pastor*. Waco: Word Books, 1977.

McCutchean, James N. *The Pastoral Ministry*. Nashville: Abingdon Press, 1973.

McEachern. *Proclaim the Gospel*. Nashville: Convention Press, 1975.

Oates, Wayne E. *The Christian Pastor*. Philadelphia: Westminster Press, 1951.

Osborn, Ronald E. *In Christ's Place*. St. Louis: Bethany Press, 1967.

Segler, Franklin M. *A Theology of Church and Ministry*. Nashville: Broadman Press, 1960.